Organising Learning in Primary School Classroom

This third edition of *Organising Learning in the Primary School Classroom* brings this acclaimed and invaluable text up to date with regard to issues such as literacy and numeracy strategies and the latest edition of the National Curriculum. It also covers recent research into effectiveness in teaching and learning and the importance of developing emotional intelligence.

The book provides teachers with a guide to all aspects of teaching practice. Opening with a look at the choices faced by a teacher when planning work in the classroom, it goes on to look at child development and considers those aspects a teacher would have to take into account. There is a chapter on the curriculum and chapters on core subjects, which cover literacy and numeracy hours and include suggested teaching strategies. Other chapters address classroom management and dealing with children with special needs or exceptional ability. Throughout there are analyses to help teachers consider aspects of classroom work. These will be invaluable not only to newly qualified teachers, but also to experienced practitioners wishing to review their work.

Joan Dean has been involved with many aspects of education, having taught in primary and secondary schools and a college of education. She has held two primary school headships and was for eleven years Senior Primary Advisor for Berkshire and for seventeen years Chief Inspector for Surrey. She has been a school governor since 1994. She is the author of over thirty books on education, including *Improving the Primary School* (1999) and *Improving Children's Learning* (2000). In 1980 she was awarded an OBE for her services to education.

Organising Learning in the Primary School Classroom

Third edition

Joan Dean

London and New York

First published 1983 by Croom Helm Ltd
Second edition published 1992 by Routledge
Third edition published 2001 by RoutledgeFalmer
11 New Fetter Lane, London EC4P 4EE

Simultaneously published in the USA and Canada
by RoutledgeFalmer
29 West 35th Street, New York, NY 10001

RoutledgeFalmer is an imprint of the Taylor & Francis Group

© 1983, 1992, 2001 Joan Dean

Typeset in Sabon by
Prepress Projects Ltd, Perth, Scotland (www.prepress-projects.co.uk)
Printed and bound in Great Britain by
Biddles Ltd, Guildford and King's Lynn

British Library Cataloguing in Publication Data
A catalogue record for this book is available from the British
Library

Library of Congress Cataloging in Publication Data

ISBN 0–415–25021–8

Contents

vi *Contents*

Analyses

Figures

1 Introduction

Janet Rogers was in her third year of teaching and was working with a year 4 class. She enjoyed her work and had settled into school well. The literacy and numeracy hours seemed to be running happily although she was worried about the lack of time for extended writing. However, she found it difficult to fit in all the other demands of the National Curriculum and to find time for aspects of personal, social and health education. She tried to keep a balance of whole-class teaching, group work and individual learning but was worried that she did not do enough to meet individual children's needs, especially those with special needs and the very able. She felt she was always chasing her tail although she spent long hours at home as well as at school in preparing and marking work and keeping records.

The deputy head, Mary Robinson, had been her mentor during her induction year and it was to Mary that Janet turned for advice about how to improve the teaching she was offering to her class. Mary suggested that Janet took some time over a holiday period to think carefully about her philosophy of primary education – the things she felt were really important and those which were less so – and also to consider the ways in which she felt happiest teaching and defining her teaching style. She could then go on to define her objectives, determine the skills she needed and analyse various aspects of her work to see if there were ways in which they could be improved. Mary also stressed that good organisation was essential if children's achievement was to be improved.

This book sets out to do just that – to reflect on philosophy and teaching style and then to analyse what is actually happening in the classroom, looking at the skills and knowledge that primary school teachers need and how best to organise your work in the classroom. Good teachers are reflective teachers. Osterman and Kottkamp (1994: 46) suggest that 'Reflective practice is viewed as a means by which practitioners can develop a greater level of self-awareness about the nature and impact of their performance, an awareness that creates opportunities for professional growth and development'. Reflective teaching also involves thinking about the feelings that were aroused by classroom situations. Osterman and Kottkamp suggest collecting observational data and analysing and reflecting on them, asking yourself questions such as 'Why did events take place as they did? What ideas and feelings prompted my actions? Did my actions correspond with my intentions? Did my actions lead to the outcomes I intended?' (p. 49).

Pollard and Tann (1987: 1) make the following statements about the nature of reflective teaching:

- Reflective teaching implies an active concern with aims and consequences, as well as with means and technical efficiency.
- Reflective teaching combines enquiry and implementation skills with attitudes of open-mindedness, responsibility and whole-heartedness.
- Reflective teaching is applied in a cyclical or spiralling process in which teachers continually monitor, evaluate and revise their own practice.
- Reflective teaching is based on teacher judgement, informed partly by self-reflection and partly by insights from educational disciplines.

Every teacher is a manager of children's learning. As a teacher you influence the children you teach in many ways. Because of you, many of them will learn things that they will remember for the rest of their lives. It is a considerable responsibility.

How you discharge this responsibility does not depend only on the person you are and the relationships you are able to build with the children and colleagues, important as these are. The ability to organise children's learning, the actual teaching skills you possess, your ability to observe, select and present material, lead discussion, assess and evaluate and reflect on your performance and so on are crucial and make all the difference between the group in which most of the children come near to achieving their full potential and one in which most are underachieving.

Each chapter in this book deals with a particular aspect of organisation, and most chapters contain suggestions for ways of reflecting on and assessing your present situation preparatory to reviewing possible ways of working and selecting those which meet your needs and those of your class.

Anyone working in education at the present time is very conscious of the pressures. Public interest in education is considerable and recent legislation has given both parents and governors a much greater say in how schools function. Good schools have always involved parents in the education of their children, and it is now essential to demonstrate the good work the school does to the local community because schools are in competition for pupils. This is time-consuming, but it pays dividends in terms of the trust and respect which can be generated and the support which can be gained. It also helps to foster children's learning if home and school work together.

The National Curriculum, Standard Assessment Tasks (SATs) and the literacy and numeracy hours have reduced the freedom of the individual teacher in the classroom. In spite of this, teachers in primary schools still have a good deal of freedom compared with teachers at later stages and compared with teachers in some other countries. It is only in English and mathematics that approaches to teaching are to some extent dictated, which still leaves a good deal for you to decide. These are vital teaching areas in which teacher effectiveness is of the utmost importance.

The way a school is managed has a considerable effect on what happens in individual classrooms, but research into effectiveness suggests that the classroom is the place where the quality of teaching and learning determines how effective the school actually is. In recent years teachers have done much more work together, planning and making decisions which affect what happens in their classrooms. Most schools also have teachers co-ordinating the work in each subject, although this poses problems for really small schools. All of this means that individual teachers lose some autonomy but gain the support of a colleague who has made a study of a particular aspect of the curriculum.

Different teachers have different styles of working. This provides variety in the school, which can be valuable and keeps the teaching dynamic in many classes. It means that there will be a variety of opportunities for children to learn. However, some styles are more effective than others and you need to be constantly assessing the way you work to ensure that children are learning as effectively as possible.

Society delegates to the teacher the task of educating children. The teacher and the child come to school bringing with them a variety of talents, experiences and influences. Children will also have formed many ideas about the world around them before they come to school and these need to be taken into account by the teacher. In school, the teacher's task is to see that the child experiences the curriculum, develops and learns. To achieve this the teacher creates a learning environment and organises time, space and resources to enable the child to learn.

Each chapter in this book offers you suggestions for reflecting on and assessing specific aspects of the situation in your own classroom. You may like to work through the book chapter by chapter, thinking out your point of view as you go along. Alternatively, you may like to select areas of your work to consider and analyse.

The profile on the next few pages is designed as a starting point for your thinking and as something to come back to after you have read this book.

Each teacher organises work to suit his or her ideas, preferences and skills and for the particular group of children he or she teaches. Analysis 1.1 is designed to help you to identify your own organisational preferences so that you can keep them in mind as you work through the book. You may find it interesting to see if you change your original ideas after considering further options open to you.

Each section of the profile represents a spectrum of possible views. There are no 'right' answers.

Analysis 1.1 Profile of organisational preferences

Tick the statement in each section which most nearly represents your views:

Pattern of daily programme

1   Each child has an individual programme matched to his or her needs. I then withdraw groups for specific teaching and do some whole-class work when it seems appropriate.
2   My main emphasis is on group work with a good deal of individual work and some class work.
3   I like to spend some time working with the whole class, some on group work and some with individuals.
4   I divide work about equally between class and group work and pay attention to individuals as necessary.
5   I work with the whole class for most of the time, following this up with group and individual work as necessary.

The teacher's use of time

1   I work with the whole class as part of the literacy and numeracy hours but for the rest of the time I work mostly with small groups or individuals, extending their thinking and helping them to plan their work.

2   I spend about half my time in whole-class teaching and the other half with small groups and individuals.
3   I spend more than half my time in whole-class teaching with some group teaching and follow up with individuals.
4   A high proportion of my time is spent in whole-class teaching with occasional group or individual work.

The children's use of time

1   I encourage children to plan the use of their time and create opportunities for them to do this.
2   I aim to have an even balance between work which matches the needs of individuals, with some choice in the order in which work is done, and work undertaken by the whole class or in groups.
3   I expect the majority of children to work at the pace of the class, but I try to arrange for the slower children to have extra time on aspects of work they find difficult. I let children choose the order of some pieces of work upon occasions.
4   Almost all my children spend the same amount of time on each aspect of curriculum and do similar work, with help if necessary.

Choice of activity

1   Much of the children's work allows choice within a carefully structured framework. I try to teach children to choose intelligently.
2   I think it is important for children to learn to choose and I build opportunities for this into the programme.
3   I like to provide a certain amount of choice as well as some compulsory activity.
4   I try to provide some choice but the majority of the work I give is compulsory.
5   I keep choice to a minimum because I believe that every child should experience a similar curriculum.

Curriculum content

1   I like to find ways in which I can integrate the concepts, knowledge and skills required by the different parts of the National Curriculum and do some work arising from children's current interests.
2   I try to provide a mixture of work, involving planned teaching, often under subject headings, and a certain amount of work arising from interests and topics.
3   I use current interests as they fit into my planned programme for teaching the National Curriculum which is more or less organised under subject headings.

4   My lessons are normally planned under subject headings because I believe this is the philosophy behind the National Curriculum.

Use of competition and co-operation

1   I believe that it is important for children to learn to work together and I plan a good deal of co-operative group work. I try to avoid competitive situations.
2   I try to encourage co-operation but use competition occasionally in situations where it seems unlikely to do any harm.
3   I use competition when I think it will motivate children. I also do some work designed to encourage co-operation.
4   I find that competition is valuable providing it doesn't get out of hand. I provide occasional opportunities for co-operation.
5   Competition is an important incentive in the classroom as in life and I believe that children need to learn to fail as well as to win. I would like to foster co-operation but don't feel that there are many opportunities for doing so within normal classroom work.

Grouping of children

1   Children often work in groups that are usually formed on a friendship basis and I aim to train them to work co-operatively.
2   I use group work a good deal, forming groups according to the needs of the work in hand. I aim to have children working together.
3   I have some work in interest groups, some in friendship groups, some in ability groups and some in groups I have structured so that they are heterogeneous. Children are encouraged to work together.
4   I normally do core subject work in ability groups. I also have occasional interest groups in topic work.
5   I prefer to work with children in ability groups when I am not working with the whole class.

Use of space

1   I use all the space I can and allow children to work in other parts of the school and move freely about the classroom.
2   I allow children to move about the classroom to collect things and occasionally I let them work outside the classroom when this seems necessary.
3   I prefer children to stay in their places except for practical work. I rarely let them work outside the classroom.

4   I like children to be in their places in the classroom where I can keep an eye on them.

Use of furniture

1   I have spaces for particular activities but other activities take place in them as well. Children normally sit in friendship groups but move to other groups when necessary.
2   I rearrange the room for practical work but I have a permanent space for books and another for messy work. Tables are grouped and children sit in ability groups for basic work but in other groupings for other subjects.
3   I tend to have one activity at a time. Children normally sit in ability groups. I like a formal classroom arrangement with tables in rows.

Use of resources

1   I make the maximum use of resources to foster individual learning. I select and make teaching materials which can be used independently of the teacher. I try to organise so that the computers are in use most of the day.
2   I like to have some good individual materials as well as materials to use with the whole class and I buy and make both types. I make good use of the computers.
3   I like to have some good individual textbooks for core subject work, but prefer to have a variety of books for other subjects. I use the computers from time to time.
4   I use textbooks a good deal, supplementing them with other materials when necessary. I use the computers occasionally.
5   The main resources in my classroom are my own voice, the blackboard, pictures to help the children's understanding and some good textbooks. I haven't much time for computers.

Records and assessments

1   I keep a forecast of my work and aim to keep a detailed record of each child's work and progress through the National Curriculum and in social and personal development and I involve the children in this.
2   I keep a forecast/record of my work, record each child's progress in National Curriculum work and note other things as necessary.
3   I keep a forecast/record of my work and a check-list of children's progress in the core and foundation subjects.

4   I keep a forecast/record of my work and a mark list showing each child's marks in the core and foundation subjects.

Work with other teachers

1   I like to work with other teachers in a teaching team or sharing thinking and materials. I learn a lot that way.
2   I like to do some work with other teachers.
3   I work with other teachers occasionally, usually when we take a group out.
4   I discuss work with other teachers but we are each responsible for our own work and development.
5   I prefer to work with my own class all the time, but I take part in staff discussion when necessary.

Work with parents

1   I try to get to know all the parents of the children in my class, to take note of what they say about their children, tell them about the work we are doing and suggest ways in which they can help. I like to have parents helping in the classroom.
2   I try to get to know the parents of children in my class and I suggest ways in which they can help. I like to have parents helping in the classroom.
3   I try to get to know the parents of children in my class and I have carefully selected parents helping in the classroom.
4   I get to know the parents of the children in my class as far as I am able but I am not keen to have parents in the classroom.
5   I believe teaching is a professional task which should be left to professionals.

Equal opportunities

1   I am conscious that that it all too easy to treat boys and girls, Black and White children, middle- and working-class children and children with disabilities in different ways and to be prejudiced about what they can do. I am constantly checking myself to see that this is not happening and aim to teach my children to value people as individuals whatever their background.

2   I am conscious that it is easy to show prejudice without being aware
     of it and I do my best to avoid treating any group or individual
     differently because of race, gender, social class or disability. I
     discourage any expression of prejudice from the children.
3   I try to avoid treating any individual or group differently because
     of race, gender, social class or disability.
4   I try to treat all children in the same way.

2 The children

Education at school is about children learning. Children are different from one another and are likely to respond differently to different approaches and treatment. Any group of children, however homogeneous, is a collection of very different individuals. It is not really possible or efficient for children to be taught individually in school, but they do need some individual attention. If, as a teacher, you are to help them all to learn, giving some consideration to individual needs, you must find enough common strands to enable some work to take place in a group or as a class. It is then possible to get the majority started and use this as an opportunity to work with individuals.

The differences among children are particularly evident at the beginning of schooling, whether this is in a playgroup, a nursery class or a reception class. They come to school with ideas and interests and ways of looking at things and with differing experience. Cohen and Cohen (1988: 49) note that children starting school for the first time have to adapt to the following:

- being part of a crowd of children, particularly in the playground;
- presence of fewer adults or unfamiliar adults at playtime and dinner time;
- organisational processes such as lining up, queuing or waiting;
- competition for adult attention – involves waiting and fewer opportunities for one-to-one conversation;
- being addressed as one of a group or class;
- restrictions on movement and noise;
- organisational constraints on time, the possibility of being last or left behind.

A very important consideration for teachers at all stages of primary education is the degree of experience that children bring to their learning. A child will only understand what you say if he can bring relevant experience to the interpretation of your words. Any new piece of work should start with a consideration of the experience which children will bring to it and the experiences to which you will introduce them. It is very easy to overestimate the experience which children have and to assume that because they use words they have the experience which enables them to understand the meaning of the words.

The process of organising children's learning so that curricular aims can be achieved involves bringing together the needs, ideas, interests, experiences and characteristics of the children with the knowledge, skill, experience and personality of the teacher within a given environment. It is therefore very important to consider what children are like and how they learn.

Child development

Teachers of children at the primary stage of education are usually very conscious of the children's development, partly because development at this stage is so rapid and partly because in the past a good deal of emphasis has been placed on child development in initial teacher training.

The importance of this knowledge for the teacher lies in the decisions which have to be made about suitable times and methods for teaching particular things to particular children. Most teachers have encountered the child who has some difficulty in tying shoe laces or forming letters who, six months later, performs these tasks easily. The problem is that in any given class there will be children at a variety of stages of maturity as well as varying abilities and somehow the teacher has to see that they all learn.

A child comes into the world with a legacy of inherited abilities, tendencies and characteristics. Throughout the years of schooling each child is developing as an individual person. Home and school environment interact with the inherited abilities and tendencies and the child discovers personal talents and abilities, interests and limitations. The adults and children around provide models and a child will test out behaviour in play and in everyday living, persisting with some kinds of behaviour and modifying or abandoning others in the light of the responses which come.

Children have also developed ideas about the world by the time they start school and these will be modified by their experience in and out of school. In science in particular, the ideas children have developed may be a barrier to observation and reasoning. Harlen (1985) describes how children cling to their own ideas in science even when experience shows them to be incorrect. In a similar way, Hughes (1986) describes the mathematical knowledge which most children have on entry to school and suggests that problems sometimes arise because children do not relate this knowledge to the language of school mathematics. It is therefore important for you as a teacher to become aware of children's ideas as a starting point for new learning. You can then direct their observation and thinking in ways which will help them to develop further.

Physical development

A child's physical attributes will have an effect on the emerging personality. A child who develops early will be at an advantage in being able to do things which others find difficult and will become more confident as a result.

This is particularly relevant in relation to the time of year when a child was born and the point at which he or she starts school. A child born in September is likely to be physically among the most developed in the class because he or she will be among the oldest. A child born in June, July or August is likely to be less well developed because he or she is among the youngest.

Mortimore *et al.* (1988) studied various aspects of classroom work in London schools, looking particularly at what makes effective teaching and an effective school. One important finding of this study was that teachers generally did not pay sufficient attention to the effects of differences in children's ages. They tended to regard the youngest children in the class as less able, rather than at an earlier stage of development. Teacher expectation is known to be important in motivating children, and, if children begin to think of themselves as less able, this is likely to affect the effort they put into their work and this in turn will affect their performance. In any case children who start school in the summer term have less time in the infant school than those who start in the autumn, and it is important that their developmental stage is taken into account.

Bennett and Kell (1989) studied four-year-olds in infant classes. They found that provision for this age group was generally not very suitable and that a large amount of time was spent on basic skills and very little on play. The time spent on play was also not very profitably used and took little account of the finding that play is more effective when adults take part in it and use it for the children's learning.

Physical development has a good many implications for teachers. Sight and hearing are not fully co-ordinated when a child starts school, and co-ordination may pose problems which will later solve themselves. It is also important for teachers of young children to be on the look out for defects not yet noticed. For example, a child may have very short or very long sight but will not realise that this is different from the norm until he or she makes comparisons with what someone else saw. Much the same is true of hearing. Colour blindness is also comparatively common in the population and most teachers will encounter colour-blind children. Children who have difficulty in distinguishing colours will have a number of difficulties in the classroom and the sooner this is recognised the better.

Intellectual development

Inhelder and Piaget (1958) describe the child's cognitive development as being in a number of stages which all children pass through at their own pace. The very young child, up to about two years of age, is in what they call the sensorimotor stage, when he or she is learning to co-ordinate movement and is discovering the world around. Children then enter the preoperational stage, which lasts until about seven years in most children. They are becoming more social but still tend to see the world as revolving around themselves.

From about seven years of age children enter a stage of concrete operations when they begin to see the world more logically but are still tied to action. Finally, often by the age of about eleven, but sometimes much later, children reach a stage of formal and abstract operations when they can reason and think systematically. They may regress to earlier stages in the face of some situations and problems.

Piaget (1952) suggested that intellectual behaviour was always involved in a person's adaptation to his or her environment. In the process of adapting, the individual uses two processes, *assimilation* and *accommodation*. In assimilating new information the child first takes it in. He then tries to relate what he perceives to his existing knowledge and understanding, which is accommodation. This may mean making adjustments to how he thinks about his existing knowledge or adjusting the new knowledge to fit with what he knows already.

Gardner (1983) suggests that human beings have a number of different kinds of intelligence. These include linguistic, musical, logical-mathematical and scientific, bodily-kinaesthetic, which includes art, and personal intelligence or ability to get on with other people. In planning the programme for children, you need to be aware of the possibility that individuals may have different types of intelligence and allow opportunities for these to develop.

Emotional development

Emotional responses are a primitive response to danger and are controlled by a different part of the brain from that which controls rational thinking. Human beings respond emotionally more quickly than they respond intellectually, and children have to learn to control their emotional responses and teachers need to help them with this.

Goleman (1996: 34) makes the point that emotional intelligence probably plays a larger part in how we do in life than intelligence quotient (IQ). He suggests that 'At best, IQ contributes about 20 per cent to the factors which determine life success, which leaves 80 per cent for other forces'. Other characteristics are important: 'abilities such as being able to motivate oneself and persist in the face of frustrations; to control impulse and delay gratification; to regulate one's moods and keep distress from sampling the ability to think; to emphasise and to hope'.

He notes that 'Much evidence testifies that people who are emotionally adept – who know and manage their own feelings – are at an advantage in any domain of life, whether romance and intimate relationships or picking up the unspoken rules that govern success in organisational politics' (p. 36).

Goleman (1996: 43) suggests that there are the following aspects of emotional intelligence:

1   Knowing one's own emotions – self-awareness – recognising a feeling *as it happens*.
2   Managing emotion.
3   Motivating oneself. Emotional self-control. Marshalling emotions in the service of a goal.
4   Recognising emotions in others.
5   Handling relationships.

If you are to help children to develop these skills, you need to find time to discuss feelings with children. Such a discussion can start with children thinking of an occasion when they felt happy or sad and you can go on to discuss situations when children felt angry. Anger can be an overwhelming feeling, particularly for young children, and many want to hit out at someone when they feel angry. It helps to discuss possible alternative ways of behaving by getting children to think through situations in which they have felt angry.

Children who not only manage their own emotions but who are also sensitive to the feelings of others make better relationships with their peer group and are more popular. Children need help with recognising the ways others are feeling and you can help this by discussing with them the ways in which people show their feelings.

They may also need help in developing social skills and learning the non-verbal language of social behaviour. You can discuss how best to get involved in a game you want to join, how to deal with someone who is angry with you or is rude to you. Discussion of bullying can be part of this.

Many schools use *circle time* as a means of involving children in discussion of these kinds of issues. This is a discussion period where the teacher asks open-ended questions to get the children to talk about matters which are important to them.

The development of the self-image

Docking (1990: 7) describes the self-concept or self-image as follows:

> The self-concept is the picture of ourselves which we carry around and incorporates all those things which are important to us – relative and friend relationships, status, material possessions, other skills and hobbies. It is learned in detail as we grow up and glean information from what others do or say to us... The self-concept is learned... It is vital that early experiences are predominantly positive and that children come to see themselves as accepted, loved and successful.

The behaviour and response of other people towards a child helps to develop his or her self-image. Initially parents start this process. A child whose parents praise and encourage him or her becomes confident in the ability to do things and is more likely to become a confident and competent adult than the child whose parents behave in a more negative way.

When the child starts school, teachers continue this process and at the primary stage much is happening that is important for the development of the self-image. The extent to which a child is praised or scolded or is acknowledged to achieve success or failure influences his or her attitudes and behaviour. All of us react positively to praise when we know it is genuine and deserved, and activities in which other people tell us we have succeeded are those most likely to be repeated. Conversely, failure tends to make us want to avoid the activity in which we have failed. In this sense the teacher reinforces some kinds of learning and also acts negatively by identifying the behaviour to be eliminated.

Askew and Wiliam (1995: 18) suggest that what is important for praise to be effective is that it is:

- *Contingent.* The praise must depend upon some particular thing the pupil has done, rather than the pupil's general performance.
- *Specific.* The praise should identify the specific behaviour being praised, so that the pupil is aware of what aspect of his or her work is being singled out for praise.
- *Credible.* The praise must be sincere; praise that follows a formula (i.e. is always expressed in the same way) or which sounds insincere is likely to be ineffective because pupils can 'see through' such praise very quickly.

Effective praise leads to the development of self-esteem, which is important for learning.

Askew and Wiliam (1995: 28) go on to say:

> If [pupils] have confidence in their ability they will expect to be successful often and, in order to gain more positive confirmation of their ability, they will seek challenges and show persistence in the face of difficulties. ... However, if they lack confidence in their ability, they will try to avoid challenges and show little persistence because they believe they are likely to fail and be 'shown up'.

Barnes (1999: 10) suggests that 'If children have low academic self-esteem, the chances are that instead of involving themselves in tasks, they already rely on other strategies to feel important. ... The pay off for them is probably to be stopped and for attention and peer approval to be directed their way'.

There is evidence that teachers reinforce some children more effectively than others. Kelly (1988), for example, in a study which reviews research into gender differences, notes that there is considerable evidence that girls get less of the teacher's attention in class than boys. This would seem to be true for all ages, ethnic groups and social classes in all subjects and for male and female teachers. Crane and Mellon (1978) found that teachers tended to think well-behaved children had a higher academic potential than those who were less well behaved. Galton and Delafield (1981) found that there was a tendency for children for whom the teacher had high expectations to achieve more praise and contact with the teacher than low achievers, who received less praise and less feedback on their work. Tizard *et al.* (1988) found that boys generally received more criticism than girls, that Black boys received most criticism and disapproval and that White girls the least criticism and least praise.

Children also praise and criticise one another and this also contributes to their learning. They are building up pictures of themselves being good at this and bad at that, able to get on well with other people or having problems in making relationships and so on. By the time they leave primary school they are already confident in their ability to do some things and worried about their performance in others.

Children's self-images are also revealed in the way they relate to others. A child with a poor self-image will expect others to respond negatively and will often contribute to this reaction by his or her behaviour.

Parsons *et al.* (1976) found that girls tended to assess their abilities as being lower than they are in actuality. Girls were also more worried about failure and more sensitive to negative information; this was evident from the age of about four.

The development of the self-image is closely related to the effect of the expectation of others for the progress of a particular child. If the child's parents or teacher demonstrate that they have high expectations of him or her, there is more likelihood that the child will achieve and vice versa. This can work for the child if the adults have high expectations which the child fulfils. He or she is then reinforced by success and starts the next task with increased confidence. There is also the complementary problem that parents and teachers can pressure children with their expectations to the extent that children eventually give up trying because they do not think they can live up to such expectations.

Alternatively, the expectations of others can give rise to an increasingly negative cycle in which the child fails, the teacher lowers expectation and the child's self-image is lowered correspondingly. Your professional task as teacher is to get the level of expectation high enough to challenge and encourage and yet be within each child's capacity.

Edwards and Mercer (1987) suggest that failure is too often seen as the property of pupils, whereas it may be the outcome of the communicative process. What is needed is a more effective structuring of what is to be learned.

There is a good deal of research evidence to suggest that teachers underestimate some children within the class and overestimate others.

The study by Mortimore *et al.* (1988) that showed teachers underestimating the younger children in the class has already been mentioned. Teachers also tended to overestimate the boys compared with the girls. Bennett *et al.* (1984) describes work in infant classrooms in which the researchers checked how well the work that individual children were given matched their ability. They found that there was a tendency for teachers to underestimate high attainers. Twenty-five per cent of tasks given to the children were misdiagnosed. At the same time teachers tended to overestimate some low attainers. Teachers in other studies have been found to underestimate children from working-class backgrounds and Black children.

The development of the self-image is also closely bound up with the physical, social and emotional development of the child. Part of the self-image will concern the child's physical appearance, and this may affect confidence and social development and the way in which the child learns to cope with personal feelings and reactions. There is some evidence that girls, in particular, are starting to become anorexic at the primary school stage. You need to very sensitive to this and try to help individuals to cope with the way others treat them and at the same time encourage children to be sensitive to each other.

Children also develop ideas about other people. Carrington and Short (1989) describe how almost half the infants in a council estate primary school thought that it was possible for people to change colour and that Black parents did not necessarily have Black children and vice versa. At the very early stages very few children saw racism as a problem about being Black, but from year 4 in the junior school almost all children recognised this. Year 6 children in particular were aware of racial stereotyping.

Language development

Language development is one of the most important areas of work for the teacher and is rightly regarded as the corner-stone of each child's education. The ability to use language determines not only the nature of a person's relationships with others and the ability to co-operate but also, to some extent, the ability to think because language is the medium of a good deal of human thought. Initially children do much of their thinking out loud and this conversation with themselves gradually becomes inner speech.

Language is also the main medium by which children learn. Edwards and Mercer (1987: 164) describe the way in which teachers have to work to achieve common understanding in the language used in the classroom. They stress the importance of classroom talk as a means of learning and suggest that what is needed is 'sharing, comparing, contrasting and arguing perspectives against those of others'. They also stress the need for children to reflect on what is being learned.

The development of language skills is far from being a simple matter. A child starting school at five has already made tremendous progress in language development. Most children, by this age, have a vocabulary of more than 2,000 words, but, more importantly, they have acquired knowledge of the structure of the language as it is used in their home environment. They can form sentences which they have never heard spoken; they can speak of the past and the future as well as the present; they know the meanings which lie behind word order, that 'man bites dog' has a different meaning from 'dog bites man', which is conveyed by the way the words are put together. They have learned the language necessary to express needs, ideas and thoughts, to ask questions, to seek co-operation from others as well as many other things. Even where the language used at home is far from standard English, it will have a structure and consistency of its own and the child will have learned to apply its rules. This is equally true for children with a different home language.

The intellectual achievement this represents is very considerable. No one intentionally teaches preschool children the rules of language, and preschool children do not know them as something to repeat but as something to apply. The acquisition of this knowledge requires reasoning power of a high order and it is interesting that one can sometimes see the process at work in the mistakes a child makes. The child who says 'mouses' instead of 'mice' or 'runned' instead of 'ran', for example, is demonstrating an ability to apply the rule correctly, but hasn't realised that there are exceptions.

We can conclude from this that children are capable of particular kinds of reasoning and abstraction from an early age if these are in context. We might go further and note that not only is there evidence of the motivation to communicate, but also many children appear to enjoy the challenge involved. It suggests that, if we can find ways of tapping motivation of this strength, the power for learning in children is far greater than we normally see in school. It also supports the view that learning is likely to be better when children are asked to reason something through rather than just remember it.

This learning and reasoning is all related in the first instance to particular situations. Children start acquiring vocabulary and language structure in particular contexts. By the time they are five, they are already using language to refer to and discuss what is not present, but they acquired and used the language initially in particular situations and generalised from these. Tizard and Hughes (1984) studied a group of preschool girls from working-class and middle-class homes and found that mothers in virtually all cases talked to children of people and situations which were not present.

The fact that children acquire language in particular situations has important implications for later learning. Young children may frequently use the same words as an adult, but give them a more limited meaning. For example, the child for whom the word 'holiday' means an air journey to foreign parts will interpret the word differently from a child whose family spends holidays at home, perhaps going out for days. The child who lives on a remote farm has a different understanding of the word 'neighbour' from the child who lives in a block of flats or in a back-to-back terrace or a council estate.

Even a teacher of older children should never assume that because a child uses particular words he or she gives them a similar meaning to that given by the teacher. Language is a way of representing the world to yourself and of talking about it to other people. Children start by talking about what is present, then develop the ability to talk about what is not present and the words gradually become the 'inner speech' of their thoughts. It seems likely that young children need to think aloud a good deal in the process of developing the ability to think silently in their minds.

When teachers talk of extending children's language they normally think first about adding to vocabulary. There is also a case for emphasising language structure and considering those words which help to organise thinking. Prepositions, for example, represent relationships among objects or people. Comparative words are also important in representing similarities and differences in relationships, and a variety of pronouns, conjunctions and other words relate the parts of what we say and enable us to express increasingly complex ideas and relationships. Discussion about the structure of language is an important part of the literacy strategy.

Words also provide a convenient way of sorting out thinking into categories; much as in learning mathematics, children sort things into sets according to their attributes. Words such as 'good', 'kind', 'naughty' are sorting words which are learned early, but the process goes on right through schooling and we expect children to be able to classify in many areas of work. For example, in geography, we classify soil characteristics, landscape types and so on; in science we classify plants, animals, substances, forces, etc.; and there are many other ways in which this process occurs in most aspects of the curriculum. It is the basis of the ability to generalise and to reason from one premise to the next and thus to be able to apply what is known to new situations.

Factors which affect learning

The major task of the teacher is to enable children to learn. While some of the factors which affect the child's learning can, at best, only be modified rather than changed, there is a good deal of evidence to show that the school and teacher have an important influence. Mortimore *et al.* (1988) in the primary schools and Rutter *et al.* (1979) in the secondary schools showed that schools make a difference. Mortimore *et al.* (1988) found that the most successful school in their study of fifty schools was better than the average by 28 per cent after differences in social background and ability had been allowed for. The least successful school was 19 per cent below the average for the sample.

The teacher who is aware of the factors that can be changed may be better placed to help a child. However, it is important not to regard these background factors as making it impossible for the child to make progress. Children in the successful schools in the Mortimore study made progress in spite of background factors.

The effect of home background

A major influence on a child's performance at school is his home background. This was clearly demonstrated many years ago in the study by Douglas (1964) which checked the IQ of a large sample of children at eight and again at eleven and related what had happened to them to their social background. Those children who came from a middle-class background increased their scores during this period, whereas the children from working-class homes stood still or decreased their scores.

In the first five years of life, children's learning in language and reasoning is substantial. They will also have learned something about the behaviour which brings approval and that which brings trouble, including some ideas about when to manifest different behaviours. They will have watched the activities of their parents and adopted some of their values and in play will have imitated them and other adults, trying out different kinds of behaviour to see what kind of response they get.

A child's home background may support school learning in a number of important ways which affect his or her ability to take from what is offered:

1   *The language of home and school*
The use of language that children experience at home may be very different from that used in school or it may be very similar. It may differ not only in vocabulary and structure, but also in the extent to which it is used to discuss ideas, respond to new experiences and talk about things. Discussion with children is very important and teachers need to consider a variety of ways of stimulating children to talk and think. Merely talking is not enough. You need to ask questions which stimulate inventiveness, use stories to introduce new ways of looking at things, encourage children to consider what a situation looks like from someone else's point of view and so on.

2   *Preschool experience*
The experiences children have been offered in the years before school are closely related to their use of language, and what they have gained from any experience will depend to a considerable extent on the way their parents have used the opportunities available. A child visiting the supermarket with a parent who knows how to use the opportunity for the child's learning may gain more than another child taken to distant places for an expensive holiday. Experience of nursery school or playgroup will also provide a background of understanding for some children.

3   *Adult interest*
Children's readiness to learn when they first come to school will also be affected by the extent to which their parents and other adults have been able to give time to them, listening to what they say and asking questions, extending their interests by sharing them.

4   *Family background*
Family size and the child's position in the family will influence the amount of adult care and conversation a child enjoys. There are now several studies of substantial numbers of children which demonstrate that the larger the family the lower the average intelligence score for all the children in the family. This is clearly described in the account by Davie *et al.* (1972) of seven-year-olds studied as part of the National Child Development Study. This documented the progress of all the children born in one week in March 1958.

It is also the case that the first and eldest child in the family tends to be more intelligent than the next and so on down the line. This sort of finding only shows up when the sample studied is very large.

5   *Social class*

Mortimore *et al.* (1988) considered the social class background, as defined by the occupation of both parents of each child in their study. The occupation of both parents was associated with achievement in reading at entry to junior school and with achievement in mathematics. Children who had fathers in non-manual work made better progress than those with fathers in manual work, but the mother's occupation did not appear to affect progress. Father's social class was also significant in oracy. Teachers in this study also noted a higher incidence of behaviour problems from children whose parents were in manual occupations.

Hughes (1986) found that there was almost a year's difference between middle- and working-class children in their knowledge of numbers. He also found that attendance at nursery school or class appeared to make little difference to this.

The study by Tizard and Hughes (1984) of working-class and middle-class girls at home and at nursery school found no significant social class differences in the number of conversations the children had with their mothers, in the length of the conversations or the number of words used by either the mothers or their daughters. However, they found that middle-class mothers used language for complex purposes significantly more than the working-class mothers. They discussed a larger range of topics with their children and a larger proportion of their conversations were concerned with topics that went beyond the here and now. They also conveyed more information to their children and used a larger vocabulary.

Tizard and Hughes' (1984) study of the language used in nursery school suggested that there was a much smaller amount of talk with adults in school than at home. On average the children took part in ten conversations per hour compared with twenty-seven conversations per hour with their mothers. School conversations were more adult dominated than at home, with the characteristic conversation being a question-and-answer session with the children just answering rather than questioning. The children asked twenty-six questions per hour of their mothers, but only two per hour of the adults at school. The working-class girls were much less likely to approach the staff with a question than the middle-class girls.

This study suggests that teachers should be careful not to take an oversimplistic view of the differences between working-class and middle-class children and be hesitant about assuming that working-class children have a more limited use of language at home. The use of language may well be non-standard and less demanding but the working-class mothers in the study spent as much time talking to their children as the middle-class mothers.

Ethnic origin

Teachers in many schools work with children from different ethnic backgrounds. Houlton (1988) suggested that they need:

> A grasp of the key factors of the cultural systems of the main ethnic groups living in Britain. At a minimum level these would include awareness of languages spoken, religious beliefs, names and naming systems, dress styles and dietary habits. For teachers working in close contact with ethnic minority children a much larger database may be needed.

He goes on to suggest that this database might include rules of etiquette, value systems, customs and traditions, child-rearing practices and family structures.

Tizard *et al.* (1988) studied the education of young children at school in the inner city, looking particularly at the development of children of Afro-Caribbean origin. Black in their study did not include Asians. They found that at the end of nursery schooling there were few differences in attainment between Black and White children and between boys and girls. During the infant school period Black girls made more progress than White girls or boys or Black boys. White boys made slightly more progress than White girls and Black boys made the least progress. They also studied the home background of each of these groups of children and found little to account for the differences in progress. The Black parents appeared to take just as much interest in their children's schooling as the White parents and were equally concerned to help their children.

Gillborn and Mirza (2000: 17) note that 'Available evidence suggests that the inequalities of attainment for African-Caribbean pupils become progressively greater as they move through the school system; such differences become more pronounced between the end of primary school and the end of secondary education'.

Gender differences

There is now a great deal on information about the differences between boys and girls. Boys tend to be behind girls in development all the way through the primary school and they also tend to get more attention from the teacher, possibly because they are more demanding. The difference in developmental level means that they are behind the girls in language work in particular, although they usually do well in mathematics and any technical subjects. Boys tend to be at the extremes of the ability range more often than girls and there are usually more boys than girls with special needs. Docking (1990) in a study of junior school children found that gender was significantly related to the length and quality of children's writing in the first year of the junior school with girls outperforming boys, and this initial superiority was maintained throughout the junior years.

Mortimore *et al.* (1988) found that girls had a more positive attitude to school than boys and more positive self-concepts. Far more boys than girls were rated by their teachers as having behaviour problems. Docking (1990) also found that, in each year of the junior school, boys expressed a much less positive view of school than girls and boys were much less likely than girls to rate themselves highly on items concerning personal anxiety.

Tizard *et al.* (1988) found that teachers tended to assess girls' ability as being lower than that of boys. Similarly, Sammons and Mortimore (1990) also found that, even though girls outperformed boys to a considerable extent, teachers' assessments of their children tended to favour the boys, although the difference was not significant.

Whyte (1988: 153) observed young children playing and found that:

> In both sexes, the tendency to conform to conventional sex-role behaviour is exaggerated when others are present. In a study set in a playroom, it was found that children who played with cross-sex toys (boys with dishes and dolls, girls with trucks and aeroplanes) abandoned them in favour of a 'sex appropriate' toy when another child entered their play-space.

Whyte also found that teachers had stereotypes about gender which affected the way they treated children. They tended to encourage the behaviour they believed existed, e.g. by complimenting boys on their strength but not girls.

Security and learning

Two further aspects of children's learning may be considered here. Children, like adults, feel secure when they are able to assess a situation and predict what might happen. In school, children are likely to feel secure when they have summed up the teacher and can guess to some extent how he or she will react. They need to know:

- what the teacher expects of them;
- how to get his or her approval;
- what they may and may not do;
- where they may and may not go;
- what they may and may not use;
- when they may or may not do certain things.

Most people placed in an insecure situation work to achieve security. The right amount of insecurity may provide motivation for learning, but insecurity which causes anxiety may be crippling. Anyone who, as a child, was taught by a teacher who appeared to be frightening will recall being preoccupied with fear and insecurity which got in the way of learning. It is a difficult professional task for the teacher to create enough challenge for the child who is confident and at the same time maintain security for the less confident.

On entry to school, most children feel some measure of insecurity and some feel very insecure indeed, however carefully they have been prepared for school and however welcoming the school is. There is also insecurity when children move to a new class with a new teacher and when children transfer from infant or first school to junior or middle school and from primary to secondary school. Studies of transfer from primary to secondary school have found a large measure of anxiety. Children are usually worried about losing their way in a much larger building and there is also usually some concern that there will be bullying.

Motivation

Part of your task as a teacher is to find ways of motivating every child in the group. This is most likely to happen when teacher, children and their parents share a common goal and can see ways of achieving it. Motivation may be intrinsic, as when a child is absorbed in a topic because of its interest to him or her, or extrinsic, when the child is motivated by a goal which is separate from the work itself – such as getting good marks, stars, praise or some other reward. A teacher should aim to use intrinsic motivation as much as possible while accepting that there is a place for extrinsic motivation.

Most people are motivated by pleasant associations with an activity. A child who paints a picture or writes a story which is praised by the teacher and by other children will try to repeat this success and the reward it brings in approbation.

Much of our thinking about library areas in primary schools over recent years has involved making a space into an attractive area for reading, in the hope that this will create pleasant feelings in children's minds so that they come to associate reading with pleasant surroundings and see it as an enjoyable activity.

Young children want to please the adult. This is a great responsibility for the teacher and you need to be sure that the efforts made to please you are worthwhile in their own right. You need to be able to justify what you are doing from an educational point of view as well as doing something to please the children and perhaps their parents.

The list which follows is a review of the ways in which people can be motivated. It may be useful in deciding what to do about a particular child or group to review the list, considering the possibilities in relation to the problem in question.

1   *Inner need*
    Human beings have a number of strong drives associated in the
    first instance with the need for food and shelter and the need to
    maintain territory and reproduce. We need to give and receive
    love, gain recognition for our contributions to a group and
    experience responsibility. When a child is motivated by this kind
    of inner need, there appears to be a greater power for learning.
    This is most evident in initial language learning, where the need to
    learn is great.

2   *First-hand experience*
    We have already noted that children's experience is limited. Seeing
    and doing for oneself is motivating, and it is important for children's
    development in all aspects of their work that they have a good
    deal of experience in looking, hearing, touching, smelling and even
    perhaps tasting, so that they build images of experience to furnish
    their thinking.

3   *A stimulating environment*
    Most primary school teachers are concerned to create an attractive
    learning environment, but it needs to be used by the teacher and
    children and it may be useful to ask yourself from time to time
    whether what you have on display could spark off work from
    different children.

4   *A desire for mastery or a problem which is challenging*
    Problem-solving or mastering a skill is an enjoyable human activity,
    as may be seen from the popularity of crosswords and other puzzles

and games of skill and particularly from children's enthusiasm for computer games. Part of your task as teacher is to offer your children opportunities to work out ideas and tackle problems within their capacity. For example, the child who has worked out the spelling rule that the vowel before a single consonant is usually long and that before a double consonant usually short (e.g. caned and canned) is much more likely to remember it than the child who is given the rule and told to learn it. Young and less able children get too few opportunities for this kind of activity, partly because their reasoning power is underestimated. They tend, as a result, to get less practice using reasoning and less chance to improve their skill. The trick is to find the level of problem which is within their capacity.

Computers play an important part here. There are many games which teach valuable skill and knowledge and there are also some straightforward teaching programmes.

5   *Competition*
Human beings are naturally competitive and most teachers use this to some extent. Even if you avoid competitive situations, the children and their parents are likely to make comparisons. Competition is motivating, but the trouble with it is that children may place too much emphasis on winning, getting a good mark or whatever the reward may be, and too little on the learning itself. The second difficulty is that some children tend to be losers every time and this is not good for their self-image and consequent attitude to work.

Nevertheless, competition is useful, especially if it is a matter of beating your own previous performance or vying with someone of similar ability. In short, competition is useful but needs to be used with care.

6   *Self-improvement*
A person who has clear goals is more likely to succeed than someone with little sense of direction. If you can help children to identify their own sets of short-term targets, their natural desire for improvement will support their learning.

7   *Co-operation*
There is satisfaction in working with a partner or as part of a group and a degree of pressure to contribute which can be motivating. The skills of working with other people are important life skills and children need to learn how to co-operate.

8   *Teaching someone else*
This can be a valuable way of working for everyone involved

because the 'teacher' has to learn first and then get another child to learn. The child doing the teaching reinforces his or her own knowledge in the process of helping someone else.

A pair of classes differing in age might work together on something such as an environmental study, with the children in the older class each having a 'pupil' from the younger class. This provides 'teachers' on a one-to-one basis, and the achievement of the older children may be judged on how well the younger children have learned. The motivation involved in this is considerable.

9   *Audio-visual equipment and computers*
There is no doubt that equipment which 'does' something is motivating. At a comparatively simple level, the tape recorder is attractive to children partly because they can control it. The most attractive and motivating is the computer, and given the appropriate software children can learn a great deal from it with very little help from the teacher. Computers are likely to become more important as voice recognition becomes more generally available.

An important aspect of motivation is the way in which children attribute their success in a task. Edwards and Knight (1994: 17) speak of the 'importance of allowing children to attribute their success to stable, controllable, changeable factors that are often within the child and their failures to unstable, controllable, changeable external causes'. Children need to be encouraged to think that success follows effort rather than assuming that one is either clever or not clever and that this determines success. They should also be encouraged to regard failure as attributable to lack of effort rather than lack of ability.

3 The class profile

The ability to observe children and interpret their behaviour is a basic teaching skill. When you get a new group of children, you need to spend time observing and talking with them in order to be able to teach them effectively.

In the past many teachers have taken the view that they wanted to see new children with fresh eyes and they were therefore not interested in what other teachers had to say about them. While this view is understandable, it is one which is no longer tenable so far as the curriculum is concerned. A teacher who wishes to start afresh is quite properly taking the view that he or she may relate differently to a child or group of children from the previous teacher and does not want to prejudice the relationship by looking at the children through someone else's eyes. Where a record is concerned with a teacher's opinion about a child and his or her potential, it makes a certain amount of sense to want to see with fresh eyes, but a factual record of the child's achievement and the stage he or she has reached is important information for the next teacher and all members of staff need to work together to see that the records that each one is keeping are really useful to the next teacher.

There are many things you need to find out in advance if you are to make the most of your first days with a new class (Analysis 3.1). It is wise to prepare by getting all the factual information you can from the previous teacher about the children you will be teaching. This is different from getting opinions, although all assessment has an element of subjectivity. You will be particularly concerned to find out the level each child has reached in the National Curriculum and, where relevant, how he or she has performed in the Standard Assessment Tasks (SATs). You also need to know such things as the books each child has read, the phonic knowledge each of the younger children possesses, the mathematical skills each has acquired and so on (Analysis 3.2).

Analysis 3.1 Assessing a new class

Where children are coming into your class from another class within the school, or from a feeder school, their records should be studied for factual information:

1 Look for evidence of general ability, especially standardised test results and SATs; note exceptionally high or low performance and any discrepancies between ability and attainment.

2 See if there are any physical problems, such as poor sight, hearing or poor co-ordination; note any children who should wear glasses or hearing aids and any with conditions such as asthma or epilepsy which may need care.

3 Note any children with learning problems, including gaps in schooling, changes of school, non-English-speaking background and so on.

4 Note any other children with special needs, including any who might have been in special schools and any with exceptional ability.

5 Note any children with home problems likely to affect the child in school.

Analysis 3.2 New children

You need to talk with the teacher(s) who have had the children previously:

1 Ask for any factual information about work attempted and achieved.

2 Enquire about teaching approaches and materials used and with what results.

3 Ask about children who appear to have special needs of all kinds, e.g. children with exceptionally high or low ability, children with problems of various kinds, children who are underfunctioning, who respond to particular approaches, who have particular skills or interests.

4 Find out what children with learning difficulties can actually do and what they actually know.

If possible, visit the children you will be teaching in their own classroom the previous term, perhaps arranging this by asking their teacher to change classes with you for a short time (Analysis 3.3). Use

Analysis 3.3 Classroom visit

During a classroom visit:

1 Identify children about whom it might be wise to know more.
2 Talk with the children about what they have been doing.
3 Look at the work of children who will be coming to you and make a special note of any who appear to be having difficulty or whose work appears to be outstanding.
4 Look at the general level of presentation of work and at what appears to be common practice.
5 Look for anything unusual e.g. the child whose presentation of work is poor but whose ideas are good; unusual ideas, points of view or use of language; unusual but persistent errors.

---

this opportunity to get a feel for the class as a group. How do they respond to questions? Are they quick with ideas and suggestions? Do they talk enthusiastically about what they have been doing?

This is only a broad preliminary to studying further all the children, but it alerts you to those who may most need study and those whose needs are likely to be different from those of the majority. It will also colour some of your overall planning and help you to remain sensitive to the fact that your class is composed of individuals. On the other hand, it is important not to let your initial summing up of children colour your expectations too much. The evidence suggests that when teachers are open about their expectations children can do very much better than when teachers' expectations are limited. It is very easy to label children prematurely. They could turn out to be very different from your initial impression and you need to keep this well in mind.

At this stage of planning it may be a good idea to look at children's ages. We saw earlier that the study by Mortimore *et al.* (1988) found that teachers were generally not aware of the different ages of children in their classes and made no allowances or differences in provision for them. It was evident in the study that teachers tended to regard the younger children as less able, although in reality they were progressing as well as older children but were at an earlier stage of development.

It may be helpful at this stage to start a loose-leaf ring file with a page for each child on which you can note things that happen which give you teaching information. In the first instance you will be noting points which have arisen as a result of your preliminary investigations. It is particularly important to do this for children who have special needs or are unusual in any way, whether exceptionally able or with particular kinds of problems. This may be the start of your record of these children.

If you teach a reception class you have a more difficult task in getting to know the children who will be coming to you except where your school has a nursery class. Other nursery classes and playgroups may also be ready to pass on information about the children. Most schools with reception classes invite mothers and children to visit the school on one or more occasions before they actually start and this may give you the opportunity to find out something about them, particularly if you get the chance to talk to the parents. If you can find out something about individual children's interests and their families you can at least start with some information which will help you to talk to new children and help them to feel at home.

Your organisation for the first few days needs to be very flexible so that you can adapt to the children as you go along. The baseline assessments of language and literacy, mathematics, personal and social development, knowledge and understanding of the world, physical development and creative development will help you to gather information which will be useful in planning teaching. This assessment also gives you a reference point for assessing how far children have progressed by the end of the year.

Whatever the age group you teach you will be making plans before the new school year starts. Try to plan your work for the first week with diagnostic work in mind. Plan fairly broad topics with work at a variety of levels and some open-ended questions. Choose, where possible, areas in which all children have a reasonable opportunity for success but which still provide challenges at various levels. For example, a story which provides a variety of work may be a good idea. It is likely to interest the children if the level is right and does not require complicated plans for organising work at a time when you are only just getting to know the children.

This early work may give you some opportunities for finding out children's interests and abilities in school work and possibly related activities out of school hours. Your prior knowledge of the able children and those with problems should enable you to pitch the work at a reasonable variety of levels and it is at this stage that your class file becomes useful. Note relevant points as they arise but don't try to do too much at once.

During the first few days with a new class you will be observing things such as the way children settle down to work, their comments and replies to questions, their first piece of writing and so on. These clues will quickly identify the problems and you will be noting the kinds of responses which particular work evokes from individuals. If you have a class other than reception, you will have information about each child's prior achievement in the National Curriculum and this will enable you to group children for any work on an ability basis.

If you have a reception class, you will be noting the children who settle into school easily and those for whom it is a traumatic change from home. You will also be getting to know parents as they bring and collect their children and using the opportunities to learn from them about each child and the parent's view of how he or she is settling into school.

In the classroom you will be noting which children choose which activities and the level of interest and concentration shown by individuals. You will be getting information from the baseline assessments you will be making and this will guide you in selecting work for the children. The need for baseline assessment means that you must be systematic in finding out about every child, studying a small number each day and recording your findings carefully and using this information to plan work.

With an older group you will need to go on from your preliminary observations to check some of them. At an early stage you can check things such as ability to concentrate and whether a child is right- or left-handed. You will want to hear each child read, and if you use miscue analysis (described by Southgate *et al.*, 1981) you will find out a good deal from the errors made. Collecting errors in written work and looking for patterns in the kinds of mistakes made is also useful.

If previous records do not tell you a great deal about children's prior achievement it may also be useful to undertake some testing. For example, group spelling tests designed to cover all the possible phonic variations may be helpful and enable you to check phonic knowledge. Tests in mathematics can be designed to give you information about children's knowledge and skill. There is much to be said for devising diagnostic tests for a number of aspects of the National Curriculum, so that you can tell what a child needs to learn, although it is wise not to do too much testing. A group of teachers might well spend time together devising test material for different aspects of the National Curriculum. Testing needs to be backed up by observation of how children actually tackle tasks in a subject such as science.

Your observation may also lead you to check sight and hearing if you see a child peering to see or holding his or her head in a way which suggests he or she isn't hearing too well. A simple check on sight is to ask a child what he or she sees at a distance and what close to. You can check hearing by standing behind a child and asking him or her to repeat what you say. If you find a child who has difficulty with either of these two senses it should be reported and parents informed about the problem as soon as possible.

A very important part of this preliminary observation process is the discussion with the child and the parents about how they view things. This should give you an idea of what motivates a particular child and help you to identify attitudes. It will also offer you an opportunity to enlist the child's interest in meeting his or her particular needs and problems and also to enlist the parents' support.

The task from then on is one of matching work to individuals and small groups. The study by Bennett *et al.* (1984), described earlier, suggested that although teachers are generally keen to try to meet the needs of individuals they are not always very good at it. Bennett *et al.* (1984) found that teachers did not easily accept that some children had work which was too easy. The main reasons for this appeared to be, first, poor diagnosis and, second, failure in task design. Another study by Bennett and Kell (1989) found that teachers tended to equate busy work with work that was well matched.

4 Effective teaching

Recent years have seen a good deal of concern with making teaching and learning more effective. There is now a substantial body of research into effective teaching and learning coming from studies in Britain and the USA. Dean (2000: 4) summarises findings made by various researchers about effective teaching as follows:

- Effective teachers prepare well and have clear goals for their teaching.
- They aim to make as much teaching contact with all their children as possible.
- They have high expectations for all children.
- They make clear presentations which match the level of the children.
- They structure work well and tell children the purpose of the work they are doing and the targets they hope the children will achieve.
- They are flexible in varying teaching behaviour and activities.
- They use many higher order questions which demand thinking on the part of the children.
- They give frequent feedback to children about how they are doing.
- They make appropriate use of praise for both achievement and behaviour.
- They keep good records of the attainment and progress of individual children and these are shared and used. Progress in learning is constantly assessed.
- Their classrooms are well organised, ordered and attractive.
- They reflect on the work they and the children have done and evaluate progress towards goals.

We might also add that good teachers are secure in their subject knowledge at a level well above that of the demands of the children they are teaching.

Hay McBer (2000) made a study of teacher effectiveness for the Department for Education and Employment. They identified three main factors within the control of teachers which significantly influenced pupils' progress. These were teaching skills, professional characteristics and classroom climate. The professional characteristics they describe as ongoing patterns of behaviour that combine to determine the things that teachers typically do. Classroom climate describes the collective perceptions of the pupils on the aspects of their environment which have a direct impact on their capacity to learn. Hay McBer (2000: 17) identify five clusters of characteristics of outstanding teachers. These are:

- *Professionalism* – providing challenge and support for pupils, developing confidence, creating trust and respect for others.
- *Thinking* – analytical and conceptual thinking.
- *Planning and setting expectations* – demonstrating a drive for improvement, seeking information about how pupils are reacting, using initiative.
- *Leading* – demonstrating flexibility, holding people accountable, managing pupils, showing a passion for learning.
- *Relating to others* – having impact and influence, good teamwork, understanding others.

Classroom climate is an important factor in pupils' progress and achievement, and a good classroom climate is something which teachers can create. The report describes the classroom climate established by outstandingly effective teachers. In their classrooms there is:

- *Clarity.* What are the aims of the lesson? How does the lesson fit into the broader subject and into the aims and objectives of the school?
- *Order.* Is there discipline, order and civilised behaviour in class? Standards of behaviour and achievement – there should be a clear focus on higher standards, not minimum standards.
- *Fairness.* Is there favouritism? Is there a clear link between pupils' performance and reward?
- *Participation.* Do pupils have a chance to join in discussion, ask questions, give out materials?
- *Support.* Are pupils emotionally supported? Are they willing to try new things and learn from mistakes?
- *Safety.* Do pupils feel safe from emotional or physical bullying or are they at risk?

- *Interest.* Are pupils stimulated to learn?
- *Environment.* Is it comfortable, clean, well organised and attractive?

Cullingford (1995: 17) describes a survey of teachers to find out which behaviours helped children to learn. The following were clear indicators:

- being clear and enthusiastic;
- using a variety of approaches and questions;
- not wasting time, yet not giving straight information;
- giving children opportunities to learn.

There was one thing that did not help – being critical.

Barnes (1999: 4) suggests that teaching should be positive. 'Positive teaching assumes that we will make the most of pupils' potential, building on and describing their successes, rather than defining their limitations.' He suggests that the teacher should try whenever possible to frame comments from a positive point of view.

Tizard *et al.* (1988) studied young children in the inner city at home and at school and concluded that the teacher variables were more important than the home variables in explaining differences in children's progress. They found that curriculum coverage and teacher expectations had important implications for progress.

The study of London junior schools by Mortimore *et al.* (1988: 250) looked at the factors associated with an effective school and which the school could control. They found that the following were important:

- purposeful leadership by the headteacher;
- the involvement of the deputy head;
- consistency among teachers;
- intellectually challenging teaching;
- the work-centred environment;
- limited focus within sessions, i.e. not more than two subjects dealt with at one time;
- maximum communication between teacher and pupils;
- record-keeping;
- parental involvement;
- positive climate.

This study also notes a number of ways in which individual teachers were effective. There was a relationship between the teacher's enthusiasm and the work provided for the children. The most effective teachers frequently involved the whole class in discussion and were skilled at doing this, which was not necessarily whole-class teaching as such. They also found that where teachers spent a high proportion of time with individuals this had a negative effect, presumably because this results in a very small amount of time for each child.

A similar finding was made by Gipps (1992: 19), who suggests that:

> All the evidence points to the fact that when teachers take as their main focus individual children most of their interactions are routine, organisational and low-level; the children, by contrast, get little teacher attention, working mostly on their own. As a result extended discussions with children about the tasks – including higher order questions and statements – are severely limited.

Recent years have seen an emphasis on target-setting at all levels, for individuals and groups of children, for whole classes, for whole schools, for local authorities and nationally. Target-setting should evolve from the assessments you make of children's progress and achievement and should lead to further planning. Both the literacy and numeracy strategies suggest short meetings with individual children at which targets for their progress are agreed and their success in meeting them subsequently assessed.

Mortimore *et al.* (1988) found that effective teachers gave rewards rather than punishments because punishment had a negative effect on learning. They spent a lot of time talking to pupils about their work and this had a positive effect on progress. They made good use of praise (but it was evident from this and from a number of studies that many teachers made only a very limited use of praise and rarely praised children for good behaviour). They created a high level of industry within their classrooms and organised work so that there was always plenty for the children to do. Their lessons were stimulating and this led to the formation of positive relationships between teacher and children.

Various pieces of research throw some doubt on what was formerly regarded as good primary practice. Bennett (1976) found that more formal teaching in the basic skills in primary schools gave better results. However, the best results of all in his study were from a teacher who worked informally but in a structured way, and boys did better in informal classrooms. There were also some queries about the nature of his samples.

Mortimore *et al.* (1988) found that children did better if lessons were concerned with a single subject, or at most two subjects, and if they were given only limited responsibility for their work and limited choice over a short period. On the other hand, there was a positive effect where pupils worked on the same task as others of roughly the same ability but at their own level. There was a negative result when the whole class worked on the same task. They also found that very high levels of pupil interaction were negatively associated with progress.

Sammons *et al.* (1995: 52) confirmed the finding of Mortimore *et al.* (1988) that teachers found problems if they had several curriculum areas running at the same time:

> Teachers can have great difficulty in successfully managing children's learning in sessions where work in several curriculum areas is ongoing. In particular, lower levels of work-related pupil communication and more routine administrative interaction and lower levels of pupil engagement in work activity have been reported in primary school research studies.

Galton *et al.* (1980) (*The Oracle Study*) found that children in a formal classroom spent more time on work activity and pupils in an informal classroom spent more time in distraction and other non-work activities.

These findings all suggest that more formal teaching produces better results. The picture is not as clear as this, however. The studies described assessed progress mainly in terms of progress in the basic skills of language and number and most primary teachers would regard their task as much broader than this. *The Oracle Study* also found that direct instruction was less effective where more challenging and complex skills were concerned. Two American researchers, Giaconia and Hedges (1982), found that children in 'open classrooms' developed high levels of self-esteem and better self-concepts. The HMI (1978) primary survey found that standards achieved in basic skills were higher where the curriculum was broad.

Galton (1989) found that many teachers who in the past regarded themselves as the kind of informal teacher described in the Plowden Report (Department of Education and Science, 1967) did not in practice work in the way that Plowden described. He found that there was a perception gap between what teachers thought they were doing and what they were actually doing. In *The Oracle Study*, for example, most of the children in the primary classes they studied were sitting in groups, but there was very little work of a co-operative nature taking place and very little of the kind of extending conversation described in the Plowden Report.

In a study of four-year-olds in infant classes, Bennett and Kell (1989) found that, although teachers often had clear ideas of what they wanted to do, the tasks that children were asked to undertake often did not match the teacher's intentions. Sometimes the task was not made clear to the child. They give an example where the teacher's intention was for a child to learn the sound of the letter 'h'. The child was given a sheet of pictures of things starting with 'h' and told to colour the pictures but nothing was said about the sound of the letter. This study also found that there was a discrepancy between the teacher's stated aims and his or her assessment of whether the work was successful. Often, work was considered successful simply because the child had completed the task, irrespective of whether any learning had taken place.

Recent years have seen a move towards a greater proportion of interactive work with the whole class and generally a more structured approach to teaching and learning. Alexander *et al.* (1992: 28) note that 'whole-class teaching is associated with higher-order questioning, explanations and statements, and these in turn correlate with higher levels of pupil performance'. However, they go on to say:

> Observational studies show that pupils pay attention and remain on task when being taught as a whole class but may, in fact, slow down their rates of working to meet the teacher's norm, thus narrowing the challenge of what is taught to an extent which advocates of whole-class teaching might well find uncomfortable.

The literacy and numeracy hours both involve interactive work with a very structured approach and a mixture of class, group and individual work. Collis and Lacey (1996: 9) stress that in interactive teaching the learner plays an active part in what is happening. They suggest that 'Learners are active modifiers of the information they receive'. They learn most efficiently when actively involved, which may mean engaging with other people or with things.

It is important to consider how children's thinking can best be developed and children need training to work in groups and individually. Wragg (1984), reporting a study of teacher education, stresses the value of higher order questioning skills. Kyriacou (1991: 38) states that 'higher-order questions involve reasoning, analysis and evaluation, whereas lower-order questions are concerned with simple recall or comprehension'. The HMI (1983) middle school study found that there was a weakness in questioning, with teachers tending to go for questions which had single-word answers. Other studies have found that higher order questions compose only a small proportion of the questions asked. A much larger proportion tend to be questions requiring recall of information.

Vygotsky (1978) writes of the 'zone of proximal development'. By this he means the distance between the stage of development that the child has currently reached and his or her potential for reaching a higher level given support from an adult or a more capable peer. Teachers work within this zone and need to create a structure which enables children to develop. Bruner (1985) suggests that the adult performs the critical function of scaffolding the learning task so that the child can internalise the knowledge involved and become able to use it in a new situation.

Collis and Lacey (1996: 33) suggest that if teachers are to be effective 'scaffolders' they should:

• provide opportunities for learning which are just a little too difficult for the students;
• offer just the right amount of assistance for them to enjoy the experience and learn from it;
• structure learning from mistakes.

Neill and Caswell (1993: 100, 101) studied the body language of teachers and looked particularly at the body language of effective teachers. They found that 'effective teachers used a wider variety of facial expressions, gestures and tones of voice'. They also found that 'effective teachers looked intently at the class more often than the others, and used head movements which are signals of involvement with a speaker: they showed their interest in what the children had to say when they contributed to the lesson'. Effective teachers smiled more and used more joking intonation. Their lessons were fun to be in.

Effective teaching should result in effective learning. In learning something new a child has to fit it into his thinking about what he already knows. Rae and McPhillimy (1985: 12) speak of this as encoding new knowledge. They suggest that 'the more elaborately something is encoded the better it is remembered'. It is important that you help children to structure their learning, relating what is being learned to previous knowledge. This does not mean that you do all the structuring for them. The actual process of structuring knowledge for yourself helps memory. You might suggest ways of grouping ideas together or thinking of other bits of information which belong with what is now being learned. At the same time you may provide a model for structuring in the way you present information.

Children also need to be encouraged to be self-evaluators. Groups working co-operatively might conclude their work by discussing the quality of what they have done. Children can work in pairs, exchanging pieces of work and looking critically but positively at what their partner has done and picking out the parts they felt were good and suggesting ways in which the work might be improved. Individual children might be asked to say what they felt was good about a particular piece of work and what they could do to improve it.

Cooper and MacIntyre (1996: 100, 101) studied the ways in which teachers and pupils felt that learning was facilitated in the classroom. They found that the following were seen as valuable aids to learning:

- teacher making explicit the agenda for the lesson;
- teacher recapping on previous lesson, highlighting continuity between lessons;
- story-telling by the teacher;
- reading aloud (by teacher/by pupils);
- teacher mediation and modification of pupil verbal input to class discussion/board work;
- oral explanation by teacher, often combined with discussion or question-and-answer sessions or use of blackboard;
- blackboard notes and diagrams as an *aide-mémoire*;
- use of pictures and other visual stimuli (for exploration/information);
- use of 'models' based on pupil work or generated by the teacher;
- structure for written work generated and presented by the teacher;
- group/pair work (for oral and practical purposes);
- drama/role play;
- printed text/worksheets;
- use of stimuli which relates to pupil pop culture.

We saw in the last chapter that a very important element in children's learning is teacher expectation. This was first confirmed in a study by Rosenthal and Jacobson (1968) in which teachers in a Californian elementary school were told, on the basis of a spurious IQ test which gave random results, that some children would make considerably more progress than others over the coming year. This was confirmed in practice. The researchers concluded that it demonstrated that teachers acted in accordance with induced expectations and children performed to meet the expectations. Although this study has been much criticised and other studies which have attempted to replicate the findings have reached different conclusions, a number of other studies provide evidence that, if a teacher believes that certain standards of work and behaviour are characteristic of a certain child and treats the child accordingly, there is a fair likelihood that the child will change his or her self-image to accord with the view that the teacher is demonstrating. Palardy (1969), for example, tested preschool children for reading readiness in September and found that boys and girls performed equally well. When the same children were tested again in March, the boys in the classes of those teachers who believed that girls were more able at reading achieved less well than the girls, whereas in the classes of those teachers who believed that boys and girls were equally able to learn to read the boys did as well as the girls.

Teachers have also been found to tend to have higher expectations of children who have middle-class characteristics. Your views about race and gender are likely to affect your expectations of boys and girls and children from ethnic minorities. It is therefore important to be self-aware, recognising possible areas of prejudice and the effect of your expectations. This self-awareness is summarised in Analysis 4.1.

Analysis 4.1 Effective teaching and learning

---

1 Have I a clear idea of relevant goals for my class and for the individuals within it?
2 Have I good knowledge of the individual needs of my children and do I plan work to match these needs?
3 Do I help children to structure their learning so that they remember?
4 Do I train children to become self-evaluators?
5 Have I a good mixture of work with the whole class, work with groups and work with individuals?
6 Do I make time for some activities arising from children's interests?
7 How much of the time are my children working profitably?
8 How many higher order questions do I ask each day?
9 Am I making a proper and consistent use of praise and encouragement to meet the goals I have in mind?
10 Have I trained my children to work independently and with concentration?
11 Have I trained my children to work co-operatively in groups or pairs? How much co-operative group work actually takes place?

12 Do I keep adequate records? Do I use these and the assessments I make to decide on the programme for individual children, for groups and for the class as a whole?

13 Are my expectations for the children I teach realistic? Have I any areas of prejudice?

5   Teaching style

Style is the way you do things as a teacher. While there are both good and bad ways of doing things, there are many good ways of teaching and each teacher has his or her own style.

At the beginning of your teaching career, you tend to draw on models that you have experienced as a pupil as well as the knowledge you have gained from training, but, as time goes on, you become clearer about your own strengths and limitations and your preferred way of working. It is perhaps worth noting in passing that most teachers, and especially the inexperienced, usually have too few models to draw upon. It is valuable to see how other teachers teach and organise, particularly at the beginning of your career.

Influences on style

Your teaching style is formed from a number of factors, of which the following are the most important.

Personality

Your working style depends, in the first place, upon the kind of person you are. For example, a person with an open and flexible personality will show this in the way he or she works.

Experience

Experience is an important factor in determining style. In particular, experience of seeing other teachers at work gives you ideas about possible ways of working, and those you choose become part of your style. Experience also affects your style in that you gradually become more sure of yourself and more confident in what you are doing.

Philosophy and aims

Your beliefs about education and what constitute good teaching and learning situations, and your values generally, will affect the way you work, however vague and unformed your thinking may be. Many teachers hold quite strong views which affect the way they work, without their being aware that they have a philosophy as such. Analysis 1.1 was intended to help you to think through your ideas about teaching and learning.

Context

Your teaching style is affected by the particular group of children you are teaching and your accommodation and resources. The same teacher will work differently with a reception class and with a class of juniors. Some things which are possible in a well-resourced school are not possible when resources are very limited.

The demonstration of style

Style is demonstrated in the way you work, particularly by the following.

The activities you decide to undertake yourself

Your style is evident in what you decide to do as teacher. The way you present material to children is part of your style. At almost every point in the day you are making choices about how you will act and these add up to style.

The use of time

In choosing what you do, you are also making choices about how to use your time and how the children will use time.

Methods of tackling work

The way you set about the tasks of the classroom is all part of your style. You may tell the children what to do, or you may have a programme where they have some choice about the order in which they undertake particular pieces of work. You may discuss how work will be done with them and incorporate their ideas, not only into what they do but also into how it is done, or you may insist that work is done as you wish. Many teachers will probably use a mixture of these methods, sometimes dictating what is to be done and sometimes giving a certain amount of freedom.

Communication

The way you communicate with children is all part of your style. You may spend a lot of time talking about how things should be done or about the actual tasks the children are doing. You may, perhaps without realising it, talk down to children or talk at a level which is stimulating because they have to think hard to follow what you are saying. You may also talk a great deal of the time or give a lot of time to getting children to talk.

Interpersonal behaviour

This is linked with communication. Teachers vary in how friendly they are with the children they teach and in how they treat children. Studies of how children view teachers suggest that they value a friendly approach and a sense of humour.

Organisation of work

Teachers differ in the way they organise work. Some teachers will choose to teach much of the National Curriculum as separate subjects whereas others will do a certain amount of integration. You may use competition or co-operative group work a good deal or very little. The extent to which teachers involve pupils in decision-making about aspects of their work also varies a good deal and some teachers do more testing than others.

Studies of teacher style

There have been a number of studies which looked at teaching style. Bennett (1976) identified a number of characteristics of traditional and progressive teachers. The progressive teacher tended to integrate subject matter rather than teach in separate subjects; involve pupils in active learning, often by discovery methods; made little use of external rewards and punishments and testing; and accented creative expression. Traditional teachers tended to teach separate subjects, stress the importance of memory, practice and rote learning, make use of external rewards with regular testing and an accent on competition with little emphasis on creative work. There were also a number of teachers who used mixed methods. Bennett (1976) compared the results using tests of basic skills and two essays, one on 'What I did at school yesterday' and the other on 'Invisible for the day', and found that on the basic skills tests the formal teachers and those who used mixed methods came out best. In the essay test the formal and informal groups did equally well, and those who used mixed methods did slightly less well. However, low-achieving boys did better in the informal classes, and the best class of all was taught informally but in a highly structured way.

The Oracle Study (Galton and Simon, 1980) looked at teaching styles in junior school classes and classified them as follows:

Individual monitors
These teachers worked mainly on an individual basis and therefore spent much time in monitoring individual progress. This resulted in their being under pressure with a high level of interaction with individual children.

Class enquirers
This group used a good deal of class teaching and teacher-managed learning with open and closed questions in class discussion.

Group instructors
Group instructors spent a larger amount of time than others on group interaction and less on individual attention, which allowed them to engage in more questioning and making of statements.

Style changers
Fifty per cent of teachers used mixed styles to meet different demands.

The group of style changers breaks down as follows:

- Infrequent changers, who gradually changed style according to the observed needs of the class group over the course of the school year.
- Rotating changers, who worked with pupils seated in groups, each working at a particular aspect of curriculum. The activities of the different groups were rotated during the course of the day or week.
- Habitual changers, who made regular changes between class and individualised instruction. This group used questioning relatively little and had the lowest amount of time spent interacting with pupils.

Each style was considered in relation to children's performance in the basic skills. In language the children of the *class enquirers* were much in advance of those using other styles, with pupils of *infrequent changers* coming second. The children of *individual monitors, rotating* and *habitual changers* scored less well.

In reading the children of *infrequent changers* did best, with those of the *individual monitors* coming second. In mathematics the best score came from the children of the *class enquirers*.

It is interesting to relate this study to the approaches being recommended for the literacy and numeracy hours which tend towards the *class enquirer* style.

The Oracle Study also looked at children's learning styles and related these to teaching styles. Four major learning styles were noted:

- *The attention seeker* – seeks out the teacher's attention more than the typical class member, constantly seeking feedback and reassurance.
- *The intermittent worker* – avoids the teacher's attention and only works when the teacher is watching.
- *The solitary worker* – spends most of the time working with little interaction with other children or with the teacher.
- *The quiet collaborator* – similar to the solitary worker in that they concentrate on work; they spend more time in routine activities than other children.

When the learning styles were related to the teaching styles in this study, it was found that the *group instructors* had the highest proportion of *quiet collaborators* and the *class enquirers* the highest proportion of *solitary workers* in their classes. The *individual monitors* and the *rotating changers* had the most *intermittent workers*.

Cortazzi (1991), in a study of the way 123 primary teachers worked, found that almost all of them often departed from their planned work to follow up an idea which the children had put forward or an event which was in the news. They gave their reasons for doing this as 'First, flexibility, second, the need for talk, the need to follow up children's enjoyment, excitement and interest' (Cortazzi, 1991: 72). The more experienced teachers did this more often than those who were new to teaching. The National Curriculum and the literacy and numeracy hours have made this more difficult to do, but there is still a place for playing it by ear from time to time.

Developing your own style

Wherever you place yourself in the various classifications in these studies, you have to discover the best way to work in the classroom for you. Your best way of working depends not only upon what you see as being important in curriculum terms, but also upon your strengths, limitations and, as we have seen, upon your personality, experience, philosophy and the situation in which you find yourself. Your age may also make a difference. We grow less flexible as we grow older, but are usually more competent and confident and able to bring wider experience to the work in hand.

Analysis 5.1 is intended to help you to work out your personal profile as a teacher. It is closely linked to the profile given in Analysis 1.1, but is concerned with the way you work in the classroom rather than with your philosophy of education. The items listed are all those where teachers tend to have personal preferences which it is sensible to take into account.

Work through the list marking your views on the statements and then look at the comments which follow. You may also like to get a colleague to mark the answers he or she thinks you would give. Sometimes the gap between your view of yourself and someone else's view can be revealing. The list could also furnish useful discussion for a group of teachers highlighting areas of difference.

Quiet/noise and tidiness/mess

Quiet and clean activities and noisy and messy activities need to be kept apart. You may do this by reserving different parts of the classroom for activities which are not compatible or by keeping such activities apart by having them at different times of the day. You need to find a middle road between being too quiet and tidy and allowing children to be too noisy and messy, and this means recognising your own style and its limitations. Too much emphasis on quiet tidiness may inhibit creativity, but a disorganised classroom where too much noise and mess are allowed is also inhibiting. It is important for a teacher to be well organised if the children are to work in an organised way. This means making rules about how materials and equipment are used and about the times when a certain amount of noise is permissible and times when everyone should be quiet. It is helpful to discuss with children the best way to work to keep the room in good order and to use some of their ideas, reviewing their success after a period.

Analysis 5.1 Preferred teaching style

	+ +	+	Av	–	– –	
I like a quiet classroom for most of the time						I don't mind noise so long as I can see that children are working
I like a tidy and well-organised room						I don't mind mess if it results in exciting work
I like to have everything well planned in advance						My best work occurs when I respond spontaneously to something which has happened
I like to concentrate on one thing at a time						I like to have more than one activity at a time upon occasion
I am normally even-tempered and patient						I get excited easily and am sometimes irritable
I like a regular timetable without too many diversions or interruptions						I like to create variety in the day or week
I think children learn best when they are not given too much choice						I believe choice to be important in motivating children to learn
I think competition in the classroom helps children to learn						I prefer to play down competition and foster co-operation

I tend to be a perfectionist							I am normally easygoing
I can't bear to be late for anything							I am a confirmed last-minuter
I work best with a class group							I work best with small groups and individuals
I prefer to have my children formally seated							I like to have children seated in groups

Preplanning/spontaneity

If you are a determined preplanner, be aware that you could just miss the moment when a particular piece of teaching might be most effective because you were so busy pursuing the goals you had planned. Edwards and Mercer (1987) studying the language used in classrooms found that teachers tend to dominate what happens in the classroom by the topics they introduce, the questions they ask and the responses they give to children's answers and comments. Up to a point this is to be expected and is part of the teacher's role, but if taken too far it prevents children from having ideas. Preplanning is most valuable when mixed with a measure of flexibility.

If you are strong on spontaneity be sure that you create situations in which children can achieve the learning necessary for the National Curriculum. You also need to make regular checks to see that all the children are getting relevant experiences and opportunities and that there are not substantial gaps in their learning or too much repetition of the things which interest you most. Spontaneous teachers need to keep good records of what happens.

One task/variety of tasks

If you normally have all the children doing the same subject at the same time, remember that they take differing amounts of time to learn the same things. You may need to have some time when the slower children have a chance to catch up while the faster ones do something different. You need to provide for this variation either by giving different work to different groups of children or by organising so that work can be undertaken at a variety of levels. You also need plenty of interesting material for those who finish quickly. Giving them more of the same simply teaches them to work slowly! You may also need material to provide opportunities for slower children which enables them to work through the same programme as others but with more information and explanation available.

If you like to have a variety of tasks going on at the same time make sure that the children are getting enough stimulus from you and from each other. Some of the studies quoted earlier suggest that there is a limit to the amount of choice which children can manage effectively.

Little choice/much choice

There is no doubt that the right amount of choice is motivating to children and can also have the advantage of training them in the process of making choices. On the other hand, choice can be overdone, with the result that children flit from one activity to another without learning very much. The Mortimore *et al.* (1988) study quoted earlier suggested that a choice of two activities at a time provided better for effective learning than a greater number. A good many of the choices made should be choices of when particular activities are undertaken rather than a choice of whether they are undertaken. Choice is also possible within a given theme. In topic work, for example, there may be several ways in which children can work to acquire the learning intended by the teacher and they may have some choice of which route they pursue. Training children to choose wisely is an important part of their learning.

Competition/co-operation

Human beings have an ancestry which needed to be competitive in order to survive and we are still naturally competitive. Even in classrooms where the teacher plays down competition, the children will create competition of their own.

Some children thrive on competition and are most likely to work well when they see themselves in a competitive situation. Others fail continually and become discouraged. The task is to get the most out of competition for those who benefit from it with the least damage for those who fail. An element of competition is useful when children are encouraged to compete with themselves or others at a similar level in simple games which create interest or give practice which might otherwise seem tedious. It is also important that children do not get the idea that it is the end that matters and that the means of achieving it is unimportant, or that what is learned is important only in terms of doing better than someone else, getting marks or rewards or pleasing the teacher. One might say that if children cheat in their learning they have gained the wrong idea of what the activity is about.

Competition may work against co-operation. There are many situations in life where co-operation is needed and school should teach children how to work effectively with other people. Researchers suggest that although many teachers give lip service to the idea of co-operative work actual examples of it are comparatively few.

Patient/excitable

Patience is obviously an advantage in teaching and it can give children considerable security to know that you will treat them sympathetically and consistently. On the other hand, excitement and enthusiasm are valuable things to offer children and enthusiasm is infectious.

The teacher who can get children really turned on by his or her own excitement is someone whom every child needs to meet. If the other side of this valuable characteristic is that you get depressed and irritable from time to time, try to organise so that you have something to switch into when you have had enough and the children are trying you beyond endurance. For example, it is often pleasant to read them a story or get them to carry on some activity which is quiet but interesting.

Perfectionist/easygoing

All teachers should demand high standards of children in all they do, but different teachers do this in different ways. If you tend to be perfectionist, be careful not to ask more than your children can give and make sure you have your priorities right. A teacher who insists that every piece of writing is done in perfect handwriting with no spelling or punctuation mistakes may find that some children write very little in order not to expose their weaknesses. This makes it very difficult to help them.

Conversely a teacher who is too easygoing needs to check that the work the children are offering is good enough and that enough attention is being paid to detail.

Never late/last-minuter

If you can't bear to be late, don't be too hard on children and colleagues who find punctuality a problem. You must, of course, teach children to be punctual, but you need to recognise that for some children this is difficult, in some cases through no fault of their own. A good way of dealing with a child who is habitually late might be to make an individual chart on which he or she marks the punctual days and seeks to improve on this performance.

If you are a last-minuter and often late, you need to take yourself in hand so that you arrive in school sufficiently early to prepare for the children and be ready when they come in. It may help to aim at a time well before school is due to begin. A late teacher is a bad example to children and a nuisance to colleagues. He or she also risks a disorganised start to the day.

Class teaching/group and individual teaching

The literacy and numeracy hours have brought the idea of whole-class teaching to the fore as well as providing opportunities for small group and individual work. If you are good at holding children's attention riveted when you wish to, you should make the most of it. Your children will probably remember the things they have done with you for the rest of their lives. However, you also need to vary the approach to match the situation and the needs of individuals. The important thing to bear in mind is making an efficient use of time. A number of studies suggest that teachers ask more thought-provoking questions when working with a whole class than when working with individuals.

Formal classroom organisation/informal organisation

Studies of the way children are seated in classrooms suggest that when children are seated in rows rather than groups more work is done. The children themselves also said they preferred formal seating. There is also evidence that although many teachers have children seated in groups not much use is made of this for co-operative work.

6　The teacher's role

Hargreaves (1994: vii) makes the following comment about the role of the teacher:

> Teachers don't merely deliver the curriculum. They develop it, define it and reinterpret it too. It is what teachers think, what teachers believe and what teachers do at the level of the classroom that ultimately shapes the learning that young people get. The ways they teach are also grounded in their backgrounds, their biographies, in the kinds of teachers they have become.

The teacher is the most important resource in any classroom and the problem is always that of trying to meet the needs of a disparate group of children. You need to reflect frequently on the extent to which you are using your time to foster the children's learning and the amount of time that children are actually working at profitable tasks. It is very easy to spend too much time dealing with matters such as finding materials for individuals or lost and broken pencils, which should be taken care of by a well-organised environment.

The developing use of computers is likely to make a difference to the role of the teacher and should eventually be able to match the learning needs of individuals very closely. It seems likely that technology will enhance the role of the teacher rather than usurp it, freeing the teacher for tasks that only a person can do.

The tasks of the teacher

Society gives teachers the task of mediating the curriculum for each child. The National Curriculum lays down what should be taught and the literacy and numeracy hours determine to some extent the way in which you should work with children, but there is still a great deal left to the individual teacher.

The tasks of the teacher include the following.

Observation of children

Chazan *et al.* (1987: 12) make the following points about observation:

> To provide the most fruitful experiences and to encourage children
> to explore and discover for themselves can only be successfully
> accomplished on the basis of careful observation of the children
> concerned over a period of time. Teachers must therefore be
> observers in order to provide the structured framework for
> learning.

You need to observe children if you are to match the teaching and
learning programme to their needs and assess learning and progress.
Much of the observation a teacher does is automatic. You note how
children are reacting to the work you are asking them to do. You use
your knowledge of body language in observing which children are
attending and which children are day-dreaming. You note how children
are succeeding or not succeeding with the task in hand. You also need
to observe more systematically and consciously. One way of doing
this is to observe a small number of children in some detail each day
or week, perhaps following this up with a discussion with each child.
There are problems about fitting this into a busy day but it is well
worth while. It is suggested as part of both the literacy and numeracy
strategies and is important in helping you to match work to individual
needs.

Another aspect of observation is your assessment of the work
children do. This may be their normal day-to-day work or specific
testing. Bennett and Kell (1989) found that many teachers did not use
assessments as a means of assessing needs, and matching work to
children and diagnostic work was generally rather limited.

The Assessment Reform Group (1999: 2) studied assessment in a
number of schools and concluded that 'assessment which is explicitly
designed to promote learning is the single most powerful tool we have
for raising standards and empowering lifelong learners'. They suggest
that:

> Teachers must be involved in gathering information about pupils'
> learning and encouraging pupils to review their work critically
> and constructively. They do this by:

- observing pupils – this involves listening to how they describe their work and their reasoning;
- questioning, using open questions, phrased to invite pupils to explore their ideas and their reasoning;
- setting tasks in a way which requires pupils to use certain skills or apply ideas;
- asking pupils to communicate their thinking through drawings, artifacts, actions, role play, concept-mapping as well as writing;
- discussing words and how they are being used.

(Assessment Reform Group Report, 1999: 8)

The organisation of the learning programme

The learning programme needs to be organised to meet the needs identified from observation, relating each day's work broadly to a plan for the week, the term, the year or the school life of the children, using interests and experiences to provide learning opportunities and checking that the necessary ground is covered. You need to be opportunist but systematic.

The work you do with your class is part of a programme for the whole school, and you need to work closely with subject leaders so that your work fits with what other teachers have done in the past and will do in the future.

The selection of learning material

Being a teacher at the primary school level is very demanding in terms of subject knowledge. You need to have a good understanding of all the subjects of the National Curriculum if you are to be in a position to select learning material which will enable individuals and groups to learn that part of the curriculum appropriate for their age and ability. This task involves not only considering how to teach the different aspects of the National Curriculum but also looking at how they can be combined so that learning in one area complements learning in another. You also need to be aware of the way in which children's interests and experiences can be used for their learning.

The presentation of learning material

Children need constant interaction between first-hand experience and other learning materials if they are to be able to transfer what they have learned from one situation to another. The provision of first-hand experience through visits, exploration of the school environment or of material brought into the classroom is basic to effective learning. The teacher's task will be to help children to become aware of and focus on aspects important for learning and help them to structure what they are learning so that it fits into a developing pattern in their minds.

You will also need to provide materials within the classroom that are designed to foster learning. Sometimes this will involve a published scheme, a book or a radio or television programme or a computer program or the material you have provided or presented. Presentation by the teacher requires skill in talking about the topic under consideration. It requires the ability to describe something in a way that captures children's interest and to give explanations which are clear and understandable. It also requires the ability to question in a way which stimulates thinking.

Matching work to children

If children are to learn well, the tasks they are asked to undertake and those they choose for themselves must match their learning needs, being difficult enough to challenge but within their capability. This is not easy to do. There is a good deal of evidence that teachers only partially succeed in matching work to children and it is certainly very difficult to do well in a large class. Tizard *et al.* (1988) found that teachers tended to give children work which was too difficult if they had good verbal skills and to underestimate children whose verbal skills and behaviour were less good.

The HMI (1978) primary survey found teachers better at matching work to pupils in language and mathematics than in other curriculum areas, and comments about not extending the most able have been made in many HMI reports. We noted in Chapter 2 that Bennett *et al.* (1984) found that teachers tended to underestimate the most able children, and Bennett and Kell (1989) found that where the youngest children were concerned there was a tendency to overestimate. Teachers were generally more prepared to accept that they were overestimating than underestimating.

It is important that teachers use the assessments they make to inform their teaching.

The structuring of children's learning

We saw in Chapter 4 that it was important to help children to structure their learning. Learning is easiest where the material to be learned is part of an overall structure and the learner can see where the new piece of learning fits in. Children in the primary school are developing structures in their minds which will form the basis of future learning. The way they organise their thinking at this stage may govern their ability to learn in the future. They are sometimes helped by being given a structure, but it is usually better to help them to form structures of their own.

For example, at one time, tables were taught mainly by rote, using one particular structure. One effect of this was that children sometimes found difficulty in using the information. We now tend to lead children to work out a number of different structures for tables including the standard one.

Another example is seen in the development of classifying skills. Children learn about sets in mathematics at quite an early age, but very often this knowledge is not applied when, for example, children go out and come back with a collection of varied objects. These could be sorted into sets according to their attributes, which is what has happened when biologists, botanists and geologists have classified the material they have found.

The view that teachers need to lead children to create mental structures has been stressed by major studies for many years. It was stated in various ways in the Plowden Report (Department of Education and Science, 1967), the HMI (1978) primary survey and in the Cockcroft Report (Department of Education and Science, 1982). The way a teacher presents material, summarises, points out links, encourages classifying and ordering and so on helps children to create appropriate mental structures.

We also saw in Chapter 4 that Vygotsky (1978) suggested that there is something which he calls the 'zone of proximal development' – the gap between what a child can learn by him or herself and what is possible with the aid of an adult. The adult provides a scaffolding or structure which enables the child to learn. The way material is presented and the discussion that goes with it are all part of these structures.

Training learning behaviour

The ability to work independently and in groups does not come automatically. A good deal of work needs to go into training these abilities throughout the primary school. With a new class you need to start with very little independent work and gradually increase the amount you expect. The study by Mortimore *et al.* (1988) quoted previously found that junior school children worked independently in a satisfactory way for short periods, possibly no more than a morning. This report also suggested that choice should be limited. What is not clear from this study is whether the teachers concerned trained their children in independent learning and whether training produced increased ability to work in this way. The teacher's attitude towards making children independent is also important.

Providing inspiration and encouragement

An important part of the teacher's role is to stimulate and interest children in whatever is to be learned. This is a valuable part of working with the whole class and is one reason why you should often work with the whole class or groups of children. You can only inspire a few children if you do this individually but you may inspire many more if you do it with everyone at once. However, individual encouragement is also needed and should be regarded as a teaching tool because children tend to repeat what is praised and encouraged. There is some evidence that teachers praise and encourage differentially. Tizard *et al.* (1988) found that White boys were encouraged more than White girls and that Black boys received the least encouragement. The less able also received less encouragement.

It is very easy to think that you do more encouraging than you actually do and particularly easy to encourage the able and offer little to the least able and the quiet child. It is helpful occasionally to try to check the number of encouraging comments you make in the course of a morning and note the children to whom they were addressed. It is also useful to go through the register occasionally, noting when you last said something encouraging to each child.

Organising a learning environment

A learning environment might be described as one which is functional with regard to children's learning. This involves:

- An arrangement of furniture that provides the optimum conditions for the work to be done.
- A layout of materials that shows clearly what is available, is arranged and marked to show function, level of difficulty or progression and can be used by children without difficulty and without a great deal of attention from the teacher.
- An organisation in which it is easy to keep materials and equipment

clean, tidy and in order and easy to check over to see that everything is in the right place.

- A discriminating use of display which provides standards to aim for, i.e. demonstrates what the teacher wants from children, and offers encouragement to those who need it most (e.g. the display of less good work from time to time to encourage an individual child as well as display of exemplary work). It should also provide materials of all kinds which interest, stimulate and extend knowledge and thinking.

Ensuring that children develop a common understanding with the teacher

Edwards and Mercer (1987) suggest that classroom discourse depends a great deal on developing a common understanding between teacher and pupils. Much conversation depends upon participants understanding the language they use in the same way and having the ability to make similar inferences from what is said. The teacher is inducting children into the language of education and is aiming to transfer his or her understanding to the children but the children's experience is shorter and different from that of the teacher and this means that misunderstandings can easily arise. You may get the impression that the children understand what you are saying only to find later that some interpreted your words very differently from your intended meaning.

Edwards and Mercer (1987) and Bennett *et al.* (1988) all found that teachers were inclined not to make clear to children their aims for the work expected. Children need not only a common understanding of the language and gestures used but also to know where they are expected to be going. This puts them in a position to know what progress they are making.

Assessing and recording children's progress and development

Teachers have always been concerned to assess how well their children are doing so that they can decide what to teach them next. The National Curriculum has made this much more important because assessment is now formally required in primary schools. The task of assessment should inform the work selected for individuals and groups.

Assessing teaching performance and approaches

The provision for effective teachers to cross the salary threshold highlights current concern with teacher performance and involves self-appraisal as well as appraisal by others. To cross the threshold a teacher must provide evidence of good knowledge and understanding of the material he or she teaches, provide evidence of ability to plan and deliver effective teaching and assessment, show that pupils are making progress and demonstrate concern with wider professional effectiveness.

At all stages in teaching reflection is an important skill. Appraisal makes a contribution to your own reflection on your work. Any new approach, whether within a single class or introduced throughout the school, should be followed after an interval by a careful evaluation to discover whether it was successful and whether there are ways in which it can be improved.

Crossing the threshold involves observation and evaluation of teaching by someone else, as does appraisal. Newly qualified teachers should also benefit from having their teaching observed. Two teachers who are both attempting a new approach may find it helpful at some stage to exchange classes and assess how each other's class has done in the agreed area of work. It can also be helpful if it can be arranged for teachers to observe each other and try to assess how far aims are being achieved.

Children are also useful assessors of your work. Discussion with children, particularly the older children, about how they feel something went and what they thought about it is a valuable part of the evaluation process. Older children can also be given questionnaires asking such questions as what they enjoyed, what they disliked, what they found difficult and what kind of classroom work they found most helped them to learn.

The knowledge a teacher needs

When, as a new teacher, you enter the profession, you bring with you from your earlier education and your training a body of knowledge and the beginning of some of the skills you will need as a teacher. The school in which you find yourself at the beginning of your career is likely to provide the largest single contribution to your professional development as a teacher from then on. Even if the school you join is not a particularly good one and the head and teacher colleagues make only a minimum contribution to your induction year, you will still learn from them – in some cases by negative example.

We have already noted that you will learn a great deal on the job by observing children, by trying out ideas and selecting those which work best for you. All teachers learn by interacting with their professional environment. You form and develop your own frame of reference by which you judge your own performance. You acquire new knowledge in dealing with the tasks which come your way. You develop skills in dealing with the situations you encounter as well as by reading, studying, in-service education and discussing work with colleagues. A good teacher goes on learning throughout his or her career.

There are a number of areas in which you need to acquire knowledge and skill. The sections below outline these and Analysis 6.1 suggests questions you may like to ask yourself.

Self-knowledge

To be a good teacher you need to be aware of your strengths and limitations and your preferred learning style. This kind of self-knowledge is a prerequisite of good teaching, especially in the primary school where teachers are expected to teach many things and where every teacher will have some areas of strength and some weaknesses.

A thought-out philosophy

Having a philosophy is not a theoretical stance but a thought-out approach to the way you work in the classroom and the day-to-day decisions you make in the course of your teaching. What you need are thought-out aims and objectives that you can use for assessing your work and for deciding on approaches and materials. It is the teachers who have the clearest ideas of what they want to achieve who are likely to achieve the most. Analyses 1.1 and 5.1 are intended to help you to work out where you stand on a number of issues.

The staff of a school also needs to have some collective philosophy so that children experience a coherent programme while they are in the school and as they move from class to class. This creates a school culture in which agreed values are fostered. Staff discussion of the philosophy and culture is not only useful in getting a school view but it also helps everyone to sort out ideas.

Child development

Initial training may have introduced you to ideas about the way children develop and learn, but knowledge in this area is constantly developing and you will be adding knowledge gained from your own observation

Analysis 6.1 The teacher's knowledge

Self-knowledge	What are my strengths? What are my weaknesses?
Philosophy	What do I believe is really important in educating children? What are my priorities? What would I like my children to remember of their years with me in twenty years' time? Can I justify what I teach and the way I teach it? What are the implications of what I believe for what I do?
Child development	Do I know enough about the normal patterns of physical, intellectual, social and emotional development to recognise the norm and deviations from it? Do I consciously use this knowledge in working with children?
Children's learning	What am I doing to help children to structure their learning? How well does the work I provide for children match the range of individuals in the class? Have my children the experience to understand fully the language I use? How many of the children in my class are not motivated for much of the time? Who are they? What interests have they? Could I use these interests to help them to learn other things? Do I provide opportunities for children to talk over what they are learning? How often do I create situations in which children tackle problems that are challenging but within their capacity?

	Do I do this for the less able as well as for the more able? How often do I use higher order questions which require thought and inventiveness? Am I helping children to learn how to learn?
Group behaviour	Am I happy with the overall behaviour of my class? How often do I praise good behaviour and how often do I comment on bad behaviour? Do I praise the same children every time? What am I doing to teach children to work co-operatively? Am I satisfied with the balance I have between competition and co-operation? Do any of my children cheat in order to do better than others or to please me? Is this because there is too much competition? Would rather more competition stimulate some of the most able in the class?
Curriculum content	In which areas of curriculum do I know least? What can I do about this? When did I last update what I know in the areas of work in which I feel most at home?

of children as well as trying to keep up to date by reading and from in-service education.

Knowledge of how children learn

Here again initial training normally introduces students to knowledge of learning, and teaching experience will add to this. Good theoretical knowledge as well as experience should guide your practice. The following points in particular are worth considering. They should be part of the background knowledge of all teachers.

1   *Learning depends upon motivation*
    A child's power to learn is considerable. It is evident from the extent of early language learning and from the knowledge that children sometimes manifest about hobbies and out-of-school interests that most children have much greater powers for learning than we can yet harness for the learning we want them to achieve. Without motivation it is difficult to get them to learn anything. They may even use their ability to avoid learning.
        Motivation can be intrinsic or extrinsic. Intrinsic motivation is that which comes from within the child. He or she wants to learn because of interest in the work in hand. Extrinsic motivation is motivation from outside the child – a desire to gain good marks or the teacher's approval. Both forms of motivation have a place but intrinsic motivation is the more satisfactory form.
        Most people, including most children, are motivated by problems which challenge but are within their capacity.
        The more you can present learning as a series of interesting challenges, the more successfully your children will learn. Such learning is often more effective than memorising because the child makes the learning his or her own by working on it. We tend to forget that children lack experience, not intelligence. Given a problem within his or her own experience, a child may solve it more quickly than an adult. Many teachers will be aware that children have taken to computers more quickly than they themselves.

2   *Reward and praise are more effective than criticism and punishment*
    This is well known and has been frequently demonstrated in research but the knowledge tends to be used in a very limited way. You can help children who have problems or who pose problems if you use praise and reward very specifically for the behaviour

you want to reinforce, doing this as soon as possible after the behaviour takes place. As far as possible the unwanted behaviour should be ignored, although this is often not possible because of the effect on other children. Brophy and Good (1986), in one study of teacher behaviour towards children typified as able or less able, found that teachers praised those they saw as high achievers more and low achievers less and criticised low achievers more and high achievers less. While this was to some extent understandable, it tended to reinforce the original typification and gave praise to those who needed it least rather than those who needed it most. This is certainly something you should look out for.

3   *It is necessary to use or talk about a piece of learning*
Learning which has not been discussed and used may remain at a rote learning level rather than being accessible to be applied in new situations. Listening and repeating are not enough by themselves if learning is to be absorbed in a way that makes it available for use. Talking about what is being learned helps to structure it and so to remember it and be able to recall it. Class, small group and paired discussion may be useful if specific tasks for discussion are given. Children learn from working together at a problem.

4   *Language means only as much as the experience it represents*
Children learn from the words of others when they can interpret them by matching them with their own experience in a way which is reasonably similar to the understanding of the person using the words. This holds true for both speech and writing. Children are also good at disguising the limited nature of their understanding, and you may think they have understood when in fact they are simply using the words without adequate understanding of their meaning.

5   *Learning needs to be made accessible and usable*
The way in which learning is acquired is important in structuring it in the learner's mind. Structuring involves matching it to what the learner already knows and helping him or her to classify the new knowledge into categories so that it is easy to remember and recall. Only if the structuring process is adequate will the learning be accessible and usable. It is not sufficient for the teacher to do the structuring for the children, although the way the material is presented should have its own structure. What is needed is help with sorting out experiences so that the children create structures for themselves.

Group behaviour

Teaching in school depends upon the ability of the teacher to manage children in groups. In the first place you have to manage a class group. You may then choose to break up the class into smaller groups for particular work and you need to be able to manage the class in this situation. A group is sometimes essential for the activity, e.g. in dance and drama, music or team games. At other times teachers form groups for various reasons. Teaching involves keeping a delicate balance between the individual and the group and using various forms of organisation to further your aims.

Group behaviour varies according to the composition of the group and the extent to which any particular group contains children who serve as models for others. An individual child can set standards of work and behaviour, both positively and negatively, and this needs to be borne in mind when forming groups.

Children not only use other children as models but are themselves controlled by the group. This control is fairly minimal at the start of schooling but gradually increases as children grow older.

You can use the desire to be part of a group to get a base for the conforming behaviour which is a prerequisite for school learning. For example, teachers often use the device of singling out individuals to get the group to follow: 'I can see that John has cleared up nicely and is ready. Come on the rest of you'. Sometimes they aim to drive a wedge between an individual and the rest of the group: 'I think you'd better sit over there, Linda, where you can't disturb other people'.

These comments signal to the rest of the class that this is the behaviour required if they, like John, are to gain your approval or are to avoid your disapproval, as shown to Linda. Research evidence suggests that teachers make far more negative than positive comments, in spite of the fact that we know that reward is more effective than disapproval. It may be helpful to count how many of each kind of remark you make in the course of a day.

A group can be strongly supportive of its members on some occasions and highly competitive on others. Both competition and co-operation can be used to help children to learn, but both create problems as well as solve them. Children can co-operate to avoid work, and competition can be counter-productive.

Curriculum content

The demands on a teacher at the primary stage are very considerable since he or she is expected to teach almost the whole curriculum. Your class may have some specialist teaching for a subject such as music but a primary school teacher is expected to teach most subjects.

Bennett *et al.* (1992) studied the extent to which teachers saw themselves as competent in the various subjects of the National Curriculum. They found that teachers felt themselves to be most competent in English followed by mathematics. Science ranked third and technology tenth and last. Webb and Vulliamy (1996) also discovered that teachers found technology the most difficult subject to teach. They suggest that teachers need subject knowledge which 'includes not only the basic concepts and procedures of the discipline but also pedagogic knowledge which includes ways of representing the subject to others through explanations, analogies, illustrations, examples and demonstrations' (Webb and Vulliamy, 1996: 60). Teachers need to be secure in their subject knowledge so that they can select appropriately from it for the particular children they teach. This is even more true if you teach younger or less able children. There is also the problem when you encourage children to undertake work which develops individual interests if you do not know enough about the subject to identify what is worth pursuing.

If you are in a medium-sized or large primary school you will have colleagues who are subject leaders who will be a source of advice and help in the various subjects of the curriculum. You need to work closely with them so that the experience each child gets of the various subjects of the curriculum is cumulative throughout his or her time in the school, with each teacher building on what others have taught. If you are in a small school there will be less of this kind of help available and you will need to develop some of your subject expertise by reading and going to courses, but the need for the child's experience to be cumulative is the same.

You need to be very honest with yourself about your strengths and limitations so far as the curriculum is concerned and all teachers need to go on learning and updating their knowledge in the areas where they are expert as well as those where they need to know more.

The skills required by a teacher

Knowledge by itself is not sufficient to make an effective teacher; you also need teaching skills. The sections which follow explore the range of skills a teacher needs and provide an opportunity for self-assessment.

Observing and interpreting children's behaviour

The teacher's ability to observe and interpret children's behaviour is crucial, particularly at the stages when children are more dependent on the teacher and are limited in their ability to express their needs.

The skills and strategies involved in observation and assessment might be classified as follows:

1   *General observation*
    A teacher, over the years, develops skills in observing children at work, coming to know the signs of underfunctioning and of learning problems of various kinds and what may reasonably be expected from any individual or group.

2   *Systematic observation*
    General observation is largely a matter of observing things as they happen. Children's performance should also be reviewed more systematically on a regular basis, working through the list of children and considering each in turn and perhaps discussing their progress with them and setting targets. This should be part of your assessment procedure. It is also important to work diagnostically with children, using such opportunities as hearing them read or discussing work with them to identify particular problems and difficulties.

3   *Using tests and check-lists*
    Systematic observation may include the use of teacher-made or standardised tests and check-lists. These require skill and knowledge in their interpretation. The national Standard Assessment Tasks (SATs) should add to the observations of the teacher as well as providing information about the stage each child has reached. In addition you need to have material which helps you to identify particular problems such as inadequate phonic skills or lack of knowledge of particular mathematical operations.

In observing any individual child a teacher might look for the following:

1   *Personality and learning style*
    There are many differences in children and the way they learn. You need to find the 'best fit' learning approaches for the particular group of children and the individuals within it.

2   *Experience and interests*
    Communication depends upon experience shared between you and

your children and the language needed to express a response to it. Any new work needs to be planned in the light of observation and conjecture about the relevant experiences that children already have and those they may need for new learning and understanding.

3   *Stage of development*
    A child's stage of development will to some extent determine his or her thought processes and specific development within subject areas. It is therefore necessary to discover how children are thinking and what their ideas are in developing any area of work. Research suggests that this is particularly important in science, in which children come to the subject with their own ideas about why things happens that are often at odds with the scientific knowledge you want them to acquire. It will also be necessary to assess specific skills as part of your assessment procedure.

4   *Abilities*
    You need to match work to individual ability on many occasions and ensure that the most able are not marking time or underachieving and that the least able or least interested are not doing less than they might because you are showing them that your expectations of them are low. There is evidence to suggest that both these groups underperform.

You also need to observe in order to assess the learning programme you are providing, the effects of your classroom environment and organisation and your own contribution. Much of this will be your own observation, but it can be helpful to ask a colleague to observe something you are doing and give you feedback.

We have already noted that children will give you feedback if you discuss with the class their reactions to the various things you and they are doing.

When you ask someone else to observe you, you have to define what you are trying to do and what you want to know about it, and this is a helpful activity in its own right. It can be valuable to do this for yourself, identifying what you consider to be success in different aspects of work and the clues which will tell you how successful you have been. Observation as a teaching skill may be reviewed using Analysis 6.2.

Skills of organisation and control

The actual process of organisation in the classroom involves selecting

Analysis 6.2 Teaching skills – observation

1	How good were the assessments of children that I made when they first came to me?
2	Do my records of the academic progress of each child give me the information that I need to help them to learn?
3	Do my records of each child's behaviour and development give me the information I need to help them to develop socially?
4	Does my use of tests and check-lists contribute satisfactorily to the knowledge I need to help children to learn and develop?
5	Do I observe individual children to find starting points for their learning?
6	Do I look for the right moment to intervene to help individuals to learn?
7	Do I discuss progress with individual children, helping them to set targets for their improvement in a regular and systematic way?
8	Do I observe in order to identify children's problems and deal with them?
9	Do I study children who are exceptionally able as well as those who have learning difficulties in order to help them learn at a suitable level?

from a range of different ways of doing things to fit your particular style, children and situation. You need to be able to anticipate likely problems and avoid them by careful planning, particularly at points of change of activity. You also need to train children to work as you think best, using the resources of time and space to full advantage. In addition you need to be able to control children as a class, in groups and individually. Very few teachers escape altogether from problems of managing the classroom and almost all beginners need to work to achieve control. Although it is certainly true that some people achieve control very easily right from the start, most people develop this ability over a period of time.

Factors involved in classroom organisation and control

There are many factors involved in good classroom organisation and control and some of these, such as grouping and the use of time and space, are dealt with in detail later in this book. The control of children is very much bound up with the organisation that a teacher sets up. The following need to be considered:

- *The quality of the classroom as a learning environment*
  Children learn from the environment as well as from the teacher
  and each other, and the way the classroom is set up for learning is
  important. It should be attractive and welcoming but also have
  much available which encourages learning. Display should be either
  encouraging children by showing their work attractively or it
  should be stimulating material which invites questions and
  exploration. There should be a good deal in the classroom which
  supports independent learning. It is useful to ask oneself whether
  children left to their own devices in the classroom would be able
  to go on learning because of the way the room is organised.

- *The use of space and resources*
  The way space is organised in the classroom has a considerable
  effect on the way children work. If resources are easily to hand
  and are organised so that it is clear which materials a child should
  use next, it is likely that there will be better concentration on the
  work in hand and fewer interruptions for the teacher.

  It is also important to try to use resources as effectively and
  fully as possible. For example, are any computers in your classroom
  out of use for much of the time? If so, it is worth considering
  whether some slight changes in organisation would give more
  children a chance to use them.

- *Grouping for learning*
  A good deal of primary school learning takes place in groups,
  although this is often a matter of children working individually
  within the group at work given to the group as a whole. There
  should also be some co-operative work in groups and some work
  where the grouping is according to ability. Grouping for learning
  is dealt with in more detail in Chapter 12.

- *The use of time*
  Time is the one resource which cannot be increased. You can only
  look for better ways of using the time that you have. There are
  suggestions in Chapter 11 for checking how you are using time
  with a view to seeing whether you are making the best possible
  use of it.

It can be frightening to find yourself not in control, and
inexperienced teachers need to remind themselves that not only can
they learn to control children but that the ability to do this – while a
prerequisite for good teaching – does not itself guarantee it. That
depends on how you use the opportunities which the control you
achieve offers. There are teachers who have excellent control, but offer

little of quality to children. There are also outstanding teachers who have had to work hard in their early days to achieve control.

There are a number of principles for classroom control which it is useful to remember:

- *Children behave badly when they don't know what to do*
  Think out the organisation of your work in detail beforehand, especially when you are changing activities. You also need to think carefully about how you are going to instruct children about the work you want them to do. This is just as important when you are working with a group of children you know well as when you are working with a new group and establishing ways of doing things.

- *Always get attention before giving instructions*
  It is a good idea to get children to look at you so that their attention is alerted and you can make eye contact with them. You may also need to find a way of attracting attention when children are doing noisy work or are absorbed in what they are doing, especially if you have a quiet voice. Establish the idea that when you clap your hands or signal in some way you want everyone's attention.

  Learn to give instructions so that each important point is reinforced and is clear to everyone. Be careful not to give too much information at once. It is often a good idea to ask particular children what the instruction was to make sure that they have grasped the message.

- *Be ready when children come into the classroom*
  The way you start work is important. It can be a recipe for trouble, and a waste of time, to insist that children wait quietly without anything to do for too long. It is generally better to establish a pattern in which everyone is expected to come in and start working at something. This may be a preplanned activity which is self-explanatory or work from instructions written on the board or on an overhead projector transparency or it may be a daily pattern of quiet work or any other regular activity. The important thing is not to leave children with nothing to do but misbehave.

  This isn't nearly as easy as it seems when you see a capable and experienced teacher at work. As with so much else in teaching, you have to work to establish the behaviour you want.

- *Be individual in calling children to order*
  It is generally more effective to pick out individuals by name when you are trying to get attention than to speak to the class generally. You can single out children doing the right things – 'I can see that

Karen is ready' – or you can comment on those who are not doing what you want – 'Peter, I'm waiting for you'. By and large, the first is more effective and you may find it useful to check from time to time what you are actually doing, so that you are not being too negative to particular children without realising it.

- *Learn to scan the class*

  Good teachers are said to have eyes in the back of their heads. Beginners often get absorbed with individuals or small groups and ignore the rest of the class. You need to look round very frequently so that you anticipate misbehaviour. This also keeps children aware that you are watching them and so helps to prevent deviant behaviour.

  The Oracle Study (Galton and Simon, 1980), discussed in Chapter 5, described one group of children as *intermittent workers* and noted that these children only worked when the teacher's eye was on them. If you scan the class regularly, very often a child about to waste time or do something unacceptable will catch your eye and settle to work again. If catching the child's eye doesn't work, try moving towards him or her in a determined way.

- *Set rules of behaviour from the beginning*

  Wragg (1984) describes how experienced teachers in his study used the first lesson with a new class. Almost without exception, they said they would use the first few lessons to establish the rules they wanted the class to follow. They varied in the extent to which they intended to dictate the rules or discuss them or work them out with the pupils, but the areas covered tended to be fairly similar. They included rules for entering and leaving the classroom, rules about work, a rule that there should be no talking when the teacher was talking and rules about property and safety.

  These were teachers in a secondary school. In a primary classroom you will still want some similar rules, and you may also want to make rules about the degree of movement around the classroom that you will allow, the numbers of children who can undertake a particular activity at the same time, occasions when choice will be allowed and so on. It may be a good idea with older children to have these rules displayed somewhere.

  You need to be consistent in dealing with children, making sure that you treat them in fairly similar ways and that you enforce the rules that you have made or agreed with the children without too many changes.

- *Work out changes in activity in careful detail*
  Most of the things which go wrong in the classroom do so in the
  process of changing from one activity to another. You can avoid
  problems by thinking out how to get from the first activity to the
  second, asking yourself what each child will be doing and listing
  the steps needed.

  Able and experienced teachers often give the impression that
  all you need to do when you change activities is to say 'It's time
  now for you to go to your number groups' for there to be a well-
  organised move round which leaves everyone in the right place in
  the least possible time. The ability to do this has been built up
  with the children and through experience over a long period. It
  takes time and effort to get children to work and move as you
  wish.

  A good deal of the ability to control a class is in the confidence
  in your voice and manner which implies that children will do as
  you wish. The trouble is that it is difficult to have confidence when
  you don't know whether what you are asking for will actually
  happen. It is possible, however, to learn to behave as if you are
  confident. Confident people are relaxed and speak confidently and
  you can learn to do this. Good teachers not only use their voices
  when they give an explanation of what they want but they also
  reinforce their words with gestures, facial expression and tone of
  voice. Smiling conveys confidence. Fumbling and self-grooming
  convey a lack of confidence, and walking to and fro is distracting.

Your organisation and control skills may be reviewed using Analysis
6.3.

Communication skills

The ability to form good relationships with children is a prerequisite
of good communication and good teaching. It is difficult to
communicate or teach well if you are not on good terms with your
children. The ability to form relationships depends a good deal on
your personality and is also partly a matter of attitudes which help
you to demonstrate to the children that you care about them and have
confidence in their ability to learn.

Communication takes place as a result of people attending to each
other. It is not simply a matter of the meaning of the words you use,
but is implicit in your choice of words and language structure to match
the listeners and the situation. (Think how you would say the same

Analysis 6.3 Teaching skills – organisation and control

---

1 Is my classroom attractive and welcoming to children?
2 Is the furniture in my classroom arranged to provide the most suitable pattern for the work being undertaken?
3 Is my classroom a learning environment in which children can learn independently?
4 Are the resources of equipment, materials and books in my classroom fully used?
5 Are the resources in my classroom organised so that they are easy to keep tidy?
6 Is each child in the class in appropriate groups for learning?
7 Do my plans include provision for children of different levels of ability and stages of development?
8 Is my time and the children's used to the best possible extent?
9 Do children start work immediately they enter the classroom?
10 Do the children in my class discuss work in pairs and small groups when this is appropriate?
11 Am I always in control of the whole group, even when I am working with individuals?
12 Can I always get full attention from the children when I wish?

---

thing to your class and to your headteacher.) It is also implicit in your tone of voice, the inflections you use, what you say and how you say it. In addition, you convey messages by movement and facial expression as well as by words and you modify your message in the light of the response you get. Your view of your listeners is demonstrated in your choice of content, vocabulary and sentence structure and in the use of pitch and pace and the use of pauses.

The children, in their turn, will respond not only verbally when you ask questions but also in terms of body language and you will read this and respond to it. There will be children who are looking at you intently and apparently taking in every word. There will be others who may be looking out of the window or at something which seems to be more interesting to them than what you are saying. There will be those who appear to be bursting to say something and others who avoid catching your eye in case you ask them something. If there are too many who are not reacting to what you are saying you will, almost without noticing it, say the same thing in a different and perhaps a simpler way.

Your task is to get the message over as clearly as possible in ways which draw an appropriate response from the children and help them to match what you are saying to what they know already. Try to tape yourself in the classroom from time to time and listen to the tape critically.

Movement is the most basic form of communication, operating from birth or perhaps even earlier. Because it is so basic and automatic, the movement message goes over even if you actually say something different. Movement and facial expression are all the time sending messages to others. Your observation of the children involves interpreting the movement messages that they are sending. Their observation of you does likewise. Very young or handicapped children often communicate with their teachers by touch.

It is often through non-verbal communication of this kind that people get across the message that they are warm and sympathetic, brisk and business-like, tired or bad-tempered, pleased or sorry and so on. Children learn to interpret these messages very early because it is important for them to recognise when mother or teacher is pleased or angry.

Eye contact is an important aspect of communication in this context. We use eye contact to signal the beginnings and endings of pieces of communication as well as to send messages to control children's behaviour. By making eye contact with individual children you can imply that they are being noticed and had better behave or that they are important and being cared for.

Communication through the environment is an extension of communication through movement. An experienced observer quickly takes in the messages which a teacher's classroom is putting over. You also send messages by the way you dress and care for your appearance. These all reflect philosophy and teaching style.

Your voice is likely to be the most frequently used form of communication in the classroom. The way you use it affects children in different ways. For example, any teacher who has tried to work with a lost voice will be aware that it is possible quite quickly to have the whole class whispering. You provide an important speech model for your children and your patterns of speech will affect theirs. You need to remember, however, that children learn to use spoken language by speaking and it is not easy to orchestrate opportunities for talking for a whole class. Paired and small group discussion provides opportunities for children to talk through ideas with others, but you also want opportunities for them to experience speaking in a whole-class situation.

Communication is a two-way process. The warm and trusting relationship necessary for good communication is something built up over time, but when you start work with a new class it is particularly important to be as responsive as you can to children's ideas and confidences. Your response at this stage to something a child volunteers may determine not only whether this particular child will risk suggesting something again, but also, if other children are listening, they too will be influenced by your reactions. A teacher who says 'My children never have any ideas' needs to look at the way he or she is reacting to the ideas they offer. It is not unusual to see a group of children silent and unresponsive with one teacher but full of ideas with another.

Trust in the teacher – once established – brings a necessary degree of security to children. As we have seen, security depends a good deal on knowing what to do, knowing the boundaries and what is expected and knowing how the other person will react to different kinds of behaviour. Security often stems from predictability.

What are the communication skills the teacher needs? The following need consideration:

1 *Presentation skills*
   Every teacher needs to be able to present material to children in ways which capture attention and help them to focus on what is important. This means making good preparation and good use of voice and gesture. It also means continually scanning the class to see how they are responding and being aware of how long you can talk before children cease to listen.

2 *Questioning skills*
   Questioning is one of the most important teaching skills. You need to think out very carefully the different types of questions you want to use so that you challenge the thinking of all the children in the class.

   Questions can be classified in a number of ways. One common classification is into open and closed questions. Another is into questions requiring recall and questions requiring thinking. Research suggests that teachers tend to ask more closed and recall questions and not enough open and thought-provoking questions.

   It is also very easy for teachers to ask 'guess what I'm thinking' types of questions and, in responding to children's answers, turn aside all answers but the one which gives the correct guess.

3 *Leading discussion*
   Leading a class discussion is a more difficult skill than it seems in the hands of an expert, partly because most classes are rather large for satisfactory discussion. It therefore requires a good deal of effort on the part of the teacher to include the whole group. A

very important part of leading discussion is the ability to draw together the points that have been made and reinforce those that are important for the children's learning. This is dealt with in more detail in Chapter 7. It is also important to respond positively to the children's contributions. Even when a child gives a wrong answer it may be possible to say something which is encouraging. Positive reactions to contributions lead children to be more ready to respond the next time and negative reactions inhibit.

4   *Helping individuals*
Whatever the organisation of the class, you will always need skill in helping individual children to move on from their present understanding. You therefore need to be good at analysing a child's thinking so that you can suggest ways forward. You also need to have the class well organised so that you are free to deal with individuals from time to time.

Your communication skills may be reviewed using Analysis 6.4.

Planning skills

Every school and every teacher needs an underlying structure for work which is clear and which allows scope for flexibility but which also has enough system behind what is done to ensure that children make progress. To some extent the National Curriculum and the associated assessment provide something of a structure, but it mustn't be allowed to become a strait-jacket. Planning does not mean a loss of spontaneity

Analysis 6.4 Teaching skills – communication

1   How well do I present material to the whole class?
2   Are my questioning skills good enough?
3   Do I ask a sufficient variety of questions and get children thinking?
4   Do I lead discussion competently?
5   Do I get children to contribute sufficiently?
6   Is it always the same children who contribute?
7   Do I get more contributions from boys than from girls?
8   Do I get more contributions from White than from Black children?
9   Am I able to draw children's contributions together to help them to learn?
10   How skilled am I at discovering how individual children are thinking?
11   How skilled am I at helping them to think on from the point they have reached?

and flexibility. It is simply that you must be clear where you are going if you want to make the most of the opportunities that arise. You also need to share with the children your view of what you are hoping they will achieve.

The planning by the classroom teacher must be set in a wider context. As a classroom teacher you are normally responsible for planning the work for your class. Your planning is part of the planning needed for the whole year group if your school has more than one class in each year, and this in turn is part of the planning for the whole school and eventually for the whole school career of your children. It is important to see what you are doing in this wider context and to know where your work fits into the overall pattern. The National Curriculum makes this rather easier to do than it was in the past.

In planning we need to be sure that some common ground is covered by all children. This will be partly ensured by the provisions in the National Curriculum. It is important to remember that objectives can be met in a variety of ways and that one activity can meet more than one objective. There is a case with older children in particular for a formal programme of fairly specific teaching, such as is required by the literacy and numeracy hours, and an informal programme which complements it by using opportunities as they occur.

Methods of planning will be discussed later, but it should be noted here that long-term planning should involve the following in some form:

1 identifying aims and objectives;
2 making general long-term plans to meet the aims and objectives which involve assessing the needs of children and making systematic reviews of their progress;
3 making broad outlines of curriculum plans;
4 setting dates or periods of time for completing different aspects of the work;
5 considering how you wish children to work and planning a training programme for them;
6 making plans for evaluation, including criteria by which success will be judged, and deciding on the records to be kept;
7 considering the books, equipment and materials which will be needed and taking any necessary action;
8 considering the first-hand experience which will be needed and planning action to provide it;
9 considering your own development and planning the necessary action to develop your own skills and knowledge.

You will also need to make short-term plans for day-to-day work which:

- will provide for children of all abilities;
- are flexible enough to include interests which may arise;
- pay attention to details of organisation and enable work to run smoothly;
- enable you to achieve your long-term aims and objectives.

Your planning skills may be reviewed using Analysis 6.5.

Problem-solving skills

Human beings develop and learn by solving the problems which face them. This is true whether one looks at problems in one's everyday life or at problems in one's place of work.

Unfortunately there is also a human tendency to regard difficult problems as someone else's fault and as something about which nothing can be done. While it is true that there are always aspects of problems which cannot be solved, the fact that there is an obstacle does not mean that a problem is insoluble.

The process of teaching and organising a class is very much a problem-solving activity for both teacher and children. For the teacher the basic problem is that of how to reconcile the heterogeneous collection of children who make up the class with what they need to

Analysis 6.5 Teaching skills – planning

1 To what extent do I state aims and objectives in planning?
2 Do I make broad long-term plans for curriculum?
3 Do I plan evaluation and record-keeping?
4 Do I work out in advance the books and materials I need and see that they will be available?
5 Do I plan adequately the first-hand experiences my children will need?
6 Do I share my plans with the children?
7 Do I think out how I want children to work and the training they may need?
8 Do I make short-term plans allowing for interests which may arise?
9 Does my planning include provision for the whole range of children? Do I make adequate provision for the most and least able?
10 Do I plan organisation in sufficient detail so that things run smoothly?
11 Do I plan for my own professional development?

learn in such a way that the optimum amount of learning takes place. The solution to this set of problems is the main subject of this book.

The development of work in design and technology has brought the idea of problem-solving to the fore for work with children but the teacher must also be a problem-solver. The skills involved in problem-solving which are evident in design and technology and which are discussed in detail in Chapter 10 are also applicable to the teacher's problems. Both teacher and children need to acquire problem-solving skills and positive attitudes to problems, and they acquire both skills and attitudes by working to solve problems.

If you are looking at the problem of how to provide for a wide range of abilities in your class, you need to start by defining the problem and then look at what you want the outcome of any action to be. You might set out the problem as shown in Figure 6.1.

There are probably a number of ways in which you could continue from this point. Two which seem particularly interesting are described below.

Force field analysis was devised by Kurt Lewin (1951) and involves considering the forces which are acting for and against you in solving your problem. Supporting forces in the situation described below might include good accommodation, a head who is prepared to let you try things and will support you financially and a class that is easy to handle. Restraining forces might be the fact that the teacher who had your class last year did nothing to encourage independent working, pressure from parents to work in traditional ways with the most able children, a lack of materials for the most able and a lack of knowledge on your part of the best way to deal with the least able children. You can then consider how you deal with each of these, looking at how you make the most of the supporting forces and at what you can do to minimise the effect of the restraining forces.

Another approach, part of which fits well with force field analysis, is described by Jackson (1975) in *The Art of Solving Problems*. He

Present state	Desired state
A small group of children have work which is at about the right level The most and least able children and some others are just occupied	All children have a programme of work which is at their proper level

Figure 6.1 Problem-solving

speaks of considering the obstacles to solving a problem, which is a little like looking at the restraining forces. He suggests working through some possible ways of tackling each obstacle. You might overcome an obstacle, go round it, remove it, demolish it, neutralise it, prove it to be illusory, turn it to advantage, buy it off, alter it, find its weakest point or wait for it to go away.

If you take the restraining forces listed above as the obstacles in your situation, you might remove one of the obstacles by instituting a careful programme of training your children to work more independently. The pressure from parents might be partly demolished by parents' meetings at which you explain what you are doing and why. It might also help to involve parents in the work you are doing in various ways so that they see for themselves that it is effective. Your head is supportive, so it would be possible to meet the obstacles about materials by buying more. However, you would be wise to analyse the kind of material you need to meet the full range of abilities that your children represent and gradually build up materials which fit into a framework, coding new material as you add it so that you are aware of what you have available. In practice, many teachers spend a lot of time making material but don't take enough time to sort out a structure so that new pieces of material fit in. If you can find time to make a structure, everything you do by way of making or buying material will fit into an overall plan.

Another possibility is to get out all the materials you have which might be relevant and look to see whether any of them could be made more self-contained and usable by children without help from you. You might like to make some bridging materials to go with another material so that a child who is less able can use it.

You might also find that you could increase materials to match some needs if you make the final end point of a project the creation of a material which other children can use. This has many advantages. It uses work already done; it can also be an interesting incentive for the children who work on it and it creates an audience and gives a purpose to the work which ties in with some of the aims of literacy teaching.

When you address yourself directly to an obstacle there are frequently possible ways forward. A useful strategy is to ask a series of questions such as 'Can I overcome the problem by looking at it in a different way, by using materials differently, by looking for time to do some basic thinking and sorting out of ideas in order to move forward, by working with colleagues, by involving parents and others, by getting children to work differently, by reorganising the situation or use of materials, and so on?' This kind of thinking is often most profitable when undertaken with others. It is sometimes a useful activity for a class of children as well as for interested staff.

List possible solutions

You will already have a number of solutions as a result of your examination of forces and obstacles and you can add to these. Write down as many ideas as you can think of, however unlikely some of them seem. Don't stop when you think of an idea which seems good but go on generating further ideas until you have quite a number. Letting your mind range over ideas in this way influences the idea you finally choose, which may be a mixture of several ideas. It can sometimes be useful to aim for a number of ideas; to set out, for example, ten ways of achieving the objective you have in mind.

If you are working with a group, one way of doing this is to pass round a piece of paper for each objective on which each person writes an idea which could be used to achieve that objective. It is better still to do this with an overhead projector transparency so that the ideas listed can be projected for discussion.

Examine solutions

The next stage is to look at the solutions you have listed. It may help to draw up a page with four columns, as shown below:

Idea	Advantages	Disadvantages	Points to note

Now take each idea and sort it out under those headings. This will lead to making a choice of possible solutions. You may want to use several of the ideas you have listed in any particular case.

Make an action plan

Include the following steps:

- Select what seems to you to be a realistic date by which you want to have achieved your objectives.
- Set down in detail the steps you need to take. It may be a good

idea to do this in the form of a flow-chart, but it depends upon the problem.

• Consider who else is involved, including the children, and note what you need to do about informing or consulting others.

Plan evaluation

It is very easy to try out some new idea and do nothing about evaluating its success except in a very casual way. When you are planning, it is much better to decide in some detail what you will consider as success and how you will know whether you have achieved your goals.

This is a very detailed way of tackling a problem. There will be many occasions when you have ideas and put them into action more casually. The point about suggesting a programme is to stress that there is always some step you can take to deal with a problem and that having some strategies for generating ideas and solutions can help. This is also a useful set of strategies for a group of teachers working together to solve a problem.

Make a point of periodically reflecting on what you have done, especially at the end of the year, to make sure that you have learned all you can from the way you tackled particular problems. Evaluation is dealt with in detail in Chapter 16.

The report of research into teacher effectiveness by Hay McBer (2000) reported in the *Times Educational Supplement* lists the following descriptions by children of a good teacher:

A good teacher
is kind
is generous
listens to you
encourages you
has faith in you
keeps confidences
likes teaching children
likes teaching their subject
takes time to explain things
helps you when you're stuck

tells you how you are doing
allows you to have your say
doesn't give up on you
cares for your opinion
makes you feel clever
treats people equally
stands up for you
makes allowances
tells the truth
is forgiving

7 Teaching strategies

Whenever you plan work in the classroom, you have a variety of possible ways of helping children to learn. The choices of teaching strategy you make are influenced by four factors:

- the particular group of children;
- the subject matter to be learned;
- the environment in which you work and the materials and equipment available;
- your own particular teaching style and preferences.

We have already looked fairly closely at the way children learn and at the consequences of different teaching styles for the teacher. Children's learning ability and the approaches most likely to be successful will vary within any class, but very often there are sufficient common elements to enable you to select an approach likely to match the needs of the majority, leaving you with some work to do to help individuals who differ.

In selecting teaching methods you need to consider not only the ability of the group and the stage of development of the majority but also the children's experience, their interests, their language, knowledge and skill and what is likely to motivate this particular group. The younger and less able the group, the more important it becomes to start from the first-hand and the practical, although first-hand experience continues to be important if a child's learning is to be carried over and applied to new situations.

The subject matter to be learned also dictates certain things in relation to teaching approaches. For example, it is difficult to teach young children very much about number in any effective way without a good deal of practical work. Geographical and historical concepts are unlikely to be established without some field work. You can't learn to enjoy poetry without reading it and listening to it.

Edwards and Mercer (1987: 126) stress the importance of classroom discourse in children's learning. They say:

> It is largely within the teacher/pupil discourse through which the lesson is conducted that whatever understandings are eventually created, are in the first place shaped, interpreted, made salient or peripheral, reinterpreted and so on. And it is a process that remains essentially dominated by the teacher's own aims and expectations.
>
> The teacher's dilemma is to have to inculcate knowledge when apparently eliciting it. This gives rise to the general ground rule of classroom discourse, in which the pupil's task is to come up with the correct solutions to problems seemingly spontaneously while all the time trying to discern in the teacher's clues, cues, questions and pre-suppositions what the required solution actually is.

This may sound a cynical view but it is firmly rooted in the writers' research in classrooms, and reflection on the way one works in the classroom tends to confirm that this is what happens a good deal of the time.

We saw in the last chapter that Edwards and Mercer (1987) and Bennett and Kell (1989) found that teachers tended not to tell children what is was they were supposed to be learning. This may have been because the teacher did not want to limit the lesson but to use ideas which came up as well as what had been planned. These writers make the point, however, that this lack of information meant that children were less able to focus their learning and that sharing with the children the purpose of what they were doing might be more effective.

The environment in which you teach obviously has some effect on the way you set about things. Lack of space may limit some activities. Lack of materials or equipment may also be a limitation. If you work in a classroom which faces a main road you may find the noise affects the way you are able to talk to the class and you may organise things a little differently to cope with this.

Chapter 5 looked at teaching style and the importance of using your style to the best advantage.

Bennett *et al.* (1984: 24, 25) suggest that there are four types of learning task:

- *Incremental.* This involves new learning.
- *Restructuring.* The pupil is 'required to discover, invent or construct a new way of looking at problems'.

- *Enrichment.* This 'demands the use of familiar knowledge, concepts and skills in unfamiliar contexts'.
- *Practice.* This helps pupils to make skills automatic.
- *Revision.* This 'demands attention to materials or skills which have been set aside for some time'.

They found in their study of primary school children that 25 per cent of tasks were incremental, 7 per cent restructuring or enrichment, 60 per cent practice and 6 per cent revision. There were considerably more practice tasks given in language than in number work. They also found that very often the task did not demand what the teacher intended. 'Almost a quarter of tasks intended to make incremental demands in fact made practice demands' (Bennett *et al.*, 1984: 33). There were also practice tasks which turned out to be incremental and there was a tendency to underestimate high-attainers.

Matching work to children is one of the most difficult tasks for teachers. The HMI (1978) primary survey found that for high-attaining children there was a mismatch in almost half the mathematics classes observed, and in some other subjects the evidence of mismatch was even higher. Desforges (1985: 102) suggests that mismatching appears to be initiated and sustained by:

1 demanding concrete records of procedures rather than evidence of thought;
2 rewarding effort to produce rather than effort to conceptualise;
3 adopting management techniques which permit rapid responses to each child's immediate problems but leave the teacher ignorant of the child's confusion or potential;
4 the teacher's inexperience with and lack of skill in diagnostic work and a taste for direct instruction, however informally put, rather than analysis.

Both Desforges (1985) and Bennett *et al.* (1984) stress the need for teachers to spend more time in diagnosing the thinking of individual children in order to discover why errors were made and to ensure better concept development.

Children may learn and teachers may teach in the following ways. These should be regarded as a collection of teaching tools from which to select according to their appropriateness for the particular children, the subject matter and the context.

Direct teaching

A high proportion of teaching at every level, but particularly with older children and adults, will tend to consist of exposition and questioning. It will almost certainly involve a good deal of questioning designed to elicit information from the children so that you can build on what they already know and the ideas they already have. The following would seem to be situations in which this approach is useful:

- It may be the most efficient and economical way of getting children to learn something and checking that they know it.
- It is a valuable way of starting and ending a piece of work. At the beginning you may want to stimulate children and interest them, or direct their attention or get the work organised. At the end of a piece of work there may be a place for drawing together what has been learned, generalising, filling gaps, questioning understanding and so on. This is what the plenary sessions in literacy and number are designed to do.
- It is a good approach for giving instructions on safety or organisation where it is important that every child understands the same thing. You will still need to reinforce your words more for some children than for others.

The success of this method of teaching and the extent of its use depends to some extent on the skills and the preferred style of the teacher, but recent developments such as the literacy and numeracy strategies have stressed the value of interactive whole-class teaching. This is a form of direct teaching where the children are constantly involved in answering questions, contributing ideas in discussion, explaining how to do something and so on.

Direct teaching involves the following.

Good preparation

Exposition by the teacher needs to be good if it is to capture interest. Each teacher puts things over in a different way, but you need to maintain a self-critical attitude to what you do and work all the time at improving your skill. This means that some work, at least, should be prepared in considerable detail.

Making appropriate notes

This doesn't mean making copious notes which you may not be able to use in the classroom, but finding the best way of note-making for you and selecting methods of planning which enable you to file and store lesson material and perhaps reassemble it for use in other ways on future occasions.

Note-making may mean setting out activities in a flow diagram. You may put notes in a file or on cards which can be reshuffled on future occasions. You may also like to make a collection of overhead projector transparencies and file them by punching holes in them and placing them in a ring binder for future use.

The number of pieces of work which you can prepare thoroughly is limited, but if you prepare a few things really well each week, selecting work which you may want to repeat at another time, you will gradually build up a stock of material.

Work which lends itself to this kind of preparation includes stories, where it is a good idea if you want to tell a story to try to see it in a series of scenes, thinking about what they would look like in great detail so that you can create pictures in the children's minds. Any topic which you want children to become involved in can be prepared in this way.

Setting the scene

When you want to present material to the whole class, try to set the scene well. Make sure the children are sitting where they can see you and try to start in a way which will capture interest and will at the same time draw on their experience. It is much the same whether you are talking to five-year-olds or fifty-year-olds: getting interest is something you need to do very quickly and it is always worth preparing the beginning and the end of a piece of work extra well.

Being ready for the work to start

It is wise to look ahead to what you plan to do after introducing your topic and to make sure that books are ready, writing materials available or whatever. It is very disappointing to create a marvellous atmosphere with a story or account of something and get the children enthusiastic and ready to go only to be brought down to earth with a bump by minor chaos resulting from not having things ready in advance.

Exposition

Exposition involves explaining, description, linking with children's experience and is an important teacher skill. Wragg and Brown (1993:

3) describe explaining as 'giving understanding to another' and suggest that an explanation can help someone understand:

- concepts;
- cause and effect;
- procedures;
- purposes and objectives;
- relationships;
- processes.

They stress the importance of good use of the voice. 'Correct use of the voice involves light and shade, knowing when to slow down or accelerate, which words or phrases to emphasise, when to pause, how to read an audience so that the appropriate tone of voice is used' (Wragg and Brown, 1993: 4). They also suggest that it is useful for children to explain things to each other.

Using questioning

Questioning is a very important teaching skill. Wragg and Brown (1993: 16) note that it can have several purposes. These include:

- finding out what the pupils already know or do not know;
- shaping the line of argument by using the pupils' own ideas;
- checking how well pupils understand what is being explained;
- eliciting concrete examples of principles or concepts;
- helping children develop a desire to enquire to learn further, once the explanation is complete.

Questions are of many kinds and some are of more use than others in developing children's ability to think. The following types of questions are common in classrooms and are taken mainly from Kerry (1980).

- *Recall questions:* These are probably the most common type of teaching questions. They are useful and necessary but should not be used to the exclusion of other types of questions. Recall questions can degenerate into 'guess what I'm thinking' questions in which you can see children concentrating on trying to guess what the teacher wants rather than on answering the question.
- *Reasoning questions:* Questions which involve thinking things through using evidence are needed in most types of school work.

Questions such as 'Why do you think that moss grows on this wall and not on that one?' or 'What do you think will happen next in the story and why do you think that?' can demand reasoning from children, especially if you follow up their replies so that you take them through a sequence of reasoning.

- *Speculative questions:* Many reasoning questions will also be speculative, but one can go beyond the reasoning involved in the type of questions given above and encourage reasoned speculation about hypothetical possibilities, e.g. 'What would happen if school ceased to be compulsory?' or 'What difference would it make if our school was on top of a hill or by the sea?'
- *Personal response questions:* These ask children how they feel about something, have no right answers and should help children to sort out their own thinking, e.g. 'How would you feel if someone damaged something you cared about a lot?', 'What should happen to people who damage other people's property?' or 'Why do you think they do it?'

Questioning should not be left to the spur of the moment. It is wise to prepare some questions in advance so that you can give thought to the kinds of questions you want to ask. It may be a good idea from time to time to tape a questioning session and then listen to the tape afterwards, perhaps with a colleague, and consider whether the questions you asked actually made the children think. You also need to consider what evidence you need to know whether you were making the children think or not and what proportion of the class this covered.

It may also be worth listening to a tape to review your responses to children. Were they such as to give children confidence to contribute? How did you deal with wrong answers? Were you able to find ways of encouraging children who gave a wrong answer and leading them towards the correct answer? Which children actually gave answers?

Holt (1984) describes how he discussed questioning with a group of children in a class with which he felt he had a good relationship. He asked how they felt when they were asked a question and got the reply 'We gulp'. Galton (1989: 73) also describes children's views about answering questions in class:

> Older pupils described the strategy where they put their hands up to answer a question and put them down again if there was a likelihood of the teacher picking on them to answer. One pupil, referring to answering a question, said, 'It's like walking a tightrope'.

This sort of evidence suggests that your responses to children's contributions are very important

You also need to give some thought to how you choose children to answer questions. It is wise to pause after giving a question to give children a chance to think and then to choose someone to answer from those with their hands up. It can be useful in a questioning session with a class of older children to get one of them to note the initials of those children who answered questions. This will give you a check on whether you are involving all the children over a period of time or whether you have a bias in choosing children to answer questions, perhaps towards boys or more able children. It is also relevant to note those children who did not answer at all.

Research suggests that increasing 'wait' time for up to three seconds after asking a question can significantly improve the quality of the answers. Askew and Wiliam (1995: 16) note that 'these effects are more pronounced for understanding concepts and principles than for simple recall of facts'.

A further consideration is how you teach children to ask appropriate questions. This is particularly important in science, where children need to learn to ask questions which lend themselves to investigation. Questioning might also be considered in relation to interviewing people and children can be asked to consider what sorts of questions get what sorts of answers. They can also be encouraged to pose questions to the class and to consider whether these were good questions for finding out what they wanted to know.

Drama may offer something here. A group of children looking at a bridge as if they were engineers from another country and studying it in order to build a similar bridge at home will ask quite different and more pertinent questions from those asked by a group who are visiting simply in order to study the bridge.

It is very easy for children to get the idea that the way teachers ask questions is the norm. Most people ask questions because they want to know the answer. Teachers are unusual in that they frequently ask questions to which they already know the answer.

Learning by investigation

We all learn better the material we seek out and work on for ourselves. Primary teachers are well aware of this and work to create situations in which children experiment and discover. Sometimes a teacher will set up an open-ended learning situation in which a group of children is taken out of school and encouraged to look for things to study as well as those suggested by the teacher.

On another occasion the teacher may want to get a particular piece of learning established and may provide specific experiences and arrange for a very specific outcome. This is most easily seen when one looks at the development of mathematical concepts, where a teacher may be providing various kinds of practical work in order to develop conceptual thinking on firm understanding. Edwards and Mercer (1987) describe teachers in this situation giving children clues about what is wanted when they don't find it out for themselves and they demonstrate how this kind of learning can degenerate into 'guess what I'm thinking'. They also show that teachers often miss useful comments by children which would have helped the learning because they are so intent on seeing that the children achieve the teacher's goals. They suggested that where this happens the learning becomes 'ritual', i.e. children go through the procedures and say the right words but do not really understand the principles underlying what they are learning. This makes the learning difficult to apply in new situations.

Investigatory learning needs to be part of a great deal of the work you do with children but there are some areas of work in which it is more important than others. It is particularly important in the development of concepts. A concept is, in effect, a generalisation made from a range of different experiences. For example, children at an early age begin to acquire one aspect of conservation when they explore what happens when you pour liquid into different shaped vessels. They need to do this a number of times before they come to appreciate that the amount of liquid doesn't change. It merely changes shape. They then need to learn other examples of conservation if they are to get a full idea of the concept.

Another example might be the idea of *old*. In order to have an understanding of the past a child needs to understand what is meant when we say that something is old. Young children use the word in several different ways – 'I am six years old'. 'My Dad has a new car. My uncle bought his old one'. 'Our church is very old'. They need to sort out these meanings through experience. In particular they need to begin to see that the term *old* is a relative one. A boy is *old* compared with his baby sister; his mother is *old* compared with him; the church is *old* compared with his grandparents, but the church in the next village is *old* compared with our church.

Acquiring this concept of age means experiencing and noting signs of age in people and objects and buildings so that it becomes possible to make judgements about age. This means making generalisations from experience and discovering the clues about age which can be used.

There will an element of telling in concept development, but if there is to be true understanding and consequent ability to transfer the learning to new situations children need to reach the point where they can formulate the concept for themselves.

The National Curriculum substantially consists of concepts. It will therefore be important to set up appropriate situations which lead to the development of the specific concepts listed in each of the subject areas. It is likely that little time will be available for completely open-ended work, but a piece of work set up to develop a specific concept will provide many opportunities for other learning, some of which will meet other curriculum requirements.

Harlen (1985) suggests that the role of the teacher in this kind of learning in science is first of all to look for questions to which to say 'Let's see if we can find out'. The question may then need to be reorganised or broken down into questions which can be investigated. In other situations the teacher's task may be as follows:

- providing problems but not instructions for solving them, then giving the children the opportunity to do the planning;
- supplying a structure for planning appropriate to the children's experience (questions to take them through the steps of thinking about variables to change, to control and to measure);
- sometimes discussing plans before carrying them out and considering different ideas;
- often discussing activities afterwards to consider how the method of investigation could have been improved;
- providing opportunities in the form of activities where simple patterns of more general trends can be found;
- enabling children to talk about their findings and how they interpret them (by questioning and listening);
- asking them to make predictions, explaining how they arrive at them and then checking them against the evidence (discussion and practical work);
- expecting them to check interpretations carefully and draw only those conclusions for which they have evidence (discussion and practical work);
- organising for the interpretation of findings to be shared and discussed critically.

This kind of learning is often particularly effective in the context of the kind of drama described earlier which requires certain learning because of the role the child has taken on. This needs careful preparation, so that each child understands his or her role and is able to identify what is needed to help in the particular role. It is easy to see how such learning could grow in this context. If children really get inside the role it will have tremendous motivation. There will also be a demand for information which is much more clearly defined than where the children are finding out simply because the teacher tells them to.

This kind of motivation is, of course, present when children investigate a real problem with an outcome to be judged on its use, but it is difficult to do this all the time and an imaginary but convincing framework can do a great deal for you and the children in terms of motivation and involvement.

Whether you use drama as part of learning or work more directly to establish a concept, your task as teacher is to draw attention to what is significant in the situation and to help children to consider outcomes in such a way that your intervention leads to the discovery of answers rather than a statement of what is to be discovered. This is difficult to do because it takes time with individuals or small groups working through questions to see where they are in their thinking.

This kind of development may also come out of direct teaching, where your skill in questioning may lead to a discovery of a generalisation. This approach is far from being a soft option and it needs very careful structuring of learning if it is to succeed.

Learning by investigation also means acquiring process skills. Harlen (1985: 159) suggests following components of process skill development in science. These skills are also needed in most other aspects of curriculum.

- Providing the materials, time and physical arrangement for the children to study and interact with things in their environment. This involves children in having the evidence of their own senses, opportunities for them to find answers by doing things, having concrete experience as a basis of their thinking and being able to check their ideas against the behaviour of real things.
- Designing tasks that encourage discussion among small groups of children. This involves children in combining their ideas, listening to others, arguing about differences and refining their ideas through explaining them to others. This kind of activity is at its most valuable when the groups are of mixed ability and the more able children stimulate others.
- Discussing their work with children as individuals and in small groups. Children can be encouraged to explain how they arrived

at their ideas and by listening to them you can find out about the evidence they have gathered and discover how they have interpreted it. This is also an opportunity to encourage children to check their findings and review their activities and results critically.

- Organising whole-class discussions. Children need the opportunity to explain their findings and ideas to others, to hear about others' ideas, to comment on alternative views and to defend their own; children also need you to offer ideas and direct them to sources which will extend their ideas.
- Teaching the techniques of using equipment and the conventions of using graphs, tables, charts and symbols. Children need to have available the means to increase the accuracy of their observations and to choose appropriate forms for communication of their findings.
- Providing books, displays, visits and access to other sources of information. Children can compare their ideas with those of others, have access to information that may help them to develop and extend their ideas and raise questions which may lead to further enquiry.

Much of what is suggested here not only leads to learning in science but also meets many of the demands of the National Curriculum for oral and other work in English and mathematics and has relevance in a subject such as history where children may be encouraged to look for evidence of what life was like in other times.

Very young children may develop concepts and skills through play but the adult needs to see that this happens. Bennett and Kell (1989) found that teachers of infants tended to regard play as a time-filler, enabling them to hear other children read. They stress that it is not enough to provide play opportunities at the reception stage, however rich these may be. The teacher or another adult needs to interact with the children, drawing out the learning possibilities. Bruner (1985), for example, notes that adult presence strikingly increases the richness and length of play. Sylva *et al.* (1980) found that young children were more likely to engage in complex play if adults were interacting with them. The adult plays a fundamental part in directing the child's attention effectively. This refers to other learning as well as play.

Learning by investigation may enable children to follow up interests and be stimulated by an experience and to have some choice in the way they respond. A group of children making a local study, for example, may record their findings in drawing or painting, model making, various forms of writing, music, movement, drama and so on. The study may give rise to mathematical, scientific, historical or geographical exploration. It will, of course, be important to bear in mind the demands of the National Curriculum and to use the experience to develop some of the concepts and skills involved. It will also be important when giving children a choice of response to see that individual children do not always choose the same way to work. A child who writes well and easily, for example, may choose to respond in writing every time, whereas a child who finds writing difficult will avoid it.

This kind of activity requires a good deal of careful thought on the part of the teacher. It is not enough just to take children to an interesting place, even if you direct their attention to some of the things which can be seen. You need to help them to acquire the skills for studying environment and recording their responses in a variety of ways.

This may sometimes involve looking for specific information and making straightforward statements about findings, perhaps using charts and diagrams. On other occasions it may involve thinking how a place made them feel and writing personally or poetically or drawing or painting, sometimes observing in detail and recording in drawing or model making; or perhaps measuring or looking for things which might be investigated further, perhaps by questioning other people or by experiment. Most visits can give rise to work in all three core subjects as well as work in history and geography, art and craft and possibly other subjects as well.

Only when children have a range of approaches and skills for making observations do they become able to use a complex environment for learning. This doesn't mean that children need training in all the skills before you encourage responses to a new environment. Skills and approaches can be built up in the course of study and during the process children will see and suggest ideas of their own, some of which you may like to help them develop. They will thus become independent observers who are not looking over their shoulders to see if they are doing what you want them to do but are genuinely investigating for themselves.

This is one of the most important approaches to learning because it can be highly motivating and can help children to structure what they are learning and acquire concepts. It is also one of the most difficult methods to use well, and creating situations in which children can make discoveries which are within their capacity but which extend their thinking is a fascinating professional task.

Learning through discussion

Most of us learn a great deal through talking and we also consolidate learning in this way. One reason why this is useful is that when you put something into words you have to think it out. The responses and questions of others to your statement may then sharpen your thinking and enlarge it. Teachers will also be very conscious that one way to learn something well is to have to teach it. Edwards and Mercer (1987) suggest that the whole process of teaching and learning is a matter of arriving at shared understandings, in particular of the language used, through shared activity and talk. In a conversation each speaker brings his or her own experience to the interpretation of the words of the other. If the experience is very different, misunderstanding is likely to follow. This can often be the case with children who may use the same words as the adult but give them a more limited meaning because of the limitations of their own experience.

Children therefore need to learn through discussion, and there is much that you can do to see that this kind of learning takes place. This is partly a matter of organisation but also a matter of helping children to become more skilled at being members of a discussion group.

We have already seen that questioning is an important part of the teacher's role as well being something we should help children to do. It is also a way of stimulating discussion, and very often you ask questions to get the children to talk in order to draw from them material useful for the learning you have in mind. However, there is some research evidence which suggests that controversial statements by the teacher are often more stimulating to children than questions. Askew and Wiliam (1995: 17) note that 'when teachers make statements in order to provoke discussion rather than ask questions, pupils can display more complex thought, deeper personal involvement, wider participation, greater inter-connectedness, and richer inquiry'.

The starting point for discussion is to think out very clearly what you hope to get from it. It may, for example, provide a series of starting points for a piece of work. It may be a way to get children to reflect on experience and generalise from it. You may also be hoping to get a lot of examples to illustrate various points and ideas.

The first task in preparing discussion is to consider the function of the discussion you plan. The next stage is to identify some key questions or statements which are likely to lead to useful conclusions. This involves thinking what experience and the language to express it your children are likely to have in relation to your key questions and statements. You can then start in areas where you know that every child will have some experience to contribute.

There are a number of important points to remember when leading discussion:

1 Look at the way you receive children's contributions. Doing this in a sympathetic and appreciative way is particularly important if you want to get a good discussion going and it would be the same if you were working with adults instead of children.

2 Remember to scan the room looking for children who have something to say and want to get in or those who are miles away and perhaps need recalling to the present. It is easy to miss children seated at the sides of the room and those who are very near you. You need to make a deliberate attempt to look at everyone in the group every so often.

3 Every teacher becomes skilled at reading children's body language and recognising when they are telling you that they have had enough. Class discussion should generally be short, unless the children are very much absorbed.

4 Much the most important task of the discussion leader is that of summarising or pulling together the ideas and the contributions that have been made, making them into a coherent whole and then possibly pushing the discussion further or moving on to some other activity. It is a vital skill for a teacher and you need to do it consciously to begin with so that you can practise the skill and improve it. It is particularly important at the end of a discussion. Many teachers build up a summary on the board as they go along but this has the disadvantage that you lose eye contact with the children. An overhead projector is slightly better for this purpose.

Discussion can also take place in small groups and there is a considerable difference between these discussions and discussion led by the teacher. When you are leading the discussion yourself you can give it direction. If you want small groups to work on their own, you need to think carefully about the brief you are going to give them so that they can use the time really profitably.

The experience of discussion in a small group with or without the teacher is a different experience from that of discussion in a large group. In a class discussion, however good the teacher, it is possible for some children to opt out and some may have developed considerable skill in looking involved when really far away.

When you are in a small group, and even more so when you are talking with only one or two other people, there is some pressure on you to participate, and the smaller the group the more true this becomes. This suggests that small group discussion has a particular value, and when something new is being learned or some experience is being sorted out a small group working with the teacher may be the best possible way of establishing learning.

There is also a case for training older children in the skills of discussion leadership, discussing with the class what is involved in leading discussion and then letting some children practise to see how well they do.

Very valuable work can be done in pairs and trios. The kind of discussion which two children might have in working out a mathematical problem together has considerable value because it requires both to put their thinking into words and the process of communication itself helps their understanding. There is also value in one child teaching another.

Learning from materials

All teachers make some use of books and materials in their work with children. Most frequently they use books and work cards to provide practice and reinforcement of learning, so that something is taught to a group or class and then children practise what they have learned in some way using materials.

A rather different use of materials is for the provision of work matched to individual needs. In this situation different children may be working through some kind of structured scheme, computer program or course book, each working at the level he or she has reached. Or each child may be working more independently with work that not only matches his or her stage of development and learning but that is also related to each individual's interests.

Work cards and work sheets have been around for a long time, but we are still at a comparatively early stage of discovering how to design materials which interest children and teach them well. Computers are gradually enabling teachers to produce really good-looking materials and this development will continue.

In making materials you need to remember the following:

1   *The materials must be motivating in their own right*
    They are most likely to be motivating if they have an element of discovery or problem-solving which is well within the child's capacity but not so easy that there is no challenge. For example, a child learning the various ways we spell the long 'a' sound is likely to be motivated if given a list of words and asked to work out the ways the sound can be spelled and then asked to find more

examples of each. This learning is more likely to be retained than a list of words to be learned because the task has demanded involvement and decision-making.

2 *Language is very important in teaching material*
The language level at which a child can work independently is much less complex both in vocabulary and structure than the language level the child can manage if the material is introduced by the teacher.

3 *The layout of a work card is also important*
Good spacing between lines of writing can make it more legible. The way things are arranged helps or hinders understanding. It is a good idea to study the way advertising material is set out and to apply some of the ideas to work materials.

4 *Good individualised learning material needs to be carefully structured so that a child can work through it in an appropriate way*
The way it is stored should also help children to see progression through the material.

Learning with computers and audio-visual equipment

Computers will gradually provide more and more opportunities for children's learning. They will, in due course, provide ways of analysing the stage a child has reached in his or her learning, match this with appropriate programs and assess and record the learning which has taken place. The programs will be designed to deal with the child's problems as they occur and do many things that can only be done by a teacher at present. Programs will be available which will teach aspects of the National Curriculum and the internet will furnish much information for children's learning. As computers become more able to deal with voice recognition they will offer even more to young children, and it seems likely that a great deal of the teaching now involved in learning to read and write and deal with early mathematics will be done effectively at the child's own pace by a computer program. Such programs will also be available for children at home in many cases, and this development will have a considerable impact on the role of the teacher. As small computers become cheaper, a sufficient number can be available in each classroom. We really need a situation where every child has a laptop computer and regards it as a combination of exercise book and text book.

Teachers already have a considerable task in selecting appropriate software for their children. There is a great deal of material which is simply offering a way of practising skills which might equally well be practised in other ways, although the element of novelty in using a computer may be motivating. It is important to look for material which really makes children think and which helps to assess what children know and can do.

It would be very easy, as computers become more available in schools and as software improves, to forget the importance of first-hand experience. It will be important to get this work into perspective and to marry it with other kinds of working which provide different sorts of learning.

Other audio-visual equipment provides many additional opportunities for learning because it can, in some sense, duplicate the teacher. Radio and television are among the oldest forms of audio-visual learning available to teachers and British teachers have access to programmes of very high quality. These can bring into the classroom experience which no child or teacher might otherwise encounter. The broadcasting authorities have access to the best of current thinking and do a good deal to consult teachers and to pilot and monitor their materials in the classroom. The video-recorder also makes it possible to use just that portion of a programme which is relevant if the teacher wishes. It is also now possible to use material from non-educational programmes if your Local Education Authority (LEA) has subscribed to this use. Radio and television are a comparatively cheap resource which can be of great value and can complement teaching of the National Curriculum very helpfully.

The great majority of broadcast programmes are made for watching or listening with the teacher rather than as teaching materials in their own right. If you wish to use radio or television as small group or individual teaching material, it will probably be necessary to extend the materials which go with the programme or provide other material to bridge the gap between use with the teacher and independent use by the children. This isn't true for all broadcasts but it will be true for a number.

The tape recorder is among the most-used pieces of classroom equipment, offering a considerable range of possibilities. It can be used for material created by the children and also for actual teaching and for various kinds of practice. It is also useful for recording interviews as part of environmental studies, and, as many children have access to cassette recorders at home, a child can record discussion with members of the family and people in the neighbourhood and bring the tape to school to share with others.

The tape recorder is also a very valuable tool for developing skill in speaking and can be helpful in teaching reading. It offers a child the opportunity to prepare reading by listening to a book on tape for later reading to the teacher. It can also be used for learning phonics. Another possibility is for a child to record a story on tape which can be typed out by a volunteer parent and used for reading practice.

At a later stage there is much to be said for putting books, stories and poetry on tape so that children who are poor readers can experience the pleasure of reading, following the reading on tape in their books. This makes available for slower readers some of the benefits that better readers are getting from reading. It also provides models of speech and vocabulary. It enables children to hear language structures which may be new to them. They will also have the opportunity to identify with people in stories and extend their experience through the text.

Such material takes time to build up, but there are often parents with an interest in drama who might help. Preparing tapes could also be an activity for older children who are good readers.

In a similar way such things as spelling, mental arithmetic and word building can be recorded for children, or a child can record the words or numbers he or she needs to learn as a personal test and then return to take the test when he or she is ready. Children might also work in pairs at a similar stage and do this for each other.

Photographic transparencies are also valuable, particularly in relation to environmental studies, and it is a good idea to build a collection of slides of different buildings, landscapes and objects which can be used on a number of occasions. These can be used with a tape recorder and a hand viewer, or they can be used as material for the whole class.

Creative work

The National Advisory Committee on Creative and Cultural Education (1999) in their report on creativity made the following statements:

> By creative education we mean education that develops young people's capacity for original ideas and action.
>
> (ibid.: 6)

> Serious creative achievement relies on knowledge, control of materials and ideas. Creative education involves a balance between teaching knowledge and skills, and encouraging innovation.
>
> (ibid.: 7)

Creativity is possible in all areas of human activity and all young people and adults have creative capacities.

(ibid.: 10)

The roles of teachers are to recognise young people's creative capacities; and to provide the particular conditions in which they can be realised. Developing young people's creativity involves, among other things, deepening young people's knowledge and understanding.

(ibid.: 10)

Primary schools in recent years have felt the pressure to achieve in the core subjects and less time has been devoted to creative activities of various kinds than was once the case. Creative work in whatever medium is important in its own right as a form of expression. It is also a medium for learning other things. Opportunities for both are needed. It is important as a teaching approach because children need to understand some things with their emotions and imaginations as well as in cognitive terms. Creating a picture or model or a piece of drama may help a child to understand what it was like to be alive at a different time or to live in a different part of the world. The experience of using implements or wearing clothes from a different period or place may bring a new understanding of people who used such implements or wore such clothes. A story may make more sense when children make a picture of it. Taking a role may make it possible for a child to enter imaginatively into learning.

It is not easy to provide for this kind of learning in such a way that all children get this kind of understanding. You need to be on the look out for opportunities in other work to complement it with creative work. In science, for example, there is sometimes the opportunity to use creatively the materials you have been using for exploration. Mathematics may be made more real by asking children to undertake such activities as taking on the role of someone who needed to measure something but had no units of measurement, or an architect who wanted to copy some parts of a building but was unable to borrow the plans.

You also need to be aware, as the report from the advisory committee quoted above suggests, that in every subject there is a chance to be creative by thinking of new ideas and ways of doing things. Subjects such as English, technology, art, drama, music and dance offer particular opportunities, but there are also opportunities to think creatively in mathematics, in science and in history and geography.

Analysis 7.1 Teaching methods

Teaching methods	+ +	+	Av	–	– –	Actual
Direct teaching using exposition and questioning						
Open-ended investigation						
Planned investigation						
Individualised learning from books and work cards						
Individualised learning with computers and other audio-visual equipment						
Class discussion						
Discussion in pairs or small groups						
Co-operative work in pairs or small groups						
Creative work						
Practice work						

You may find it useful to analyse your preferences for teaching approaches using the matrix in Analysis 7.1. Make a profile of the extent to which you think you use each method, marking the appropriate column. Then make an analysis of what you actually do over the course of a week and compare the two.

Conclusion

The intention of the last five chapters was to help you to analyse your role as teacher and look at alternative strategies which can be used in working with children. The information about your style and preferences form a background for your decisions about how to organise your teaching.

8　The curriculum

The main concern of this book is classroom organisation, but we need to consider what we want to organise before we can consider how to do it. Many studies suggests that *how* children learn is probably as important as *what* they learn. The way work is organised affects the extent of each child's contact with the teacher, the opportunities and resources available and the actual learning which takes place, both by conscious intent on the part of the teacher and also as a hidden curriculum with its own values and assumptions.

There are many definitions of the word curriculum. The National Curriculum, for example, might be defined as the intended content of children's learning. However, children learn a great deal in school which is not intended directly or even not intended at all. The definition of curriculum used in this chapter includes all the learning which a child does in any aspect of his or her school life. This might be seen to include at least three kinds of activity.

The taught curriculum

This is the usual meaning of the word curriculum. It covers all the teaching and learning which goes on intentionally and deliberately within the classroom and elsewhere during the school day. It is the work which those outside the school recognise as what the school is in business to do and is largely covered by the National Curriculum.

The institutional curriculum

Any organisation teaches those who work within it about its way of life, its culture, its values and codes of behaviour – *the way we do things here*. Sometimes this is done explicitly, as when a teacher tells children how to behave in particular circumstances or talks about school rules. Sometimes it is implicit, as when children are praised for behaviour which accords with the views and values of the head and staff or scolded for behaviour which is not in accord.

Schools are usually very clear about the patterns of behaviour required from teachers and children, partly because the immaturity of the majority of the school population requires the support that this offers. The patterns of behaviour demanded of children teach them many things and probably should be discussed much more by teachers so that shared values are reinforced and differences recognised. This learning is sometimes less effective than it might be because of inconsistencies in what is demanded by different teachers. Children also find themselves unwittingly behaving in ways which teachers dislike, but which may be acceptable at home. For some children, school life can be fraught with problems in working out the demands of the institutional curriculum.

The institutional curriculum also includes opportunities for taking responsibility and for leadership and for working with others. It includes the social learning that goes on in the playground and in the classroom, the learning which takes place at lunch and in assembly and all the attitudes developed as a result of the way a child is treated in school by teachers and by peers.

The hidden curriculum

Some parts of the curriculum are hidden, not only from the children but also from the teachers. Much of what we now list under the institutional curriculum was once part of the hidden curriculum. As soon as we become conscious of it, it is no longer part of the hidden curriculum, which is, by definition, hidden. Since it is hidden, a school cannot control it, although by discussing what may be hidden it may be brought into the light of day.

It is therefore possible that there is learning going on which you don't know about. Is the child who is able, for example, learning to work slowly because finishing first brings more of the same? Are children learning to give you the answers they think you want rather than seeking a thought-out answer? Do some children get the impression that they are unimportant because they are, for example, not good at mathematics or games or writing? Do some children get the impression that reading, writing, mathematics and possibly science are the only things that matter? Do girls feel inferior to boys or conversely? Do children get the impression that it is better to be White than Black?

Factors affecting the curriculum

The curriculum that a school offers is determined by government by means of the National Curriculum. However, it is affected by the views of the LEA, the school governors, the headteacher and the teaching staff. Thus, although the National Curriculum is laid down in some detail, it is very far from dictating all that an individual teacher or school does.

Teachers affect the curriculum because each teacher has a particular personality and teaching style and a particular set of skills and knowledge to offer and is free to select material to teach the National Curriculum and anything else which he or she thinks will be appropriate for the particular group of children. Teachers work with three sets of variables:

Variables which are predetermined
- Current educational thinking.
- Current national policies and needs.
- The National Curriculum.
- Children and parents:
  - social and educational background;
  - ability levels.
- School building and facilities.
- Head and staff of the school:
  - background and experience;
  - ability;
  - staffing ratio.

Variables which can be influenced but not determined
- Parental expectations of the school and the child.
- Support from parents.
- Support from governors.
- Behaviour of children.
- Attitudes of head and colleagues.
- School organisation.
- Interpretation of the National Curriculum.
- The literacy and numeracy strategies.
- School schemes of work.
- Use of buildings, facilities and resources.
- Money available.

Areas of self-determination by teachers
- Vehicles for curriculum:

   – e.g. choice of books, materials, approaches, some subject
      matter.
- Use of time within the classroom.
- Use of learning space.
- Use of resources.
- Teaching skills and knowledge.
- Teaching methods and approaches.
- Children's learning.

These areas are not separated very clearly, but you are most likely
to be using time effectively if you concentrate on the last section.

The whole curriculum

The National Curriculum specifies:

- The core subjects of English, mathematics and science.
- The foundation subjects of art and design, geography, history,
  music, physical education and technology and, at the secondary
  stage, a modern foreign language.
- Information and communications technology as a statutory part
  of teaching in all subjects except at Key Stage 1, where it should
  be introduced but is not statutory.
- Language requirements should be considered in all subjects.
- Citizenship is a statutory requirement from 2002 in secondary
  schools.
- Personal, social and health education is a non-statutory
  requirement at all stages.

Teachers should be aware of legislation for equal opportunities
regarding race, gender and disability. The National Curriculum also
includes statements about the values to be inculcated regarding self,
relationships, society and the environment.

In addition to the requirements of the National Curriculum, all
schools must teach religious education according to the local Agreed
Syllabus or the Diocesan syllabus.

Language

Each subject discipline has its own language, its linguistic register, and
even when subjects use the same words they may not be using them
with the same meaning. For example, at an early stage, children discover

that, when they paint, the primary colours are red, blue and yellow and they learn how to mix these colours together to make another colour. At a later stage in science, however, they learn about the colour of light, where the primary colours are different and they have to adjust to the difference in meaning.

We tend not to think very much about this kind of problem and yet it is relevant from the earliest stages. A child at home learns that the postman brings a letter. At school the same child has to learn that a letter is something different.

There are many such linguistic traps for children and it is often valuable to list the words and language you want to use for a given piece of work and ask yourself what experience the children will need to understand them fully. This would be a useful thing to do with each part of the National Curriculum.

If you teach very young children you are more likely to be aware of this than if you teach older children because young children force you to recognise the inadequacies in their understanding. They often give you clues to their thinking in the mistakes they make or in what seem to be amusing sayings. For example, the child who defined 'less' as 'downer' partly understood the word, but one could not be certain that her understanding would be sufficient for understanding a phrase such as 'less space' or a more abstract phrase such as 'less hope'.

If you teach older children the problem is still with you and is possibly increased by the fact that children learn to disguise their lack of understanding. It is important to ask questions to see whether language is really understood.

Thought about language as part of the framework in major areas of knowledge must also include thought about the use of symbols in mathematics and science, the language of movement in dance and drama, the language of shapes and forms in art, sounds in music and so on. Each subject area not only has its own linguistic register or way of using language but also has its own forms of expression which need to be studied and understood so that they can be used.

Concepts, knowledge, language and skills

One breakdown which can be applied to most subjects is a division into underlying ideas or concepts, knowledge or information, subject-specific language and skills.

Each subject discipline has a set of techniques and skills required for its study, and these too can be listed although they are best acquired in the context of their use. If the emphasis is placed on concepts, the skills often come naturally. For example, children acquiring the concept of area by counting the squares that are covered by a leaf are not only practising counting in whole numbers but are also likely to find ways of adding fractions to account for the parts of squares covered. In writing, children are most likely to persist in practising if they want to express something on paper, and this motivation has to be reconciled with the need for appropriate teaching and practice of letter formation.

Cross-curricular learning

Schools also need to be concerned with skills which go across the curriculum – communication, numeracy, study, problem-solving, personal and social skills, health education, information and communications technology, economic and industrial understanding, citizenship, environmental education – and with aspects of subjects which are cross-curricular.

Communication

Communication skills are clearly an important part of the National Curriculum, running through all the subjects. A child should learn to communicate and receive communication using movement, language, mathematics and graphics, adequately and appropriately for different people, situations, purposes and topics. The development of communication is highly relevant when one looks at organisation since children cannot learn unless they and the teacher can communicate with each other. All aspects of living involve communication and the teacher who is clear about what the children might learn incidentally will find opportunities at all times of the day for using the ordinary work of the classroom to foster learning in this area.

The word *communication* tends to be used in schools in relation to language. It can be looked at much more widely, however, and this will be particularly important in technology, where communication is often through drawings and diagrams. All the higher forms of animal life have sophisticated forms of communication and human beings are no exception. We differ from other animals, however, in the primacy afforded to language, particularly as a way of representing experience to ourselves and others, and we use language as an important and integral part of our thinking. It also enables us to co-operate and achieve collectively more than any individual can achieve alone.

This stress on language tends to make us less aware of other kinds of communication, particularly that transmitted by movement.

Movement communication is present before language and it continues to be an essential part of the way we relate to other people and communicate with them. Teachers of young children, in particular, need to be aware of the importance of body language for communication because they both read this kind of communication made by their children and themselves use it to help children understand what they are saying. Facial expression, gesture, movement of the body and extensions of this, such as the way you dress and organise your environment, all communicate something about the kind of person you are, the mood you are in, the kind of relationship you see yourself having with the children and so on.

Children explore a great deal of this in play, and school can take this further as children grow older in work in drama and in talking about how people behave in different situations. Children are also discovering how other people react to them and part of the response will be demonstrated by movement and facial expression which the children learn how to read.

Teachers of children from ethnic minorities may find that their children have a different body language from that of the indigenous population. This can sometimes lead to misunderstanding when a child shows in his or her movement something which has a different meaning at home from that expected at school. This is particularly true of Black Caribbean children, whose body language is often misinterpreted.

A further extension of this is graphic communication. One might argue that the way people dress and organise their environment is a form of graphic communication in that other people draw conclusions from appearances. Teachers of younger children will be aware that children not infrequently use drawing, painting and modelling to express their feelings and reactions.

At the other end of the range of graphic communication is the use of maps, graphs, diagrams, tables, charts, and so on. It is particularly relevant to work in technology, where drawing is often needed to explain ideas. These are all part of the communication process, complementing language and sometimes communicating more effectively than language since graphic communication can show more easily than words how things relate to one another. For example, a map shows more than a verbal account of how to get there. It can also be seen all at once, whereas verbal instructions have to be heard or read in sequence.

Certain kinds of organisation within the school will give children better opportunities for practising this kind of learning than others. For example, if children are expected to work collaboratively on something, a good deal will be learned about communication within the group and this will be complementary to the language learning taking place.

Numeracy

Being numerate requires us to have the skills which are widely needed in everyday life. The basis of those skills is acquired at the primary stage of education. The skills will be learned in mathematics lessons but may be practised across the curriculum. Technology and science will involve measurement and calculation. Geography will involve map-reading skills; history the use of a time line. Calculation may be involved in art from time to time as in block printing where children will need to work out how many prints can be fitted into a sheet of paper.

In recent years calculators have changed our needs. Many jobs that require calculation now involve the use of calculators or computers. Neither can be used intelligently without understanding, however, and it is important that children develop understanding and skill in using these aids as well as the ability to calculate without them.

The calculator and the computer enable a child to perform many calculations quickly so that patterns can be seen which might not be evident if all the calculations had to be carried out manually. This enables children to reach a level of understanding which was difficult to achieve before calculators were available. Calculators also make it possible to use more real-life problems in which the numbers involved would be too difficult to manage if the calculation had to be carried out manually.

Study skills

Today's children will need to go on learning all their lives, and it is therefore important for them to acquire the skills of study and that they learn to work independently. New technology makes study skills important because, if you have a world of knowledge to choose from, how you seek it and what you actually do with it becomes as important as remembering parts of it. There is much to be said for regarding the ability to learn without a teacher as a major aim for education to be achieved by most children by the time they leave school. Very few would pass a test in this at the present time because we are not really geared to this idea. We generally pay too little attention to the process of learning and give children too little help with it. In one way, the National Curriculum should make it easier to concentrate more on process because content is decided for us. In another sense, however, teachers may be hesitant about giving children opportunities for learning independently because of the need to cover the content.

We use the word *learn* for several different activities. Sometimes we are asking children to memorise something, e.g. 'Learn those spellings'. Sometimes we are describing a more complex process involving different kinds of learning, for example 'We are learning about conservation', and sometimes we are talking about doing something, e.g. 'John is learning to turn a back somersault'. These are three rather different approaches and children need to know how to tackle all three when required.

The extent to which your children are able to work independently has implications for the way you organise your work. If you want time to work with small groups and individuals, you need to do all you can to train children to work profitably without constant reference to you.

Although the information explosion makes learning by heart less necessary, there is still a great deal which we all need to remember, and children need to memorise some things. They need help with this process, although it is often easier to memorise when young than it is later. Most people remember best when things make sense or can be grouped or classified in some way or associated with something else. Learning to spell correctly also depends on teaching children to group things which have to be memorised, to look for associations and write as well as say the words being learned. One may remember the feel of writing something.

Where understanding is involved, the business of grouping and seeking patterns and rearranging the material becomes essential. We understand something only when we make it our own by working with it and using it. Children need a great deal of help in learning how to structure things for themselves. Work which asks them to put things in groups or order of priority or to select things which go together or contrast with one another, all work involving sets, work which looks for patterns in numbers or spelling or involves the use of flow charts or other forms of graphic layout all contribute to the ability to learn and understand.

Doing also has an important place in understanding and learning. Physical activity is often more easily remembered than mere words. It is interesting, for example, that a hairdresser, who, in the course of a week, may work on eighty or ninety customers, rarely forgets the way each customer likes her hair done. This is quite a remarkable feat of memory and illustrates well the way in which the memory of movement helps other forms of memory.

There is a need to learn movement skills in work such as art, craft, needlework, cookery, physical education, science, technology and handwriting. We normally teach most of the skills involved in these activities by demonstration. It seems likely that the computer will eventually be helpful here, and we should certainly teach children to work out practical tasks from written instructions since this is a very necessary skill for adult life.

There is much to be said for setting out for children what has to be learned and discussing with them possible ways of learning it. Children need the skills for independent learning and these involve having some idea of how to set about the learning process in different contexts.

This stress on process makes classroom management a very complex business, and the pressure to complete what is required by the National Curriculum can make teachers feel that there is too little time to be concerned with how children learn, so long as they learn. This is a short-sighted view which in the long run works against helping children to achieve their maximum potential. Where children are involved in considering the learning process as well as the learning content, teaching becomes a more exciting business because they will come up with ideas you haven't thought of and the detective work of finding out how they view things can be very challenging.

The skills involved in study are numerous and complex, but it is possible to identify some of them and to look for ways in which children can acquire and practise them. They include the following, although this list is by no means exhaustive:

1   *Investigating*

You can find out from your own observation and experiment, by asking other people, by turning to books and printed material, by using a computer or perhaps using television or videotape. Most people use observation and questioning more than they use other sources and we need to take this source of information seriously and teach children to use it well.

Children need to learn to make observations of various kinds. This involves learning to use the tools that extend the senses, such as lenses and microscopes, and the tools that help us to measure, such as rulers, clocks, weights and so on. These are all extensions of observation. They also need to learn to use the tools of analysis, from simple graphs to databases and spreadsheets.

Asking questions to get information is also a skill to be learned. Field study work is important in providing such opportunities and this has implications for organisation since it is difficult to develop questioning skills if you don't have the opportunity for asking questions of anyone except the teacher. Children need to learn that some questions bring more information than others and that you need to ask the right person, i.e. someone likely to know the answer. Children also need to learn to ask questions in a tactful way. Practice in this kind of skill can be given as homework where children ask questions of their parents and grandparents perhaps about what life was like when they were at school.

2 *Sorting, classifying, ordering, generalising, making and testing hypotheses*
When material has been collected, learning may involve sorting and classifying it and putting it into some sort of order for presentation or to see if there are generalisations which could be made or further questions which could be explored. It may be possible to find ways of applying what has been learned, perhaps to deal with a situation or to do or make something. As a result of sorting material, patterns may emerge which could be tested as hypotheses or problems could present themselves which could be investigated.

This again has implications for the way you teach and the way you organise. If you do not provide children with opportunities to do their own sorting and classifying with help from you, they will not acquire these skills.

3 *Planning*
You will also need to teach some planning skills. Children, as they grow older, can be encouraged to produce plans for the work they are doing, sometimes working in small groups or pairs, probably following a demonstration of how to do this, building up a plan on the board. The plans can be written lists or topic webs with lines and arrows linking together various parts of the plan. This kind of plan will need to be turned into a list in due course because the work has to be carried out in real time, there must be a priority order and there will need to be discussion about the order in which work might be done.

You can go on from there and encourage children to estimate how long a piece of work may take and then check to see how long it actually does take. The next step is to plan for increasing lengths of time, so that older children are eventually planning their work for some time ahead. However, you need to take into account the fact that research suggests that planning for too long a time ahead can be counter-productive.

There should be a good balance of teacher-directed and whole-class and group work and work in which children, as they grow older, have an increasing degree of choice about how they set about things and make plans for themselves.

4   *Evaluation*

A further and very important learning skill is the ability to evaluate your own and other people's work and behaviour. Young children starting school depend very much on the adults in their world for views on what is good or bad, right or wrong. Parents tells them that this is good and this is naughty and they gradually internalise these views. When they start school their teachers do much the same thing and the children internalise their teachers' views also, sometimes finding that there is a conflict between what is considered good or naughty at home and what is considered good or naughty at school.

As they grow older children learn to set their own standards and to make judgements using both the standards they have been given by adults and their own emerging judgement. The teacher can do a great deal to help this development by discussing work and trying to help children identify criteria for making judgements and then matching work and behaviour to them. It is also helpful if you make clear to children the criteria you are using to assess their work. Research suggests that children tend to regard presentation as the major criterion used by teachers for assessing work rather than the ideas expressed and how they have been used.

Problem-solving

Problem-solving, like language, is a skill which can be practised right across the curriculum and problem-solving strategies can be applied to many aspects of the daily life of the classroom. This is discussed in detail in Chapter 6 and in Chapter 10 in relation to technology.

Personal and social education

There are many skills involved in personal and social education and you need to be concerned with them throughout all your work in the classroom.

1   *Self-knowledge*

We looked at the way children develop in Chapter 2. Throughout the years of schooling each child is developing a view of him or herself which is made up from the reactions of those around, both adults and children.

Initially a child's parents are very important in forming an early self-image, but teachers are also very powerful at the primary stage and the peer group plays an increasing part as the child grows and develops. It is very important for the teacher to recognise that this is happening and that his or her recognition of progress and success counts. It is also essential that you see that there are opportunities for every child to succeed in some way and for every child to take responsibility and contribute to the class community.

A child also needs to know and come to terms with his or her own strengths and limitations. Children need a range of opportunities, encouragement to try new things and help and support in overcoming difficulties. It may be helpful to recognise a difficulty frankly with an individual child and together make a plan to overcome it so that you can genuinely praise each step taken.

The development of self-confidence is closely related to the development of the self-image. Children need to be confident in themselves as people, in their ability to learn and tackle new tasks successfully and in their relationships with others.

You need to help all children to develop a confident attitude to at least some part of their activity. The secret of this is to match tasks to the level at which a child who tries can succeed. This is not easy, but it is more important for some children than for others and you can see very quickly those who lack confidence and need success. In the first days with a new group it is worth concentrating rather more attention on these children so that they achieve fairly early and gain confidence in you and become ready to try new things. Your reaction to their ideas and contributions is crucial in the early stages.

Children are influenced not only by the example, teaching and behaviour of teachers but also by their peer group. We tend to forget the learning that goes on between child and child. Parents often have this in mind when they choose to send a child to one school rather than another. This is not necessarily because they think the teaching is any better but because they want their child to be with children from similar families rather than learning a way of life from other children which they see as alien.

2   *Ability to live and work with others*
Learning to work with others is an important part of the curriculum. The ability to do this is a valuable skill in adult life and involves a number of subskills.

We want all children to be socially competent, knowing what to do in different situations. There is also a case for seeing that all children learn the conventions of social behaviour, such as greeting people, making and responding to introductions, thanking someone, making a complaint politely, making an enquiry and so on. The teacher's example is important here, but there is also a need for specific teaching and plenty of opportunities to practise. Drama lessons may well offer this kind of opportunity.

In adult life the majority of people have reason to work with others to an agreed end from time to time. We want children to be able to get on with others and live and work with them to achieve group goals, sometimes leading and sometimes following. There are skills involved in this which are discussed in Chapter 12.

We also want children to be sensitive to others. Sensitivity is closely linked to the ability to see through the eyes of another person. A teacher needs to find ways of extending children's understanding of how things look from other points of view. Stories are often a help and it is worth trying to make a collection of stories which help to develop such understanding. Drama or role-play games in which each child has to study the part he or she is playing and see things from the point of view of a particular character may contribute.

Discussion about this is important and it is often possible to use the occasion when a particular child's behaviour has hurt someone else to get that child and others to see how it looked from the other person's point of view. Very young children find this difficult to do, but development is likely to come from encouragement to think about other views. As children grow older they need continued help and constant encouragement to view things in this way.

Social education as well as religious education must include moral education. Moral behaviour is sometimes confused with obedience to a particular set of rules. While we need some rules to regulate the way we do things because life would be very difficult without them, mere obedience to them is not really enough because they can never cover all eventualities.

A person who is acting morally needs to be able to weigh up the facts in a moral situation, look at it from different points of view as well as his or her own, generate or refer to principles and see if they fit the situation, and then make a choice and act with intention.

At the primary stage of education teachers can do a great deal to help this development. At the beginning of the primary stage, children need to be bound by the rules of the adults in their world, whether parents or teachers, because they are not yet ready to generate their own rules for living. By the time they leave the primary stage, some are already examining the principles offered by adults and thinking deeply about how to deal with moral situations in their own lives.

3 *Developing a framework of meaning for life and a value system*
Children start to develop a framework of meaning and a value system during their years at school. As they grow they gradually develop their own frame of reference by which they make judgements about people, events and things. Everything that happens to them contributes to this, rather as it does to their self-images.

Initially, children take on the values and ideas of their parents, and these are gradually modified and developed as teachers and other adults and children put forward different ideas. Eventually, children reach the point where they have an internal set of references which they use to make judgements about new people and new situations.

Each person's frame of reference constitutes a view of the world and life, and, where people have widely differing views of what constitutes *good*, their views may be difficult to reconcile. You may find, for example, that the parents of some of your children have views about bringing up and educating children which are very different from your own, particularly if they come from a different culture.

Those with religious faith accept with it a set of values, many of which they make their own, so that the values enshrined in their faith become part of their frame of reference. There is an important sense in which Christian values are part of the frame of reference of most British people because they are part of British history and culture and much of our thinking is rooted in the values of Christianity. This may change as the other cultures in our midst influence the way we think.

Health education

A good deal of health education is incorporated in the science curriculum and some aspects should be dealt with as part of physical education. Children should learn about the importance of regular exercise and its effect on their bodies and on their health. At Key

Stage 1 children learn about parts of the body, growth and development, personal hygiene and rules for keeping safe. At Key Stage 2 they learn about a healthy lifestyle, the onset of puberty and the physical and emotional changes this may bring about. Teaching about drugs, including tobacco and alcohol, can be introduced at this stage.

Primary schools have a choice about whether to include sex education in the curriculum in addition to the teaching about reproduction, which is part of the science curriculum. It is important to get this in context, stressing the need to provide a loving and caring environment for children.

Citizenship

Citizenship is not a compulsory part of the curriculum at the primary stage but children need to know something about how democracy works nationally and locally and this is reinforced if the teacher uses opportunities which arise to make democratic decisions in the classroom and then relates this to democratic decision-making elsewhere.

Some aspects of citizenship are likely to be covered in the history programme, which should introduce children to some of our historical and cultural background and that of other groups and nations. It is important also that children know something of how people behave in groups and something about the way our society functions, including its institutions and practices, the way we are governed, the need to generate wealth and the way present-day life differs from that of the past. Children also need to learn about the part played by industry and the rule of law. Some of this may come from relevant visits or visitors, such as the police or members of the fire service.

Children should be introduced to those values in our society which are commonly held. There will be many opportunities to introduce the values of the school which are part of wider values. These values will be evident in the way teachers deal with children and encourage children to deal with each other and with other people and the way the school tackles children's misdemeanours. Assembly is traditionally a way of reinforcing values.

In today's multicultural schools there are considerable problems about putting over values because different groups within our society have different values. However, there is a good deal in common on which early work may be based. As children grow older it may be possible to discuss some of the differences.

Environmental education

One of the most important issues for children to learn about at the present time is that of the environment. They need to know what is happening to the world in terms of the greenhouse effect and the human behaviour which is creating it. They also need to be concerned about maintaining an environment in which we can live in comfort with areas for leisure and recreation as well as places for work. We need to give thought to the way we want our towns and cities to develop. Much of this work will come in geography and in science and some in technology.

In thinking about the environment it may also be sensible to think about human behaviour and ways in which we might change it. Discussion about issues such as graffiti and vandalism, football hooliganism and drugs at the primary stage might have an effect which would be difficult to achieve when children are older.

Multicultural education

Schools in areas where the population is ethnically mixed have usually done a great deal to help the various groups appreciate each other. There is much work in celebrating each other's festivals, helping children to understand other points of view and generally respecting and tolerating differences. This may not always be successful but there is no lack of appreciation of the need for such work to be done. There continues to be a need to combat racism in all its forms, and every school needs to consider how incidents of racism should be dealt with and how children can be helped to realise its dangers.

There is a different and more difficult task to be done in schools where there are few children from ethnic communities, and there is often a lack of realisation that in these circumstances there is also much to be done. The Swann Report (Department of Education and Science, 1985: 236) makes the following comment about attitudes in schools:

> A major conclusion which we feel must regrettably be drawn from the findings of this project, is in relation to the widespread existence of racism, whether unintentional and 'latent' or overt and aggressive in the schools visited. ... The project revealed widespread evidence of racism in all the areas covered, ranging from unintentional racism and patronising and stereotyped ideas about ethnic minority groups combined with appalling ignorance of their

cultural backgrounds and the facts of race and immigration, to the extreme of overt hatred and 'National Front' style attitudes.

Children in 'White' areas, and their parents also, often have a very limited idea of people of other nationalities, especially those who are Black, and the school has an important job to do in broadening this view. Contacts with schools where there are substantial Black populations would be valuable, but there should at least be discussion about people who are different in various ways, including stories and films about other nationalities and some work on festivals.

Education for equal opportunities

Concern for equal opportunities for everyone whatever their race, gender, social class or disability is important in all schools. Most young children come to school with fairly firm ideas about male and female roles. In most households it is still the mother who stays at home while the children are very young, although this is changing, and she is therefore the person with the time to undertake the household chores and feed the family. Small children naturally take this as the norm, as is evident from the way they play in the Wendy house and elsewhere. A view of women as subservient to men is also reinforced in many schools where the headteacher is male.

The school has a substantial task to do in helping children to appreciate that women need not take the background role but can offer many of the contributions made by men except those which require physical strength. Boys need to appreciate that men are no less masculine if they are sensitive to others and take their share of domestic chores.

This task is made more difficult by the fact that children are themselves trying to sort out their own roles as future men and women. Boys are under pressure to seek macho behaviour and avoid anything which has overtones of the feminine. Girls experience less pressure in some senses but are growing up in a society which is very uncertain about the role of women and this makes life difficult for them.

There is also a need to consider issues of equality where children with disabilities are concerned. Are they being treated in the same way as other children as far as this is possible? Are they getting all the opportunities that other children have where they are able to gain from them? Handicapped people are continually surprising us with the things they can do.

A further area in which there is the need for equal opportunities is in social class. It is easy to favour middle-class children by giving them more opportunities for taking responsibility, more praise, more opportunities in the classroom, and so on.

You need to be constantly watching the way you work with children. Do you ask more questions of boys than girls or vice versa? Do you make more critical comments about behaviour to Black Caribbean children than to others? Do you always have higher expectations of middle-class than working-class children and is this always justified? Are responsibilities around the classroom equally distributed among girls and boys, Black and White, able-bodied and those with disabilities, middle-class and working-class children?

Preparation for adult life

It might be argued that all education is about preparing children for adult life. It might also be said that certain aspects of this preparation, such as preparation for employment, marriage and parenthood, are really the province of the secondary school as it is then that children begin to look forward to adult life and experience work related to possible careers.

Yet preparation for adult life is really a continuum which starts before school and continues into the nursery school and reception class, with children playing out the adult activities they see taking place, such as shopping, cooking, caring for the home and children, visiting the doctor or hospital and so on. Some of these activities become more directed as children grow older and they may experience cookery or sewing or perhaps gardening or caring for animals and learning about how babies are born and grow. None of this is a very conscious preparation for marriage and parenthood, but it is a starting point and a valuable contribution that is likely to affect later attitudes.

Schooling at any stage may be regarded as induction into the adult world. Part of the induction process is introducing children to their cultural legacy, teaching them about their past and that of other groups, reading and telling stories, hearing about great men and women and events. This is one of the reasons why the study of history is important.

Children learn a great deal about living with others at all stages in their schooling and the ability to share, to work together, to take responsibility, to lead and to follow are all useful parts of learning to be a member of a community.

A further aspect of adult life which has its roots in the primary school is the development of leisure interests, skills and hobbies. This involves opportunities for learning to enjoy music, dance, drama, art,

Analysis 8.1 Cross-curricular themes

Complete this analysis by marking where the subjects of the National Curriculum meet the aims listed

		English	Mathematics	Science	Art	Geography	History	Music	Physical ed.	Religious ed.	Technology
Cross-curricular topics and skills	Communication										
	Numeracy										
	Information technology										
	Study skills										
	Problem-solving										
	Personal and social education										
	Health education										
	Citizenship										
	Environmental education										
	Multicultural education										
	Equal oppotunities										
	Preparation for adult life										

practical opportunities for developing craft skills and playing games, the development of interests such as reading, stamp collecting, electronics, photography, astronomy and many other likely and unlikely studies, depending on the enthusiasm and skills of teachers and anyone outside the school willing to be drawn in.

Teaching and learning are not tidy pursuits. A good deal of important learning goes on outside the curriculum and much that is important is apparently learned incidentally. No teacher can do everything and none of us can do everything at once. The value of considering a set of aims is that it gives you a frame of reference for your teaching and enables you to look at what you are doing from a wider perspective from time to time.

The list in Analysis 8.1 is intended to enable you to consider where the various cross-curricular areas fit in with the subjects of the National Curriculum.

9 The core subjects

English

The teaching of English has undergone a considerable change in recent years through the introduction of the National Literacy Strategy and the literacy hour. The strategy suggests that literate children should:

- read and write with confidence, fluency and understanding;
- be able to demonstrate a full range of reading cues (phonic, graphic, syntactic, contextual) to monitor their reading and correct their own mistakes;
- understand the sound and spelling system and use this to read and spell accurately;
- have an interest in words and their meaning and a growing vocabulary;
- know, understand and be familiar with some of the ways in which narratives are structured through basic literary ideas of setting, character and plot;
- understand, use and be able to write a range of non-fiction texts;
- plan, draft, revise and edit their own writing;
- have a suitable technical vocabulary through which to understand and discuss their reading and writing;
- be interested in books, read with enjoyment and evaluate and justify their preferences;
- through reading and writing, develop their powers of imagination.

Over the past thirty years or so, some important developments have taken place in our knowledge of language. In particular the tape recorder has made it possible to study language as people actually use it, giving us valuable insights which have implications for teachers. We have become aware that we use language in different ways according to our background, the particular situation, the persons to whom we are speaking, the subject matter and so on. We each use language in ways which are personal to us. Your language initially developed from your background, upbringing and education and most of us retain traces of the speech of the area in which we grew up, sometimes as accent, sometimes in the tunes of our speech and the language structures we employ. Children starting school may find that their teachers and other children speak in much the same way as their parents or they may find that language is used in a different way in school from the way it is used at home – so different in some cases that children have difficulty in coming to terms with it. There may also be children whose home language is not English.

Each group of people – the family, the friendship group, the social class, the professional work group, the nation – has uses of language which are peculiar to it, i.e. the language register. We also use language differently in different social classes, and in Britain this is very marked. The use of language in this way is a mark of membership and a way of excluding those outside the group – which is why it can be very difficult to persuade children from a working-class background to use language in a middle-class way; their use of language identifies them with the home and their peer group and pressure to change language may be seen as a threat to personal identity.

The National Curriculum for English makes it very clear that teachers should work towards all children acquiring standard English, not with the idea that there is something wrong with whatever variety of English a child may use at home but because this is the most widely used and widely understood form of the language. Using standard English does not mean acquiring a middle-class accent. It refers to a standard use of grammatical constructions and use of words.

We need to stress in school that adopting standard forms of English is necessary and appropriate for some purposes, but does not mean abandoning other ways of talking at home or with friends. The individuals who are in this sense bilingual in the different ways they can use language have an advantage. They can feel at home and be accepted by a much wider variety of social groups than would be the case if they were unwilling to extend their use of language in this way.

Appropriateness of language use is a very useful concept for teachers. If we want to help children to use language in ways which match situations and purposes, we need not appear threatening or apparently condemning of the language they already possess if we ask them to extend their language knowledge and skill and learn to select the language behaviour they need for a particular situation.

In this context it is helpful to seek out opportunities to match language to real circumstances. The teacher is a very particular kind of audience or readership because it is his or her task to read what children write and listen to what they say. Teachers usually read or listen in the classroom not because they want to know, in the sense that the reader of a book may want to know about its content, but in order to assess a child's ability or progress, to see what help is needed or what has been learned. The child reading or writing for the teacher is thus in a different position from the adult speaking or writing with a particular purpose which affects the nature of the communication.

When we speak or write, we try to match the language we use to our purpose, situation and its recipient. We use language differently in speaking to children as distinct from speaking to adults and try to find language they will understand. We use language differently in writing to apply for a job from the way we use it in writing to a friend. Talking to a group is different from talking to an individual. Giving instructions is different from persuading and so on.

These variations are reflected in our choice of content, vocabulary, language structure and form, in the way we speak, in our body language of gesture and facial expression. In writing we have fewer variables but still match language to likely readership. It can be useful to look at language with these variations in mind and consider where children have the opportunity to practise the variety of language this suggests.

This is more difficult to do than it seems at first. It is easy to feel that the need is being met by writing letters for practice or writing as if one were someone else. This kind of work is necessary and has a valuable place, but children really need the discipline of working from time to time for a real audience or readership, who will read or listen only if the material is right. Many opportunities for this may be found as part of other aspects of curriculum. For example, children may plan to interview adults in connection with a local study and may need to write letters to arrange this and also to plan and undertake the interviews. Inviting a visitor who has valuable information to give into the classroom offers similar opportunities, plus a need to think about how to make a visitor welcome and the questions which might be asked. Some topic work can be planned with another group of children, perhaps much younger, whose understanding of language will need to be taken into account. Making books for younger or less able children is also a useful task.

HMI (1996–7) looked at standards in English in primary schools. They found that good or satisfactory progress had been made in 90 per cent of schools, with work weakest in years 3 and 4 and strongest in year 6. There was a 10 per cent gap between the performance of boys and girls at Key Stage 1 and this widened to leave boys even further behind at Key Stage 2.

Medwell *et al.* (1998: 8) studied the work of effective teachers of literacy and found that they tended to:

- believe that it is important to make it explicit that the purpose of teaching literacy is enabling their pupils to create meaning from text;
- centre much of their teaching around 'shared' texts, i.e. texts which the teacher and children read or wrote together;
- teach aspects of reading and writing such as decoding and spelling in a systematic and highly structured way and also in a way that made it clear to pupils why these aspects were necessary and useful;
- emphasise to their pupils the functions of what they were learning in literacy;
- have developed strong and coherent personal philosophies about the teaching of literacy which guide their selection of teaching materials and approaches;
- have well-developed systems of monitoring children's progress and needs in literacy and use this information to plan future teaching;
- have extensive knowledge about literacy, although not necessarily in a form which could be abstracted from the context of teaching it;
- have had considerable experience of in-service activities in literacy, both as learners and, often, having themselves planned and led such activities for their colleagues.

In 1999, HMI made an interim survey of the effects of the National Literacy Strategy (HMI, 1999a) followed by a further survey to evaluate the first year of the strategy (HMI, 1999b). They found the following strengths:

- All the schools in the sample were implementing the policy in all age groups and teachers were positive about it. Workloads for teachers were high.
- Teaching was satisfactory or better in 80 per cent of lessons.
- The best teaching was in years 5 and 6, where whole-class teaching of text and sentence-level work was good in two-thirds of lessons.
- Reception class teachers were implementing the literacy hour as soon as possible and the children were responding positively.
- The teaching by literacy co-ordinators was much better than that of the rest of the staff.

- Teaching of shared reading was the most successful part of the hour and was well taught in almost 90 per cent of lessons.
- The headteacher's leadership was satisfactory or better in 85 per cent of the schools receiving intensive support from their LEAs.
- Training by LEAs had been well received.

Weaknesses were as follows:

- Word and sentence-level work was the weakest part of the hour. The teaching of phonics was omitted in some lessons and was unsatisfactory in others. It was improving at Key Stage 1, but was only taught well in about half the classes.
- Insufficient attention was being given to word-level work in years 3 and 4. There was no phonics teaching in one-third of the year 3 lessons observed in the interim survey.
- Insufficient attention was being given to shared and guided writing.
- Independent group activities were weak in one-fifth of the lessons and good in only two-fifths.
- Too few teachers used the plenary session to reinforce teaching points and review the lessons' objectives.
- The performance of boys, of whom in 1999 only 46 per cent achieved level 4 in writing as compared with 61 per cent of girls, is worryingly low.

HMI (1999b) report that 'The framework for teaching has raised teachers' expectations, increased the pace of their teaching – particularly of reading – and brought about a substantial improvement in teachers' subject knowledge' (HMI, 1999b: 8). They note that teachers have moved from the practice of attempting to hear children read individually as often as possible to one in which pupils are more often taught to read more directly as a group. They suggest that the following developments are needed:

- more training for teachers in how to teach writing effectively, particularly the teaching of grammatical awareness and sentence construction;
- more emphasis on the teaching of shared and guided writing;
- further training in the teaching of phonics at Key Stage 1 and more systematic attention to phonics in years 3 and 4;
- consideration by teachers of how pupils can apply and develop in other subjects the skills they are learning in the literacy hour;

- consideration by schools of the best way to use assistance by other adults in the classroom.

Mathematics

The National Numeracy Project stated that numerate pupils should:

- have a sense of the size of a number and where it fits into the number system;
- know basic number facts and recall them quickly;
- use what they know to figure out an answer mentally;
- calculate accurately, both mentally and with pencil and paper, drawing on a range of strategies;
- use a calculator sensibly;
- recognise which operation is needed to solve a problem;
- be able to solve a problem involving more than one single-step operation;
- know for themselves that their answers are reasonable;
- explain their methods and their reasoning using correct terminology;
- suggest suitable units for making measurements, and make sensible estimates of measurement;
- explain and make sensible predictions from the numerical data in a graph, chart or table.

Hughes (1986) found that children started school with more knowledge of mathematics in practical situations than most reception class teachers were aware of. He suggested that teachers should talk to parents to find out about what their children seemed to know and could do. He also noted that children appeared to have considerable difficulty in translating between their everyday language and mathematical language and that this difficulty persisted well into the junior school. The trouble is that for children the phrasing of mathematical problems can be ambiguous. He gives as an example of the kind of difficulty which some children encounter the child who was asked 'What is the difference between 6 and 11?' and gave as the answer '11 has two numbers'. When this was marked wrong, she answered that 6 was curly and 11 was straight. This exemplifies the kind of difficulty which children meet over language. The child in question was giving everyday meanings to the mathematical question when what was wanted was a mathematical interpretation.

Hughes goes on to suggest that many difficulties arise from the use of the mathematical symbols +, −, × and ÷. Children come across numerals in many contexts outside school, but the mathematical symbols are, for children, peculiar to the classroom and they may take a long time to link them with their experience. This suggests that it might be a good idea to look for ways in which these symbols could be used in as many practical contexts as possible.

Askew and Wiliam (1995) write of the importance of finding out how pupils are thinking perhaps by asking them to write about what they have learned. Many pupils have misconceptions or intuitive methods, believing, for example, that subtracting a larger from a smaller number gives the answer nought. You need to find out how children arrived at incorrect answers if you are to help them to overcome their difficulties. Askew and Wiliam (1995: 20) go on to say: 'Knowledgeable teachers questioned pupils about problem-solving processes and listened to their responses while less knowledgeable teachers tended to explain problem-solving processes to pupils or observe their pupils' solutions'.

The ability to use calculating skills in a practical setting depends to some extent on the acquisition of concepts. A concept is acquired when a child has met a range of examples and non-examples and can use and apply the underlying idea. Discussion can be helpful in developing concepts, with children being asked to find examples and non-examples. Practical work is also important.

Askew and Wiliam also found that using a computer to teach particular topics resulted in more rapid learning and higher achievement. They make the following comment about this:

> The crucial feature in evaluating educational software appears to be the tension between the extent to which the software supports and constrains the activity of the pupil. Using computers allows the teacher to create an environment for the pupil where the options open to the pupil are limited, so that the pupil is pushed into thinking about using a particular aspect of mathematics (constraint). At the same time the software allows the pupil to do things that would be difficult without the computer (support).
>
> (Askew and Wiliam, 1995: 34–5)

They also note that co-operative group work has a positive effect provided there is a shared goal for the group and individual accountability for the attainment of the goal. They suggest that near-mixed-ability groups containing perhaps high and middle attainers or middle and low attainers are the most effective. There should also be a balance of boys and girls in the group.

Askew *et al.* (1997) studied the work of effective teachers of numeracy and categorised teachers into three orientations – the connectionist orientation, the transmission orientation and the discovery orientation.

They found that the connectionist teachers emphasised the links between different aspects of mathematics. The transmissionist teachers demonstrated a belief in the importance of routines and procedures and stressed the importance of pencil and paper methods for each type of calculation. The discovery-oriented teachers tended to treat all methods of calculation as equally acceptable and valued pupils' creation of their own ways of doing things, basing work on practical approaches. Overall, they tended to find the connectionist teachers to be the most effective.

They listed the characteristics of effective teachers of mathematics. These included the following:

- a coherent set of beliefs and understandings which underpinned their teaching of numeracy;
- a belief that being numerate requires a rich network of connections between different mathematical ideas;
- a belief that almost all pupils could become numerate;
- a view that discussion of concepts was important, particularly in revealing the pupils' thinking processes;
- attention to careful monitoring of pupils' progress and the keeping of detailed records.

The National Numeracy Strategy Framework (Department for Education and Employment, 1999) also lists the characteristics of teaching which leads to better numeracy standards. These come about when teachers:

- structure their mathematics lessons and maintain a good pace;
- provide daily oral and mental work to develop and secure pupils' calculation strategies and rapid recall skills;
- devote a high proportion of lesson time to direct teaching of whole classes and groups, making judicious use of textbooks, worksheets and information and communications technology (ICT) resources to support teaching, not to replace it;
- demonstrate, explain and illustrate mathematical ideas, making links between different topics in mathematics and between mathematics and other subjects;

- use and give pupils access to number lines and other resources, including ICT, to model mathematical ideas and methods;
- use and expect pupils to use correct mathematical vocabulary and notation;
- question pupils effectively, including as many of them as possible, giving them time to think before answering, targeting individuals to take account of their attainment and needs, asking them to demonstrate and explain their methods and reasoning, and exploring reasons for any wrong answers;
- involve pupils and maintain their interest through appropriately demanding work, including some non-routine problems that require them to think for themselves;
- ensure that differentiation is manageable and centred around work common to all the pupils in a class, with targeted, positive support to help those who have difficulties with mathematics to keep up with their peers.

A survey by HMI (1996–7) suggested that at that time there was a need for more direct and whole-class teaching, more frequent oral and mental work, clear targets with suitably demanding expectations and more monitoring and review of progress analysing performance against benchmarks. To some extent these issues have been addressed by the National Numeracy Strategy (HMI, 2000).

The interim evaluation of the National Numeracy Strategy by HMI (2000) found that schools had made a good start with the strategy with the quality of teaching good in about half the lessons seen. There were weaknesses in the progression from mental to written mathematics and work with fractions, decimals and percentages. Teachers also found it difficult to achieve an appropriate level of differentiation, particularly where the range of ability was wide. The plenary session was the weakest part of the lessons seen, with only four out of ten lessons satisfactory. Teachers did not always leave enough time for it and often did not use it to identify and correct errors and misconceptions and reinforce teaching points.

Science

A number of writers stress the importance of taking children's initial ideas into account when working with them in science. Children develop ideas of why things are as they are from a very young age, and if they do not have opportunities to investigate these ideas errors may persist and will be very difficult to overcome later. It is important that they understand from an early stage that scientific knowledge is continually subject to modification as more becomes known through investigation. The question 'Will it always happen like that?' following an investigation should gradually lead children to the idea that there can never be a certain answer to this question.

Science requires a way of thinking about evidence which is relevant in other areas as well. For example, evidence is very important in learning history and the idea that something may be the case increases as more evidence is gained applies here as well as in science. Work in geography on the nature of the earth has very strong links with science – in fact the boundary between science and geography is not a clear one. Technology is perhaps more involved with science than any other subject and much work within it will be the practical outcomes of the applications of science. Food technology is also related to science and provides the opportunity for considering why foods behave as they do, what happens when we cook food, what happens when food decays, what our bodies need for nourishment and growth and so on.

The making and testing of hypotheses is also a way of working which can be applied to any area of curriculum. Considering and predicting what happens if you take particular actions and then checking to see if the prediction was right is relevant in many aspects of daily life and is something which may often be the subject of classroom discussion.

Harlen (1985) gives useful summaries of what may be expected by way of scientific work from children of different ages. This review of development has application in other parts of the curriculum. The following is an abbreviated version of her statements:

Five- to seven-year-olds

1   They cannot think through actions but have to carry them out in practice.
2   They can only see from their own point of view. They need to move physically to see from another's point of view.
3   They focus on one aspect of an object or situation at a time, e.g. their judgement of the amount of water in a container will take into account only one dimension, often the height the liquid reaches, not the combination of the height and width of the container.
4   They tend not to relate one event to another when they encounter an unfamiliar sequence of events. They are likely to remember the first and last items in a sequence but not the ones in between.
5   The results of actions not yet carried out cannot be anticipated.

Seven- to nine-year-olds

1   They begin to see a simple process as a whole, relating the individual parts to each other so that a process of change can be grasped and events put in sequence.
2   They can think through a simple process in reverse, which brings awareness of the conservation of some physical quantities during changes in which there appears to be some increase or decrease.
3   They may realise that two effects have to be taken into account in deciding the result of an action, e.g. if a ball of Plasticine is squashed flat so that it gets thinner as well as wider, it is not any bigger overall than before.
4   There is some progress towards being able to see things from someone else's viewpoint.
5   They can relate a physical effect to its cause.

Nine- to eleven-year-olds

1   They can to some extent handle problems which involve more than one variable.
2   They can use a wider range of logical relations and so mentally manipulate more things.
3   They show less tendency to jump to conclusions and a greater appreciation that ideas should be checked against evidence.
4   They can use measurement and recording as part of a more systematic and accurate approach to problems.
5   They can go through the possible steps of an investigation and produce a possible plan of action.

Edwards and Knight (1994: 60) write of the teacher's role in helping children to develop concepts in science. The teacher's task is:

• to have an idea of which concepts are to be improved;
• to know which alternative concepts children are likely to hold;
• to provide situations in which children may be encouraged to notice discrepancies;
• to use that observation to get children to suggest an explanation;
• to get them to play with the explanation, making fair tests of it;
• to get them to apply and consolidate their conclusions.

They go on to suggest that the teacher needs to help children to see and understand, 'sometimes by drawing attention to what children have done, sometimes by asking for ideas, sometimes by asking if there are alternatives that might have advantages and sometimes by getting children to compare and evaluate what they are doing' (Edwards and Knight, 1994: 61).

Science and mathematics both require substantial time to be devoted to them, but there will be opportunities for practising both in many aspects of the curriculum.

Opportunities for scientific investigation will arise as part of other work on many occasions. An environmental study will provide many opportunities for studying plants and animals and perhaps looking at soil and rocks. A study of a historical building could lead to an investigation of how people raised stone before modern equipment was there to help them or it could offer the opportunity to study the effect of weathering on materials.

HMI (1996–7), studying science in primary schools, found that standards had improved and compared favourably with standards achieved by children in other countries. Four-fifths of pupils achieved or exceeded the expected national standard at Key Stage 1 and more than two-thirds at Key Stage 2. Attainment was similar to that in English and better than that in mathematics. Teaching was good in 40 per cent of schools and at least satisfactory in 90 per cent. The least satisfactory area of science teaching was the use of information technology to collect, store, retrieve and present information. They also found that assessment procedures were often inconsistently applied and not incorporated into planning.

10 The foundation subjects

Art

Art has much to contribute in the teaching of other subjects and in topic work but it is important that it is explored as a subject in its own right. Four areas need exploration. Children need experience of drawing at first-hand and this can usefully be part of other work, although encouragement to draw anything and everything is also needed. Second, they need to explore what different media will do, in both two and three dimensions. Third, they need the opportunity to think about putting these skills together to make compositions of one sort or another in both two and three dimensions. Finally, they need to study the works of artists and to explore some of the ideas and techniques they see used.

The teacher's role in the exploration of media is to provide opportunities. It is then to set problems which encourage exploration. For example, you may ask children to make a picture or pattern using as many different reds as possible, making the colours by mixing red with every other colour in differing amounts. You might ask for a pattern or picture using as many different textures as possible or get children to explore ways of representing the texture of things around them. With clay you might ask children to move in particular ways and then make figures doing exactly the same thing. Or you might ask children to explore surface textures in clay, perhaps making them by impressing the clay with different objects.

You can also encourage children to look at the relationships of the things they put into their pictures or creations. You can encourage them to make first-hand observations of the objects they draw or make, or feel how a person might look by moving themselves in similar ways.

In looking at pictures with children you can draw their attention to the way in which the artist has used texture or arranged the shapes in the picture. They can then go on to try to use similar techniques in their own work.

HMI (1996–7), looking at art in primary schools, found attainment and progress good in 30 per cent of schools, with the best teaching in year 6. They note that where standards were high pupils explored a wide range of materials in two and three dimensions, such as paint, clay, pastel, collage and modelling materials. In such classes pupils began to develop observational drawing skills from an early age. They found that assessment was weak compared with that in most other subjects.

Design and technology

We noted in Chapter 6 that Bennett *et al.* (1992) and Webb and Vulliamy (1996) found that technology was the subject in which teachers felt least competent. HMI (1996–7) found that, while work in this subject continued to improve, standards achieved were lower than in most other subjects, mainly because teachers lacked subject expertise and often failed to provide a programme which built successfully on earlier knowledge. There was also a dip in attainment in years 3 and 4. On the other hand, pupils' attitudes were generally positive.

These findings are not very surprising, given that this subject has only recently been part of the curriculum. It will take time for teachers to develop the knowledge and skill needed and for schools to develop resources.

Technology has a very close relationship with science, but whereas science is concerned with the pursuit of knowledge through investigation technology is concerned with meeting human needs and with making things and requires pupils to apply their knowledge and skill to solving practical problems. It is also concerned with working with others as a team.

The basic concern of technology is problem-solving and the processes used can be applied to other areas of work and to teaching. Problem-solving was discussed from the teacher's point of view in Chapter 6. Problem-solving for children requires similar steps. These are as follows:

1 *Define the problem*
   This is a necessary starting point for all problems. It might be the problem of how to make a bird-table which the squirrels cannot reach or a problem in the classroom, such as difficulty in keeping some areas tidy or a problem of everyone wanting the same things at the same time. You need to work with children to help them to make statements about what the problem really is. We saw in

Chapter 6 that it is often helpful at this stage to consider what you wish the outcome to be.

2 *Examine the problem further*
This is a matter of discussing the nature of the problem and the needs which it must be designed to fit. It might be a matter of defining the social setting of a problem or discussing the range of materials which might be used or discussion of why the problem arises. In some cases a good deal of research will be needed to find out about the needs and the situation which the design must meet. If we take the problem of the bird-table, children will need to find out what squirrels can do and what would make the bird-table inaccessible to them while meeting the needs of birds.

3 *Define your objectives*
It is very helpful in problem-solving to know exactly what it is you are trying to do in as much detail as possible. If we take the problem of keeping an area of the classroom tidy, it may help to discuss what should be available in that area and in what sort of order and try to define what is meant by 'tidy'.

These three items provide the design specification.

4 *Consider possible solutions*
Here, children need to be encouraged to find a number of alternative solutions before settling on one. It may be a good idea for them to work in groups, each group trying to make as many suggestions as possible. This may be the stage with some problems for sketching ideas.

5 *Examine solutions*
The next stage is to examine the possibilities and problems of each solution. Children need to look at such things as practicality, ease of making or doing, the cost in terms of materials and the extent to which each solution meets the criteria set out in the design specification.

6 *Select a solution*
If this is a group decision it will need a good deal of discussion and the final decision might be made by voting or by discussing to the point of consensus. Whether it is an individual or a group decision, it will involve careful weighing of the points arising out of the consideration of possible solutions.

7 *Make an action plan*
It is valuable to get children into the habit of making action plans for work in hand and this is particularly relevant where problem-solving is involved.

8 *Make an evaluation plan*
Evaluation should be part of the planning with any problem-solving activity and should take into account the criteria which were part of the design specification.
9 *Carry out the project*
10 *Evaluate the result against the criteria defined*
Children should be encouraged to consider their work and look to see whether anything could have been done differently or improved.

Part of the work in technology will involve evaluating one's own work and that of other people. Different artefacts may be discussed, looking at what they were designed to do and consideration given to how effectively they do it. Children may also be involved in finding out how things work. They need to learn how to use tools and devise mechanisms that make things move.

The teacher's role in technology will be to define the parameters within which work takes place. In many cases it will be the teacher who identifies the problems to be tackled, although children should be encouraged to identify problems as well. It is important to define tasks in such a way that there is ample scope for children to solve them in their own way, selecting materials and tools as seems best to them.

Geography and history

Over the years there has been a good deal of discussion about how far schools should be concerned with knowledge in these subjects and how far with the interpretation of evidence and empathy with people who live in other places or lived at other times. There would seem to be a need for some emphasis on both.

Both history and geography require an act of the imagination to understand the way different people have lived or do live in the world today. Children easily get the impression that people who live differently from them are in some way odd and a variation from the norm. Since children's experience is limited, it is important to provide as much first-hand experience as possible and to complement this with videotape and television programmes. Fieldwork is an essential part of these subjects and visits to museums can be valuable. Drama may help in enabling children to imagine what life was like at another time or in another place and a visit to one of the museums where children are incorporated into a drama about a particular period in history will be immensely valuable.

Geography must involve learning how to use globes and maps and the characteristics of places and the effect of different places on the people who live in them, and also the effect of people on the places in which they live. Children can share information about their own environment with children in other locations in other schools through e-mail.

HMI (1996–7) looked at the teaching of geography in primary schools and found well-organised and managed field studies and good practical work in the school grounds and elsewhere. There was good development of investigatory and mapping skills, particularly in years 5 and 6, and children enjoyed their work. They found weaknesses in some schools where geography was only taught infrequently and skills were not well developed and there was a lack of use of information technology. There was also a dip in attainment in most schools in years 3 and 4.

History involves learning how to find out about the past from various sources and children should learn to place events in chronological sequence.

HMI found that history teaching compared favourably with that in most other subjects and they felt that this was mainly owing to the fact that teachers' subject knowledge was good. This led to good progress and a high degree of enjoyment of the subject in many schools.

Planning for progression was weak in a number of schools in both these subjects, as was assessment.

History and geography may be incorporated into topic work, but it will be important to have a clear idea of the historical or geographical learning which is intended.

Information and communications technology

Information and communications technology should be an integral part of every subject area. It is not statutory to use it in other subjects at the beginning of schooling but it becomes so at Key Stage 2.

Children need to become familiar with the keyboard from an early stage and use word-processing as a means of drafting work as often as equipment makes it possible. They also need to learn how to make and use a database and spreadsheet and opportunities should be sought to make this part of work in different projects. As laptop computers become cheaper they will play an increasing part in education and it is likely that many programs will be devised which assess what children already know and then set out to teach new knowledge. This has considerable implications for teachers.

Skills involved in meeting the National Curriculum criteria include presenting information in various forms – text, images, tables and graphs, sounds, desktop publishing. The use of e-mail can provide opportunities for genuine correspondence with children in other schools and, in some cases, other countries, and this should help children become sensitive to readership and provide opportunities to exchange and share information. Using the internet should provide opportunities for discussing how to evaluate information, questioning accuracy and looking for bias.

The HMI (1996–7) study of standards in primary schools found this the least well-taught subject of the curriculum. Teaching was good in only 20 per cent of schools and progress good in only one-sixth. This was caused, on the one hand, by teachers' own lack of knowledge and, on the other, by the lack of suitable equipment and software. Work did not cover the requirements of the National Curriculum in many schools. Pupils lacked skills and strategies for searching systematically for information and there was a need for greater reinforcement of previously learned skills. Many teachers were uncertain about what needed to be taught and the expectations they should have of pupils. On the other hand, pupils' enthusiasm and self-esteem rose markedly when they worked with information technology.

Music

Music teaching has changed radically in recent years, partly as a result of electronic music-making. There is now also a much greater emphasis on composition. Singing is still important and children need to sing a wide variety of music and learn to play different tuned and untuned instruments and compose rhythms and tunes for them. There should be good opportunities for playing with and to others and discussing critically both performance and composition. Children need eventually to learn to read music but this is probably best approached by asking children to invent methods of writing down the music they make up and then gradually introducing more formal ways of writing.

It is also important for children to listen to a wide range of music and discuss their reactions to it and to the music they compose.

Physical education

Physical education should serve two important purposes in school. It is concerned with achieving and maintaining fitness and it is also concerned with helping children to move in a controlled way. There is a good deal of concern at the present time about the fact that children are taking less exercise than in the past and the long-term effects of this for their health. This makes the subject of particular importance. Physical education also aims to teach the beginnings of games skills which may form the foundation for activity in adult life, in a society where much work is sedentary. There should be opportunities both to create dance and to perform dances from other times and places. Swimming is an important element in the physical education programme. Children should be encouraged to look critically at their work in all aspects of physical education and consider ways in which movement could be improved.

HMI (1996–7) found that in most schools pupils made good progress in games, gymnastics and dance, although there was a tendency to repeat known skills rather than seek to improve them. Teaching was good in nearly half the schools and at least satisfactory in 90 per cent. The least satisfactory aspects of the subject were assessment and recording, which was not well done, with records of children's progress rarely kept. Athletics and outdoor and adventurous activities also tended to be neglected and a common failing was the lack of attention to involvement of pupils in a cycle of improvement and skill development. They noted that good physical education teaching was characterised by clear task-setting, challenge and a focus on skill learning.

There is a tendency to regard physical education lessons as separate from the rest of the curriculum. There is a need to make links in many ways. In physical activity, a teacher can see whether children are understanding the language he or she is using in a way which is more difficult elsewhere because in physical education they have to respond directly to instructions. Many mathematical words come into physical education – fast, slow, circle, line, shape and so on. It is also important to observe children's movement in the classroom and about the school and to consider the implications of the way children move at other times.

Religious education

Religious education is not an easy subject to teach in a pluralist society. On the other hand, the presence of children of different faiths in a school gives the study of religion a reality which is more difficult to achieve when all the children are at least nominally of Christian background or of no faith at all.

Religious teaching in schools other than church schools is teaching about religion and the part it plays in human history. An understanding of Christianity is essential for an understanding of British history and customs. An understanding of Judaism, Islam, Sikhism, Buddhism and Hinduism is necessary to understand present-day British society and also to understand what is happening in different parts of the world, as well as for understanding world history.

Religious education in schools other than voluntary schools is governed by Agreed Syllabuses devised by local Standing Committees for Religious Education (SACRES).

Religious education is also concerned with moral education, although this needs to be pursued in many other contexts as well. Children need to know the moral basis of Christianity because it is the moral basis of much in our society. At a later stage in education they may learn about the moral ideas of other religions.

HMI (1996–7) found that religious education was taught to a satisfactory or better standard in 90 per cent of schools but was good in only about 20 per cent. Years 5 and 6 made better progress than years 3 and 4 and teaching was slightly better at Key Stage 2 than Key Stage 1. The quality of teaching was inconsistent. Teachers generally had the necessary knowledge but lacked the confidence and expertise to teach religious education effectively. There was a tendency to emphasise the facts about religion rather than beliefs and values. Assessment of performance was also weak and rarely related to specific objectives. There were fewer good standards of attainment and progress than in other subjects and the teacher tended to have low expectations of pupils. The teaching of religious education was rarely monitored although subject leadership was improving. Pupils' attitudes were mainly positive.

11 The learning programme

A good teacher is always searching for the best way of using the time, space and other resources available for the children's learning. The National Curriculum places a certain amount of pressure on teachers to cover the ground and this makes it even more important to use resources well, which makes planning especially important.

Planning is needed both for long-term and for day-to-day work. Some of the planning may be for topics which may be subject specific or cross-curricular and some for straightforward subject teaching such as the literacy and numeracy programmes. As teacher you have to find the best path between making all the decisions yourself and leaving too much to the children. If you decide exactly what is to be done and how it is to be carried out, the children may learn some things extremely well, but they will not become independent learners. You may also miss the inspiration which children can bring to work when they have a measure of freedom about how to do it. If, on the other hand, you leave too much to them, they will lose the inspiration which you bring to them as teacher and they may not learn what you intend. You need to plan flexibly so that your plan can be adapted to changing circumstances.

Different pieces of work provide differing opportunities for children to contribute ideas about learning. In some situations you need to dictate fairly fully what is to be done and what is to be learned and how the learning is to be carried out. In other situations there can be much more freedom and the opportunity for children to choose and develop ideas of their own. Some of both approaches are needed.

When you first start work in which there is a good deal of freedom to choose with a group of children for whom this is new, they will need a lot of help if they are going to do any of the planning for themselves. At this stage you could discuss with them possible ways of working. A question such as 'We need to learn about how living things differ from each other – how do you think we might set about it?' may bring useful suggestions. It may be useful to plan some discussion in pairs or small groups. There will be much work where you plan in more detail, but planning should often be shared with the children with the teacher adding in ideas and suggestions. This approach should help children to become independent learners and to think how learning might take place.

As teacher, you need to plan at three levels:

- long-term planning for the year or term;
- teaching plans for pieces of work which may spread over several weeks;
- planning for day-to-day work.

The first of these will not involve the children to any extent but the other two types of planning may do so.

Long-term planning

Every teacher needs to plan on a long-term basis as well as from day to day. You need to plan work for the whole year, using various approaches to the National Curriculum. An important planning task is to consider your objectives in broad terms at the long-term planning stage and then to consider the time-scale of what you plan to do, noting the points at which you hope to introduce new material. These need not be too definite and it is useful to set in earliest and latest dates so that you can allow for the stage the children have reached and their readiness to move on to another piece of work. You may also need to plan in co-operation with other teachers of the same year group.

There is a great deal of research evidence to suggest that the teacher who has clear objectives is more likely to be a successful teacher than one who has not defined work in this way. The National Curriculum makes the setting of objectives more important and at the same time gives a clear lead in defining the learning tasks.

It may also be helpful to consider what use might be made of the computer for planning and for recording. It may be helpful to store outline plans so that you can come back to them and update them when you are working with a new group.

Finally, in long-term planning it is important to consider your objectives for training children to work in the organisation you have in mind. What do you need to do to train them to become independent learners? How are they going to acquire learning skills? These can all be acquired as part of the learning which is in hand, but you need to be conscious of what is involved and how you can help them to develop the necessary skills. These were discussed in Chapter 8.

Your teaching plan for a piece of work

Whether you are planning work within a particular subject or as a topic it is a good idea to start by setting down your objectives which will be based on the National Curriculum requirements. These may be from one subject or more than one subject and should include objectives for training children as independent learners as well as subject knowledge. They should be stated in a form that enables you to see easily whether they have been achieved.

In the past there have been many occasions when teachers have taken advantage of something topical or something which interests the children and used this as a stimulus to help them to learn. Local events such as the fiftieth birthday of the school, new school buildings, national and international events and annual events can all be used for learning within the National Curriculum. While this should not be the main way of working, partly because of the time element, opportunities should be looked for and used. However, it is difficult to ensure progression and coverage of the National Curriculum if work is too opportunist. The development of scientific understanding, for example, requires progression in the ability to identify questions which could be investigated and ability to apply scientific thinking to the investigation, and there is a similar need for progression on most subjects. If progression is to be achieved, it must be planned.

Topic work

Although the National Curriculum is set out in the form of subjects, teachers are free to introduce some work in the form of topics or projects provided that the required subject-related skills and concepts are developed. Cross-curricular work can be an efficient way of working in that the same experience may provide material for learning in more than one subject. It also shows how subjects are related to one another. Young children tend to learn from everything that happens to them and project work seems a natural way of learning, but as they grow older the work can become more subject specific.

It is perhaps worth considering at this stage what topic work offers as a learning medium. In the first instance, a topic helps to place learning in a context. Children learn about a number of related things at the same time and this makes it more likely that the learning will be retained. A good topic will involve a strong element of first-hand experience as well as a variety of different approaches to learning. Children will observe, question, use first-hand experience, use computers and use books to find out; they will write, draw, paint and make models. The teacher will give them information and lead them to form appropriate concepts. They will also develop and practise skills of various kinds. They may also learn to work together if group work is part of the activity. All these approaches help to reinforce learning.

There are also some problems about topic work. Different children may undertake different tasks and it is then difficult to be sure of who has learned what. A child may get a biased view of a particular topic because he or she has chosen particular aspects of it to work on. Topic work tends to make continuity difficult because of the different tasks children have undertaken and it is difficult to ensure progression in the context of a topic. You have to allow for each of these difficulties, mainly by the care with which you record what each child has done. With older children it will be possible to ask them to do some of the recording of the ground they have covered on a particular topic.

Aspects of planning

Whether you are using a topic as the basis of your teaching in a particular area or are dealing with a specific subject directly, the following need consideration in planning:

- Children's existing experience
  - What have the children already experienced on which I can build?
- First-hand experiences needed
  - What experiences must I provide for the children so that they understand the work we shall be doing?
- Language
  - What words and phrases will children need to understand the work we shall be doing?
  - What new language will they learn as a result of this work?
  - What varieties of language can be practised? (Formal and informal modes, transactional language, expressive language, poetic language.)
- Knowledge
  - What do I hope children will know at the end of this piece of work?

- Concepts
  - What do I want the children to understand at the end of this piece of work?
- Skills
  - What should children be able to do as a result of this piece of work?
- Creative work
  - What creative work might grow out of this work?
- Outcomes
  - How will the learning be demonstrated?
  - How will I evaluate what has been learned?

This pattern of planning can be used for whole topics or a series of lessons on a particular subject. The plans given below set it out as a form which could be adapted for use.

This type of plan gives you a clear picture of what the outcomes of your work might be but does not limit the possibilities which may emerge. With a new group you might plan the broad areas in which they might be working. For example, you might plan the field work involved in the *living things* project described below and discuss with the children what they might see and what they might collect. You then feed in ideas such as the quadrat as a means of helping observation. Gradually, you build up a list with the children, rather like the lists on pp. 159, 161 and 163, and you can then add to this ideas from the lists you have prepared yourself. Although the outline is given here in detail, in practice quite a lot of the items might be those suggested by children.

From there, you go on to plan which children should undertake which tasks. Some of the organisation here will be a matter of children choosing tasks which interest them and some tasks may be allocated taking children's abilities and interests into account.

Bennett and Kell (1989) found that teachers do not always judge what has been achieved in terms of their original intentions. The same study also suggested that teachers often do not make it clear to children what is the object of a given piece of work. If children are to be partners in their own learning, it is essential that they know the purpose of any work they do. The National Curriculum makes it important to judge work in terms of intended learning.

The conclusion of any piece of work is important for learning. Both the literacy and numeracy strategies suggest ending the lesson with a plenary session which draws together what has been learned and looks forward to the next lesson. HMI (1999a,b) found that this was the least well-used part of the lesson. Teachers did not always have a clear understanding of the purpose of the plenary session and sometimes they did not leave enough time for it.

The conclusion of any piece of work should therefore demonstrate what has been learned in a way that enables you to assess whether you achieved your intentions. In planning, you need to decide how the work will be concluded. Will there be an exhibition or talks or presentations by groups of children? How will you draw things to a close and what important points do you need to bring out in doing this?

Short-term planning

In addition to planning long term and planning major pieces of work, you will need to make plans for day-to-day teaching. The more experienced you are, the less detailed these plans need to be, but the need for planning remains, however long you have been teaching. The following need to be prepared in advance:

- *The range of activities and objectives you intend to pursue during the day*
  It is essential to think clearly about these since some will need careful preparation of the classroom.
- *The provision you intend to make for the range of pupils*
  Some activities will be for the whole class; others will be for different groups and individuals.
- *Questions you plan to ask in relation to the activities planned*
  We have already noted the importance of questioning. Higher order questions, in particular, need to be considered in advance because it is often difficult to think of such questions on the spur of the moment.
- *The resources you will need*
- *How you plan to undertake starting, changing activity and clearing up*
  If you are experienced and your class is well trained this needs no preparation. Inexperienced teachers would be well advised to plan starting, changing and clearing up very carefully because these are times when things can go wrong.
- *The children for whom individual help may be needed*
  You will have identified some children from previous work who will need extra help or perhaps different materials from the others. You may also need to consider the needs of the more able children.

Will they need more challenging work or work to extend their thinking or work to go on to if they finish before the other children?

- *The children whose work you plan to check*
  It is a good idea to have a systematic plan for checking the work and understanding of a few children in detail each day.
- *How you will assess the effectiveness of the work you have done?*
  It is a good idea to identify some success criteria for your day's work.

Theme outlines

Figures 11.1–11.6 give outline plans for work on three themes which arise from National Curriculum requirements. The themes are communication, materials and living things.

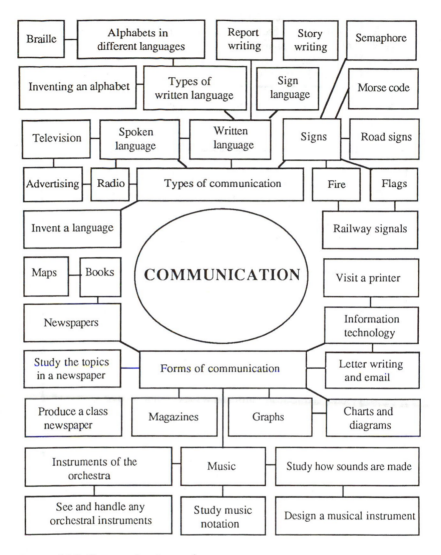

Figure 11.2 Communication web

Existing experience	Tv and radio; observation of forms of communication; use of telephone; signs and symbols in environment; possible experience of other written language symbols; sounds of musical instruments	
First-hand experience	Opportunity to handle musical instruments; experimental work making sounds; visit to printer; observation of signs and signals	
Language	Names of forms of communication e.g. books; graphs; newspapers, maps etc.; words connected with sounds and the way they are made e.g. vibration; names of types of communication. e.g. signs, braille, language of the deaf etc.; know something about musical notation; know something about how to match speaking or writing to an audience or readership	
Knowledge	Know how musical sounds are produced and the types of instrument making them; know how advertisers capture our interest; know the ways in which we communicate over long distances	
Concepts	Sound is produced by vibration; vibration is caused in a variety of ways; we use many forms of communcation which are not dependent on language , e.g. road signs; we speak and write in a different way according to the audience or readership	
Skills	Work with a group on a communication task; collect information about types of communication and organise it as a block graph; write about findings using full stops and capital letters correctly; prepare and give a talk to a specific audience (e.g. children from another class), matching the talk to the audience	
Creative work	Invent a language; invent signs; create a newspaper; devise musical instruments; devise advertisements	
Outcomes	Exhibition and presentation to another class; class newspaper	

Figure 11.1 Analysis of thematic material for topic on communication

Existing experience		Observation of plants, birds and animals in environment; plants grown in classroom; keeping of pets; observation in gardens and parks; television wildlife programmes
First-hand experience		Visits to field, woodland, pond; growing plants in the classroom; keeping small animals in the classroom; observation in school environment and home areas
Language		Names of plants and animals; names of their parts; words describing plants e.g. deciduous, evergreen. Words describing what animals do e.g. hibernation; descriptions of animal movement; words describing animals homes and their young; explain work being done; relate events in the life of a plant or animal to other children
Knowledge		Plant and animal life cycles; some of the habitats of different plants and animals; some of the food chains of different animals; the effects of season and weather
Concepts		Basic life processes are common to all living things; living things grow and change over time; different living things require different habitats; a habitat must have appropriate conditions for the plants and creatures that live there; plants and animals can be classified in various ways
Skills		Making classes and sorting; devising questions for research; making and using a database; speaking to the class; using lenses; making tables/bar charts; recording over a period; making and using a quadrat; drawing and naming parts of animals and plants
Creative work		Making pictures of the areas studied and of plants and animals using different media; writing poems about the areas studied and setting them to music; drawing plants and animals as they grow; writing stories about animals which include knowledge of their life style; making leaf prints; making lino blocks from drawings of plants and animals; printing fabrics with them
Outcomes		Exhibition of what has been discovered; talks by individuals and groups about their findings; making of books; sharing of creative work; class discussion about what has been learned

Figure 11.3 Analysis of thematic material for topic on living things

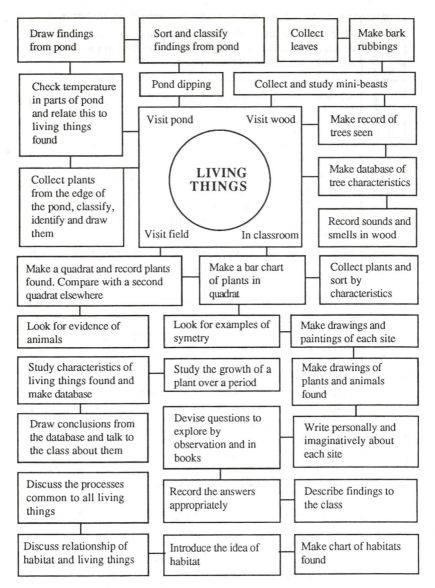

Figure 11.4 Topic web on living things

Existing experience	Experience of a variety of materials in everyday life - fabric, food, furniture, materials, building materials, use of yarn in clothing, knitting, woodwork, experience with clay
First-hand experience	Visit local street and small manufacturing unit e.g. a pottery; bring in fabrics, dig clay, collect sheep's wool, collect similar sized twigs of different woods, survey buildings, visit building site
Language	Names of different fabrics, dye plants, stones, woods etc. Transparent, opaque, porous, inflamable, saturated, flexible rigid, man-made, natural material Discussion of how to test materials; presentation to others of findings; use of books and computers to find out; writing of reports on findings
Knowledge	Sources of different materials; their characteristics; uses of different materials
Concepts	Some materials are natural and some are man-made; different materials have different characteristics which determine their use
Skills	Testing materials for different characteristics, e.g. hardness/softness, flexibility etc.; making bricks and pots, making dyes; spinning; weaving
Creative work	Making a picture with stones; making bricks and pottery; making dyes and using them; making a fabric collage; spinning and weaving; writing about how different materials make you feel
Outcomes	Exhibition of work; discussion of experiments and findings; planning for presentation to parents

Figure 11.5 Analysis for topic on the theme of materials

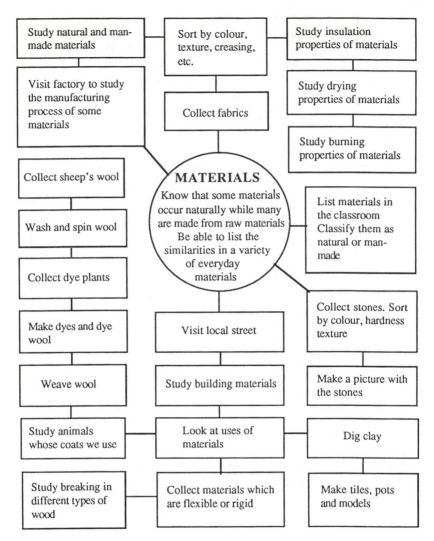

Figure 11.6 Topic on materials

12 Classroom management

The range of children in a school is decided by the LEA, which determines the age groups that a school caters for. The way children are organised within the school is the decision of the headteacher and staff. Classes and groups can be formed on the basis of age, ability or stage of development or achievement in a particular activity. Children can also be grouped randomly or by friendship and family. Teachers can work solely within one class or they can take some subjects with another group or they can work with other teachers taking joint responsibility for a group of children.

The way you organise work within the classroom has a hidden or partly hidden agenda which should be considered from time to time so that it ceases to be hidden.

The extent to which you work with the whole class or with individuals or groups affects the kind of contact you have with each child. Your organisation also has implications for the development of study skills and independence in learning. The extent to which you encourage competition or co-operation will affect attitudes to learning and to other people. Encouraging children to work together or compete with one another will have implications for social behaviour and the extent to which children eventually come to regard others as fellow workers or rivals.

The way a teacher organises work is a very personal matter and there are many good ways of working, each with its own collection of strengths and disadvantages or pitfalls. No one way of working suits everyone. At the same time there is a certain amount of research evidence which suggests that some ways of working yield better results than others, and Chapter 4 listed some of the findings of research about effective teaching.

HMI (1997), studying the teaching of number, found that the more effective teachers had a good balance of teaching the whole class, work in groups and individual work. Less effective teachers tended to have too much emphasis on individual and group work. They also found that effective teachers ended the lesson with a plenary session summing up what had been learned and checking how much children had understood. These approaches have been incorporated in the numeracy strategy which primary teachers are now following.

Classroom routines

If teaching and learning is to take place, it is essential that the classroom is well organised. Bennett and Kell (1989) described poor classroom organisation which showed itself in a lack of pupil involvement, children wandering about, lack of interest or motivation and poor use of resources. Children played about without the teacher apparently being aware of it. The same study was critical of some of the use of play activities in the youngest classes where children were fighting, throwing things about and generally working with a lack of purpose.

Cleave *et al.* (1982) noted that in their study there was three times as much queuing to see the teacher in infant classes as there was in the nursery.

These descriptions identify a number of things which can go wrong. Children will not work well if the work they are given lacks purpose in their eyes or if they are unclear about what is being demanded. Clarity in giving instructions is essential for a well-organised classroom. There also needs to be structure in what is required so that children know what to do when they have finished a piece of work. A classroom in which there are long queues to see the teacher is a badly organised room where children are wasting time.

Bennett *et al.* (1984) found that queuing was a considerable problem in the classes they studied. Some teachers operated a dual queue system where they heard a child read on the one hand and at the same time marked the work of others. Children spent a great deal of time queuing to see the teacher, who, consequently, had too little time to work with groups or to assess adequately the problems of the children they heard reading.

Wheldall and Glynn (1989: 51) made a study of queuing in the classroom. They found that 'On average about three children were observed to be waiting at any one time, varying from zero to twenty-one children waiting in classes of approximately thirty children'. They also found 'that the mean length of time spent waiting was about one and a half minutes, but this was highly variable, ranging from zero (when children received immediate attention) to over thirteen minutes.

... A quarter of the teachers were observed to have at least one child in their class waiting for more than ten minutes'.

This is not an easy problem to solve. Many teachers like to mark work with the child present, but too great an emphasis on this makes it difficult to work with groups of children. It may be better to mark a smaller proportion of the work with the child present, selecting a few children each day for this purpose and marking other children's work outside the classroom. Children should also be encouraged to look at information around the classroom and ask advice from other children before going to the teacher for spellings or similar information. When you are working with a group it should be accepted that there will be no interruptions and that children should move on to something else if they are unable to complete the work without your help. This is easier in a team-teaching situation or one where you have a teaching assistant who can deal with the rest of the class while you are teaching a group.

An important part of children's learning is how to learn. There is a case for discussing with children how they set about a particular piece of learning. In learning spellings, for example, children often feel that they should learn by simply repeating the letters of the words. It is better if they are encouraged to look for patterns in spelling. Which words are like other words? Can words which are alike be grouped? Are there any rules which can be learned? For example, do they know that words ending with 'y' change the 'y' into 'ies' when the word becomes plural? Can you put them in a position to work this out for themselves? What about words ending in 'ey' such as donkey or monkey?

Children can also be encouraged to think about planning their work. They may set out the outline for a story after doing something similar with the teacher. Groups and pairs can be encouraged to plan work on a topic.

Part of independent learning involves being able to make good use of books and the internet. Children need to be taught how to use catalogues and indexes and content lists and how to scan a page searching for the information they need. The more you can help children to become independent learners, the more you will be able to direct your time where it is most needed.

Children also should be involved in helping to manage the classroom, perhaps looking after different resources, caring for classroom pets, seeing that materials are properly tidied away after use and so on.

Another important point is that of monitoring. The teacher needs to be aware of what is happening in the classroom at all times. Kounin

(1970) identified various aspects of teacher behaviour which were effective in managing children. He called one of these 'withitness', which he describes as 'the teacher's communicating to the children by her actual behaviour that she knows what the children are doing or has the proverbial eyes at the back of her head' (Kounin, 1970: 81). He also noted that effective teachers were able to deal with more than one thing at once and moved smoothly from one activity to another. The habit of scanning the room and catching the eye of children who are not on-task or who need help is an essential teacher skill. Monitoring also involves being aware of the work that children are doing and how it is going.

A well-organised classroom has routines, so that children feel secure in knowing what to do. You need to have rules about the following:

- *Movement about the room*
  Children should know when they are allowed to move freely about the room and when you expect them to sit at their tables. They also need to know how many people are allowed to undertake any one activity at the same time.
- *The things for which they need your permission*
  This needs to be made very clear to children from the beginning. Most teachers would expect to have to give permission for children to leave the classroom, although where there is working space outside further definition may be needed.
- *What to do when they come into the classroom first thing in the morning and after breaks in the day*
  You may want them to continue with the work in hand or have some other task for them to do, but they need to be clear about what is required.
- *When they are expected to be quiet*
  There will be times in the day when you want quiet. There will also be situations when you want attention from everyone. You need to have an understood signal for quiet, such as clapping your hands or raising one hand, and you should insist that everyone stops and listens when you give this signal.
- *What to do when they have finished the work they are doing*
  Try to avoid the situation where children come to you every time they finish a piece of work. If you give them more than one piece of work at once, the occasions when they need to come back to you will be fewer. You may also be able to provide some materials that have a structure which makes it clear what comes next, and there may be materials about the classroom from which children

may choose when they have finished other work. At the same time you need to keep track of some individuals who may avoid coming to you at all. If everyone is kept busy it becomes possible to call on those you want to see.

Forms of organisation

There are a number of different ways in which a class can be organised for learning and you need to select your approaches to suit the material to be learned and the mood of the class.

Whole-class teaching

The literacy and numeracy strategies have made the case for an important place for whole-class teaching which is interactive and involves individual children while maintaining the attention of the whole class. It is useful in number work, where individuals can be involved in answering the different parts of the problems the class is discussing. The introduction of big books has made whole-class teaching of reading more of a possibility. A good teacher can also do much to stimulate and inspire children in a class group. It is particularly useful for starting a new topic and for drawing together the work as a topic nears completion.

Class works at the same subject at different levels

The numeracy and literacy hours and some other studies are likely to involve work in groups after the initial introduction, sometimes with different work set for each group and the teacher working with each group in turn and sometimes with everyone doing the same work but at a level determined by his or her ability. This requires good organisation to keep everyone going so that you are free to work with a group at a time. It can work best if your materials are set out in an order which children recognise. Children need to know what to do if they need your help but you are teaching a group. There should be alternative work for them to do so that they can get on with something useful until you are free to help them.

Children work on individual programmes

There is a place for this, particularly in topic work where children may have a choice of activity, but the evidence described in Chapter 4 suggests that children make less progress in this form of organisation if it is too widely used.

There is, nevertheless, an important place for individual work which may involve any of the following situations:

1   Children work at individual tasks which may be chosen by the child or given by the teacher. These tasks could arise from topic work or a class activity or be a development of the child's own ideas. Individual work is part of the literacy and numeracy strategies.
2   Children work at their own pace through a structured scheme of work. This may mean that everyone is doing English or mathematics but the actual work each child is doing may be different. This should not replace direct teaching as a class or in a group.
3   Children work at individual tasks which are part of a group activity. Each child's work contributes to the groups' findings or presentation.

Individual work in one or other of these categories would seem to be most appropriate for:

*   A situation in which there is a wide range of ability within the class, but a common theme. For example, an environmental study might involve a variety of different questions and working plans so that the work could be matched to the ability of the children.
*   Learning which needs to be step by step, such as those aspects of mathematics which are concerned with individual understanding and practice.
*   Learning which is matched to individual need and differentiates children according to their ability, stage of development and the stage they have reached in the work in hand and in the National Curriculum.
*   Providing individual opportunities for creative and practical work, although this may contribute to a common goal.

Children work together in pairs or groups

The smallest group is a pair and this is usually very easy to arrange without rearranging seating. Children can be encouraged to help each other, check each other's work, discuss how to tackle a problem, plan together for written work, teach each other and so on. You need to be alert to possible time-wasting but much valuable work can be done in this way.

Group work might be divided into two broad categories. The first is grouping by ability, in which the teacher may work with a group at a time giving them work matched to the ability and stage of development of the children within the group. Both the literacy and numeracy strategies involve this kind of grouping and the number of such groups should be kept comparatively small, probably no more than three or four groups in the class. If there are too many groups you will not be able to deal with them adequately.

The second kind of grouping is grouping for co-operative work. Here the groups should be small – four or five children in a group would be a good size.

Collaborative group work has much to offer as a way of learning. Children working together in a group can generate more ideas than individuals working alone. There is some evidence that self-confidence and self-esteem are improved. Working together can be enjoyable and children can sometimes help each other very effectively. Group work can also free the teacher from some demands because children can use the members of their group as a point of reference rather than always turning to the teacher for information. The ability to work in groups is also an important skill for adult life where much work involves working with others. School should train children to do this as part of preparation for adult life.

Group work can vary in the degree of collaboration involved. In some classes children are seated in groups but work individually. Children can also work individually on elements of a task for a joint outcome such as the production of a group story or newspaper or the making of a set of objects as in a mathematical activity. This requires a certain amount of co-operation. In a fully co-operative situation children work jointly on a task for a joint outcome or discuss a topic together.

The role of the teacher during co-operative group work is to monitor unobtrusively and encourage children to put forward their ideas. It is important not to join in in ways that discourage children. Delamont (1987: 40) found that children resented any takeover. She quotes a child who comments 'You have put all that work into it and then the teacher suddenly changes it'. It is not an easy role for the teacher and requires great sensitivity.

Bennett and Dunne (undated) analysed the conversation which took place in groups studying different aspects of the curriculum. They found that when children were genuinely working together task-related talk was very high, averaging 88 per cent of the time, being highest in technology and computer tasks and lowest in language work. Children working in groups where they were expected to achieve the task demonstrated much greater involvement in their work, and the amount of task-related talk was 22 per cent higher than in groups where children were working individually. Language tasks, in particular, appeared to generate a good deal of abstract talk, although this might be the effect of the nature of the tasks set. Talk about action predominated in all the groups. The majority of teachers in Bennett and Dunne's study were delighted with the perseverance of even the youngest children and of children with the lowest ability. They felt that the children produced better results than usual in the action tasks. In addition, more able children tended to take on the role of the teacher, leaving the teacher free to stimulate by asking questions and encouraging higher order thinking.

Children can be organised for learning in groups of many kinds, varying in size, composition and permanency. Each type of grouping has its advantages and disadvantages for particular activities and particular children and there is a place for work on an individual basis, work in a variety of different groups and work as a whole class.

Group size

Teachers in the past have had very little opportunity to consider the size of group that is likely to be more or less suitable for different activities, unless they happen to have been in a team-teaching situation. More classes now have some help from teaching assistants or volunteer parents and this may have a bearing on the way that children are grouped. Teachers need to ask whether a particular size of group is the most efficient and effective way of teaching a particular thing or of providing opportunities for practice and discussion of a particular topic or achievement of a particular task. Groups can be as follows:

Pairs and trios

This form of grouping is easy to organise, has a good deal to offer and is probably insufficiently used. A pair of children tackling a mathematical or scientific problem may benefit considerably from talking it through. This not only helps the mathematical or scientific learning but it also makes demands on the child's language ability. This also applies to the situation where one child teaches another.

Small groups (six or fewer)

Groups of this size are valuable for a variety of activities. It is a good size of group for the kind of collaborative work which might be the outcome of a topic or environmental study. Groups of four may be a good size for reading, with each group reading from a book chosen to match the group's ability.

Large groups

A large group can be anything from a class group to the whole school. A large group does not lend itself to discussion as well as a smaller group and it is much easier for a child to opt out in a large group. On the other hand, there are activities such as aspects of music and dance where the large group provides an experience of involvement and participation which is very valuable. Large groups require much more detailed preparation than small groups.

Analysis 12.1 is intended to help you to consider group size in relation to different kinds of activity. The heading items give you possible group sizes, and some suggested kinds of activity are listed in the first column. You will need to select from these activities those which are appropriate to your situation and add any others which seem to be relevant. Then tick the appropriate cell for the type of group which seems most suitable for each particular activity. As with many of the analysis suggestions in this book, it may be valuable to discuss this with other teachers.

In considering what may be appropriate grouping for different activities it is useful to consider grouping from the child's point of view. We actually know very little about how children view the groups they are in. Does a five-year-old, for example, know all the children in the class? At what stage does an assembly of the whole school have meaning for a child and to what extent are some children frightened by being part of such a large group?

In a small group it is difficult for an individual to opt out or day-dream. While too much day-dreaming or day-dreaming at the wrong time may be a nuisance or worrying, there may be a case for providing some opportunities for children to be inactive and to think. This is probably more difficult in today's active classrooms than it was in traditional settings, where class teaching sometimes became a background for a child's own thoughts. Times are needed when everyone is quiet not only for the teacher's peace of mind but also in order to allow the children to reflect.

Analysis 12.1 Grouping for learning

	Indiv-idual	Pair/trio	4–6	7–9	Whole class	50+
Direct teaching						
Studying text						
Working on mathematical problems						
Mental arithmetic						
Science experiments						
Practical work in technology						
Discussion						
Listening to radio/watching TV, film						
Listening to the teacher reading						
Drama						
Topic work						
Practical music making						

The formation of groups

Another important question about grouping for teaching concerns the criteria by which the groups are formed.

Different kinds of groups are needed for different purposes and different activities and it is better not to have groups which are too fixed. Ability groups for working with the teacher may be fairly stable over a period but even these should be reviewed every so often so that children can be moved to a higher or lower group if their progress warrants it. For other purposes groups should be variable so that children have experience of working with a range of different people.

There is much to be said for structuring the groups for collaborative work so that there is a good mix of abilities and there is some evidence that mixed-gender groups do better than single-sex groups, although as the children grow older they tend to be negative about this. Dunne and Bennett (1990) found that both high and low attainers worked well in mixed-ability groups. Groups of high attainers worked well but groups of low attainers did not. This seemed to be because of a lack of understanding of the task and low-attaining pupils in low-attaining groups were not drawn into the task as they were when they worked in mixed-ability groups.

Grouping for class management

There are many situations where the teacher needs to divide the class in order to undertake particular activities. This kind of grouping is very common in physical education and in art and craft activities because there may be a limited amount of space and equipment which has to be shared. It is also necessary to group children from time to time in order to make the teacher's work easier. For example, you may wish to demonstrate or show something which cannot be seen properly if the group is too large.

Grouping by age

Primary schools tend to group children in classes by age when the school is large enough to do this, but there are many schools in which children are in mixed-age classes. Teachers need to be aware of age differences whether the class is of a single age group or a mixed-age group. We saw in Chapter 2 that Mortimore *et al.* (1988) found that teachers were not sufficiently aware of age differences among children in the same class and made little allowance for this.

A child's date of birth may have all sorts of consequences for his or her education. A child who is among the oldest in the class may appear to do well and this can be motivating. A child who looks mature may be treated as older and is thus encouraged to behave in more mature ways.

A child who is one of the youngest may be stimulated to emulate the older children and thus make good progress. On the other hand, such a child may become depressed about doing less well and develop a self-image which suggests a person who is not very competent and consequently may cease to try very hard. Mortimore *et al.* (1988: 163) also found that teachers 'were found consistently to have judged pupils born in the summer months as being of lower ability and having more behaviour difficulties. Younger pupils themselves were found to have a less positive view of school than their older peers'. When a child is small and immature as well as being young, teachers and others will speak to him or her as to a younger child and their expectations may be lower than the child's ability justifies. There may therefore be a case for grouping by age in classes containing only one age group.

Grouping by ability

Studies of ability grouping suggest that teachers need to be aware of underestimating the less able, who tend to do better in mixed-ability classes. Teachers have also been shown to believe that they review ability groups and move children from group to group more often than they actually do.

The attitudes and expectations of the teacher and the school make all the difference to the way children view ability grouping, whether this is by sets across a year group or within the class. A good teacher can make each group feel that they are special and deserving of the best attention. It is also important that the school encourages more able children to be sympathetic to less able peers.

Ability grouping may be the most efficient and effective way of teaching some things, offering the right level of group stimulus to the children and using your time most effectively. For example, some aspects of work in mathematics may best be carried out in ability groups, although there is also mathematical work which can be carried out effectively in a mixed group. There is a particular case for sometimes working with the most able and the least able in separate groups.

Other work may gain from a mixed-ability group. This is particularly true of the creative types of work such as art and drama and the content, although not necessarily the presentation, of personal writing.

Friendship groups

Most of us like to work with our friends and there will be occasions when friendship groups work well. There are some caveats, however. At the junior stage friendship groups will nearly always be single sex and there may be occasions when a mixed group would be preferable. Research suggests that mixed groups tend to work better than single-sex groups. There is also the problem of the child whom no one wants and the group where one dominant child does all the work. You may need to do some engineering in these cases.

A teacher needs to use a mixture of groupings, sometimes forming ability groups or groups at the same stage of learning, sometimes deliberately structuring groups – so that children learn from one another – and sometimes using friendship groups. This enables children to gain from the differing contributions of other children.

Questions to ask about grouping

The questions you need to ask in planning grouping might be as follows:

Which activities need homogeneous groups?

Mathematics is one area which is commonly expected to need homogeneous groups. Some activities can be undertaken with the whole class and children can follow them up according to their ability, perhaps with differentiation into groups with different tasks. Nearly all work benefits from discussion and you need to consider what can be discussed as a class and in groups.

Reading is another area where you will need ability groups, with each group reading a particular shared text matched to their ability.

It could be argued that physical education and music are subjects where work might be more effective if children worked in groups of similar ability, but it is unusual to find this.

Which areas of curriculum gain from being undertaken in a mixed-ability group?

Most creative work provides a situation in which a mixture of abilities is possible and often useful. Inventiveness and creativity are not solely the province of the more able and this is likely to become particularly evident as the technology curriculum develops.

Any area of curriculum where pupils are asked to work collaboratively can be undertaken effectively in a mixed-ability group.

Topic work and work in history and geography, environmental studies and science all lend themselves to mixed groups.

Does the organisation I provide offer children a chance to work in different kinds of group in the course of time?

If different types of group offer different learning opportunities, this suggests that it would be beneficial for children to have experience of different types of groups over a period. There should also be an opportunity to work with different children over a period.

Am I training children to work together rather than alongside each other?

Children will work together without a great deal of encouragement as they grow older, but their ability to do this is likely to develop more quickly if they are given encouragement and training in the skills of corporate working.

Training children to work in groups

Working with a group towards a common end involves a different set of activities from working alongside others with similar tasks. It requires certain skills and is important for adulthood.

Children need training in working together if the intention is to do co-operative group work. Teachers of infant classes are usually concerned about the way children are reacting to each other and training in group work skills starts here with such elementary tasks as learning to share, to take turns and to listen to other people and try to see their point of view. Children advance from this stage to develop readiness to contribute to common goals and to sink personal differences in order to achieve something. These continue to be necessary skills as children grow older.

Training may involve discussing with the class how to listen to each other in a group and how to encourage each other to contribute. After a session of group work, groups can be asked to consider how well the group did these things. Was there anyone who did not contribute anything? Why was this? Were everyone's ideas considered? How did the group come to conclusions?

Some thought needs to be given to the skills of leading a group, and children can take it in turns to be leader. Good group leaders make sure that everyone has a chance to contribute and is listened to. They sum up what has been said from time to time and move the group on when people seem to be getting nowhere. They are sensitive to people wanting to say something and encourage everyone to contribute. Groups might consider at the end of a session how successful their leader has been. Some useful tasks for group leaders to practise in the context of a piece of group work might be the following:

- *Getting ideas from the group*
  A group leader gives shape and direction to discussion about a task and the action required, e.g. a group leader asked to prepare the group for a visit to a local farm might start by getting the group to list what might be available for study at the farm.
- *Sharing out the tasks*
  When the lists of possibilities have been made, the leader has to see that the tasks are reasonably distributed. This is more a matter of saying 'Who would like to do this?' than of telling others what to do. It will include seeing that all the tasks are covered and that they are fairly distributed, taking into account the particular people in the group.
- *Pacing the work*
  The group leader needs to keep track of what is happening and to see that anyone left behind is helped to catch up. He or she may also need to discover whether anyone finishing early has a further contribution to make.
- *Encouraging and supporting*
  Encouraging others is an essential part of leading a group and often makes all the difference between a person who leads well and is accepted as a leader and a person who cannot get others to follow him or her. Very few people do this without being made aware of its importance and you need to encourage children who are leading groups to tell others that they are doing well or to thank them for contributions. The teacher's example will be important here.
- *Considering the way the pieces fit together*
  If the group is to present its findings to others, the form of the presentation has to be agreed and the leader will need to keep a running check on how the various contributions fit together and how each contributes to the whole, bringing the group together to discuss this.

The existence of a leader in a group implies the existence of followers. If a group is to work well, its members must accept the leader's role and work with him or her. This can be difficult for children who are natural leaders, but it is an important piece of learning for them. As many children as possible should have experience of leading a group so that they can learn the skills involved. You need to make a point of praising children for being good group members.

It is also worth considering the other roles which children may play within a group and discussing how best to fulfil them. Roles might include:

- secretary: to record group answers or materials;
- spokesperson: for reporting to the class;
- evaluation: to keep notes on the group process – how well individuals in the group are working together; to lead any evaluation at the end of the session.

The contribution of classroom support

Many teachers now have a certain amount of support in the classroom, sometimes from paid classroom assistants and sometimes from volunteer parents. There may also be support assistants employed to help particular children with special educational needs. It is very important that these valuable resources are fully used.

All assistants, whether employed or volunteers, need to be briefed fully on the tasks they undertake. Ideally they should be trained in tasks such as hearing reading, overseeing children involved in practical activities, extending the learning involved in play activities with very young children and so on. There may be some training offered at school level or even by the LEA, but you will almost certainly need to do some training yourself from day to day, explaining how best to tackle the tasks that you are delegating.

Each day you need to plan exactly how you are going to use the services of your assistant at each stage of the work. You also need to brief those involved in supporting your work as teacher on what you are aiming to do, how you are going to set about it and what the role of the assistant will be. It is also a good idea to try to find some time at the end of a session to talk over how things went, using this as an opportunity to get some feedback from someone who has been observing and also to discuss any difficulties the assistant has encountered. During the lessons you need to be alert to such difficulties and ready to intervene or offer advice later.

Classroom organisation is summarised in Analysis 12.2.

Analysis 12.2 Classroom organisation

---

1 Do I have an established classroom routine which children follow?
2 Do I have the right balance among class teaching, group and individual work?
3 Are my children really learning to work in groups?
4 Is the grouping that I am using satisfactory for its purpose?
5 Do the children have the chance to work in a variety of groups?
6 How well am I able to match work to individual children?
7 What opportunities do I offer children to contribute to the planning of their work?
8 Are they becoming independent learners?
9 Have I the right balance between teacher-directed work and choice by children?
10 Am I providing enough opportunities for discussion in pairs, small groups and as a class?
11 Am I making the best use of any support I have from support assistants or volunteer parents?

13 The use of time and space

Organising work in the classroom involves not only managing the children and planning the curriculum but also managing time, space and resources. Time and space are finite and cannot be expanded. You can only plan to make better use of them.

The use of time

The National Curriculum and the literacy and numeracy hours have created a pressure on time for teachers. There is now a great deal to do in the time available, and, since a primary teacher usually has considerable freedom to plan the programme of work in a way that seems best for the children within the constraints which have been created, the use of time requires a good deal of planning. There may be fixed points because of shared use of some facilities or because the school does some specialist teaching and teachers now have to incorporate the literacy and numeracy hours, but generally speaking teachers still have a good deal of time in which to plan their programme as seems best to them.

Since time is finite and you cannot get any more of it, you need to be very conscious of how you and the children are using it. While it is almost certainly impossible to organise so that you and your children are always using time to the best advantage, this is, nevertheless, the goal you should be trying to achieve.

The problem about organising time in the classroom is that the time individuals need for learning and the practice they need are so varied. The mixture of class, group and individual work needs to allow for this. Your aim is for every child to be working profitably with no one simply occupied because you haven't time to deal with him or her. This means that for much work you will need to provide a variety of levels or provide work which can be carried out at different levels according to ability.

Studies of the use of time

Tizard *et al.* (1988) found that in the top infant classes in their study less than half the day was devoted to work activity. Forty-three per cent of the day was spent on routine activities such as registration, toilet visits, lining up, tidying up, meals and playtimes. During the part of the day when children were learning, they were actually on-task for 66 per cent of the time.

Hargreaves (1990: 78) found that on-task behaviour was better in small primary schools. In his study, he found that:

> The striking feature of both the infant and junior levels is the high level of task work. Seventy-one per cent of observations were task-focused, and this increased to 80 per cent if routine task-supporting jobs, such as sharpening pencils or ruling lines, were included. Only 13 per cent of the observations were counted as off-task or distracted behaviour such as chatting or day-dreaming. In the Oracle study (Galton *et al.*, 1980) the equivalent proportions were 64 per cent task work, 17 per cent routine jobs and 19 per cent distraction.

Alexander (1992: 69), in the course of evaluating a project in Leeds that set out to improve performance in primary schools, found that on average children in the classrooms in his study spent:

- 59 per cent of their time working;
- 11 per cent on associated routine activities (getting out and putting away books and apparatus, sharpening pencils and so on);
- 8 per cent waiting for the teacher or other adult;
- 21 per cent distracted from the work which had been set;
- 1 per cent other (unspecified).

Mortimore *et al.* (1988) found that there was a significant positive relationship between the time spent with the teacher interacting with the class and progress in a wide range of areas.

Overall the studies of the use of time appear to suggest that the amount of time spent on-task is more limited than most teachers would like. There would seem to be scope for improving the use of time by both teacher and children.

The teacher's use of time

As a teacher, you are responsible for the way you use your time and the children's time. It is not easy to fit in all the aspects of the National Curriculum and it is important to consider the areas in which one subject overlaps with another; how, for example, the National Curriculum in English can be met through work in geography and history and other subjects as well as in English lessons, where mathematics is part of work in science and technology and so on. It is also important to consider how the time available in the week and the term can be broken down to ensure that every subject is getting a fair share of attention.

How you use your time depends also on your teaching style, but it is very easy under the pressures of day-to-day classroom life to believe that you should be using time in a particular way and end up using it completely differently, sometimes without realising it.

A good starting point, therefore, may be to work out how you think you ought to be using your time and your children's time, perhaps using the log sheet in Analysis 13.1, and then to check how you are actually using it. Most studies show some differences between what teachers think they are doing and what they actually do, so don't be surprised if this is true for you.

It isn't easy to find a way of recording how you are using time because of your involvement in what is actually happening. The ideal would be if you and a colleague were able to observe each other and note the use of time against a check-list. Most teachers are likely to have to do this for themselves, however, and you will need to find a way of recording that you can manage to use in the classroom. One possible starting point is to have a tape-recorder running for a time, recording what is going on. You can then listen to it and decide on the categories of activity which could be checked with a list as you work. Another approach to recording is to go through your list at each break in the day, estimating the time you spent on different activities. It may also be possible if you have a classroom assistant or parents helping you in the classroom to ask one of them to note brief details of how you are using time. Analysis 13.1 suggests recording day by day so that you can see whether you have a different pattern of using time on different days. You may want to change the titles in the cells or add more. You may also like to note the time spent on routine activities which do not contribute to the children's learning.

Children's use of time

Studying your own use of time will inevitably involve studying aspects of the way the children are using time. How you set about studying

Analysis 13.1 Teacher's time log

Complete this analysis by writing in the amount of time spent in each activity:

Name ....   Date ....

	Class or group activities						Contacts with individuals			
	Talking/listening to class or group	Questioning/discussion	Leading practical work	Organising activity	Radio, TV, films	Other activities	Explaining to individuals	Talking/listening to individuals	Checking work, hearing reading	Other activities
Monday										
Tuesday										
Wednesday										
Thursday										
Friday										
Totals										

this must depend partly on the age group you teach and whether the children are able to make some observations of their use of time for themselves, perhaps as part of mathematical work on time.

It may also be possible to co-opt some outside help in making detailed observations of what a sample group of children is doing at agreed intervals. College of education students or education department staff are often interested in undertaking this kind of study and it can be helpful to have someone with whom you can discuss children's use of time.

The involvement of children in studying their own use of time might become part of graphical representation. This kind of study may help children to concentrate more. The log sheet for children, which follows in Analysis 13.2, can be adapted for your particular class.

If possible give every child a copy of the log sheet and discuss what each item means. Bring in a pinger egg timer and set it to ping at regular intervals – every ten minutes might be a good starting point. Give a child the task of resetting it each time it pings. When the pinger goes everyone puts a tick in the column which shows what he or she is doing.

Although this may seem to be a bit disrupting, what you may find is that the number of children doing what they should be doing when the pinger goes actually increases because they want to be able to write down that they are doing the right thing. Ideally you want to do this on several occasions over a number of weeks, so that you get a fairly typical pattern.

When you have put together the overall findings they can be discussed with the children, who can consider how they can increase the amount of time they are on-task. It may be an opportunity to discuss with older children possible ways of studying and to provide an opportunity for each child to choose the order of some work and discover his or her best way of working. We all have our own ways of using time and we need to know whether we work best in short or long spells. Children may like to set personal goals to improve their patterns of working, and it may help them to identify and state something they plan to improve and to keep a log of whether they are achieving this. It is all part of the process of becoming an independent learner.

Further investigations and action

These exercises will almost certainly throw up things you will want to do something about. Your areas of concern will be to some extent

Analysis 13.2 Children's time log

	Listening to the teacher	Answering questions/class discussion	Working in a group	Writing	Reading	Mathematics	Practical work	Using a computer	Talking about work	Talking about other things	Getting ready to work	Doing nothing in particular	Getting help from the teacher
Name .... Date .... When you hear the pinger, tick the column which says what you are doing.													
1													
2													
3													
4													
5													
6													
7													
8													
9													
10													

personal to you, but the following suggestions for considering your findings may be useful. If you made a statement earlier about the way you thought you should be using time, this will give you a useful yardstick against which you can assess how well you and the children are doing.

Consider the balance of class, group and individual work

A recent study of children in year 7 asked children in a questionnaire what teaching approaches they felt did most to enable them to learn. The results showed a strong preference for class discussion, work in pairs or small groups and practical activities. Individual work scored lowest, and exposition and explanation by the teacher came midway. Although this was a secondary school study its findings would seem applicable to at least the older children in a primary school.

The grouping of children for learning was discussed in the previous chapter. Here we are looking at whether the balance of grouping you are using is the best for your class in terms of the time spent in each kind of organisation. This means studying the differences in children. These include not only differences in ability, skill and knowledge, but also differences in learning style. There are normally considerable differences in the way boys and girls respond.

The following may help you to take your analysis a step further. Select a time when you are working with the whole class using exposition and questioning and discussion. As soon as possible afterwards go through the class list classifying children as follows:

- those for whom what you did was probably exactly right;
- those who had either learned what you were doing already or could have learned it much more quickly;
- those who needed more work and explanation before they grasped what you were talking about.

Most of your children will come into the first category and you will probably have made use of those who knew it all to stimulate the others and make them think, perhaps also asking open-ended questions which challenged the thinking of the most able and took their thinking further. Those in the third category will have made a start which you will be planning to follow up.

If you can honestly say that this is what happened in your class then you have probably spent time profitably. But if you find that you have quite a number of children in the second and third categories, then you should consider whether you might have done better to teach them group by group.

You might also look out for differences in reaction from boys and girls when you are teaching the class. Do you get equal contributions from both? What seems to stimulate each group? What interests do they each demonstrate?

You also need to consider whether the time spent in group and individual work is being well used. There are a number of ways you could look at this:

- Take a point in the day when everyone should be working individually and look around the class noting how many children are really engaged and involved in what they are doing, as far as you can tell. Do this several times over a period. Note the children whose names occur most frequently among those not involved and consider whether a different form of organisation might do more to engage them.
- Note over a period of time which children respond best to teacher-stimulated and -directed activities and which do better given more freedom to work on their own.
- Listen to what happens when you ask a group of children to work together at something, thinking about the skills involved in group work and considering how you foster them (see pp. 179–80).
- Set up an experiment by selecting two very similar topics and then deal with one as a piece of class teaching and the other on an individual or group work basis. Check at each stage how many children are fully involved in learning in each case.
- Ask each child to do a week's work in one notebook, differentiating in your own mind which pieces of work arose from class work and which from individual or group work. While written work is by no means the only way or even the best way of assessing what children are learning, this will nevertheless give you valuable information. It will show how much each child actually does in a week and the notebooks can be kept and used in this way perhaps once a term. This provides a very useful long-term record.

The outcomes of these investigations into the use of time may not change your practice all that much and, of course, you can never cater equally well for all the children. Nevertheless, they should provide some food for thought and perhaps a greater awareness of the children who would benefit most from different approaches. This may give you some criteria for deciding how to set about a piece of work.

Study the occasions when you are speaking or reading to the whole class

The value of these activities lies mainly in the extent to which you can stimulate interest and thought. The review suggested above, when you check through the register thinking about what children have gained, is probably among your best checks on the value of whole-class activity, although you need to remember that some of your inputs may not have immediate outcomes but yet have important long-term benefits. Much reading and story-telling might come into this category.

If you are near the beginning of your career, you may have doubts about your ability to stimulate children in a large group. The skills involved come with practice. It is easiest to stimulate others if you are enthusiastic yourself.

Examine your work in questioning and leading discussion

This is a most valuable way of supporting children's learning. You need to consider whether you do enough of this kind of activity or too much and whether you are happy with the quality of what you do. Stimulating questioning at the right moment which demands thought and goes beyond questions which are a matter of recall may do a great deal to help children assimilate their learning and explore ideas. The ability to draw thinking together through discussion is also valuable.

Further investigation here must be concerned with quality as well as quantity and you may find it helpful to tape two or three sessions for analysis. You may like to turn back to pp. 94–96, where there is an analysis of the different kinds of questions which you can use to help you analyse the questions you actually asked. You can also speculate about what was achieved perhaps looking at the following:

- Which questions got the most response and which the least? Why do you think this was? If you changed some questions a little would you get a better response?
- How many children actually gave or wanted to give answers? It may be useful to make a seating plan and tick each child who answers a question. This will give you several pieces of information. It will tell you which children actually answered questions and which children were silent or not called upon. You will also be able to check whether there was any pattern about who answered and speculate about whether this was the result of your selection of children or lack of contribution from some children. Do the

children who contributed most, for example, come from any particular part of the classroom? Are you unwittingly missing some children because of where they are sitting? There is some discussion of this on p. 96. Are girls answering fewer questions than boys and is this because of your selection of children to answer or the natural behaviour of the two sexes?

- What was the quality of the answers given by different children? What does this tell you about them?

- How did you respond to children's answers? Were there any children who might hesitate to respond again because you were not encouraging enough? How did you deal with incorrect answers or answers which did not contribute to the work in hand?

- If you go through the register, for which children can you say that this session was a valuable use of time? For whom was it of some value and for whom was it of very little value? How many would have learned more from personal reading? How many didn't need the session anyway? Could you, by better planning, better questioning and better follow-up, have increased the number for whom the session was valuable?

Study the time spent on organising children, space and materials

Many of the studies of the use of time in school show that teachers spend quite a lot of time on this kind of activity. Mortimore *et al.* (1988) found that on average the teachers in the Inner London Education Authority (ILEA) junior school project spent about a tenth of their time on classroom management. We saw earlier that Tizard *et al.* (1988) found that in top infant classes much time was spent on routine activities. This is time which it is in everyone's interest to reduce to the minimum.

It isn't easy to check the detail of this type of use of time, but you can note how long clearing up takes and consider whether there is any way in which you could do it more quickly and efficiently. You can also study the extent to which your organisation is making you use time inefficiently. If you keep a copy of the list in Analysis 13.3 beside you during a morning or afternoon and tick it when you deal with any of the matters listed, you will begin to see where some of your time goes and you can then consider whether you can reduce the time you are using for these kinds of activities.

Using this list should help you to see which activities are using too much time. Each of the activities can be considered in turn:

Analysis 13.3 Where time goes.

Tick the appropriate box each time you do one of these activities:	
Tell children what to do	
Explain work to an individual who hasn't understood	
Answer a child asking what to do next	
Answer a child asking where to find something	
Answer a child raising a query about work, e.g. spelling, maths problem	
Answer a child checking that (s)he is doing the right work	
Answer a child asking permission to do something	
Make a disciplinary comment	
Other	
Other	
Other	
Other	

Tell children what to do
The following points might be considered:

- Could you more often give children their work in writing, particularly where you are providing different work for different groups? Even with quite young children you can build a vocabulary which allows this to some extent and the instructions can give reading practice. With older children more can be done, and this too will provide practice in reading comprehension.
- Could you organise materials so that their sequence is more evident to children? In a number of areas of work there is a sequence and if children know, for example, that the blue mathematics group is working through the next four cards or exercises in the book they can get on without coming back to you at frequent intervals to check on how they are doing. This gives you time to intervene and direct your attention where you think it necessary rather than using your time at the children's behest.
- Children who have genuinely developed skill in working in groups will often turn to each other to ask questions which in other circumstances they would ask the teacher. This is to be encouraged.

Explain work to an individual who hasn't understood
The best way to cut this down is to look at the kinds of questions that children are asking you and then to use the information about problems that this gives you to modify the way you give out work. It may be, for example, that the language you are using is too difficult, perhaps not so much in vocabulary but in language structure. You may also be unwittingly referring to things outside the children's experience. You may be giving too much information at once and it will help to have some of it in writing so that a child can check it over when you have finished speaking. Preparing work on overhead projector transparencies so that you can leave it up after you have talked about it may be helpful.

Another approach is to get a child who has understood to explain it to one who hasn't but in such a way that it is clearly seen as the responsibility of explainer to see that the child to whom he or she is explaining really has understood.

Answer child asking what to do next

This links with your arrangements for giving work to children. However, there will be children who are working individually, who need your guidance. There will also be the attention seekers, who ask questions in order to make contact with you. However, if you start getting a lot of questions on a particular aspect of the work then you should take a look at the following:

- Your organisation and the way you give children their work.
- The need to train children to work independently. We noted earlier that there is a need to train children in study skills. You need to identify the way you want children to work and make sure that they gradually become more independent.

Answer child raising query about work

Some such queries are inevitable, but you need to minimise them. The following are very common queries:

- *How do you spell…?*
  There are various ways of dealing with this. You can encourage the use of dictionaries and word lists. For some children it may be useful to ask another child before asking the teacher, although one has to watch for the problem of some children being constantly interrupted in their work.

  You can also ask children to have a go before they come to you or suggest that they write the word in rough, without worrying about spelling and then discuss it with you when the rough draft is finished before going on to make a finished copy. There will also be spell-checkers on your computers for children to use and there are freestanding spell-checkers now on the market which allow the writer to check the spelling of a word.

  If you press children too much about always spelling correctly, they will tend to use only words that they know they can spell. This makes it more difficult for you to help them enlarge their spelling vocabulary because you can't tell easily what is in their spoken vocabulary. An approach which encourages children to have a go allows you to pick on words on which the child should concentrate attention.

- *How do you do this sum?*
  This is more difficult than spelling because you really need to explore a child's thinking and level of understanding in order

to help. If you are getting many enquiries about a particular piece of work, however, you are obviously pitching it at the wrong level for a number of children.

It is also helpful to try to note the types of query you get over how to do something. It could be a matter of not understanding the language involved, inadequate number concepts or understanding of number operations or one of several problems. By generalising from the range of queries, you can often improve the ability of children to cope without recourse to you.

• *What does this mean?*
  Try to get children to rephrase this as 'Does this mean x?' This encourages them to try to understand before coming to you.

Answer child checking that he or she is doing the right work
The children who constantly turn to you to ask this kind of question tend to be the children who are a bit insecure. You need gradually to build up their confidence in themselves and in you, so that they know that you won't be cross with them for doing the wrong thing. It may be a good idea to check at the beginning that children who tend to ask this kind of question have understood and at an early stage, if possible, make encouraging sounds about what they are doing so that they know they are doing the right thing.

Answer child asking permission to do something
A teacher normally expects children to ask permission to go out of the classroom unless there are work areas adjacent, but as you work with a group of children you should be able to reduce the number of other occasions for asking permission to a minimum. Note the occasions when children ask permission and see if you can organise so that some of these requests are not needed.

Make disciplinary comments
These include both telling a child not to do something and praising a child for doing the right thing. There is a lot of evidence to show that the latter is more effective than the former and that it is used more rarely. As your class gets to know you there should be a declining need for negative comment, although there will always be children who need to be restrained from time to time.

It is also useful to look at the children to whom you offer each kind of comment. It is not unusual to find that some children get negative comments all the time and research suggests that these tend to be more often boys than girls and more often Black Caribbean boys than others. If you find that this is so, you need to look for situations in which positive comments might be made, because quite often some children will misbehave in order to get attention and attention for doing the right thing may satisfy this need and reduce the number of occasions when negative comments are needed. Remember that behaviour which attracts positive comment is likely to be repeated while behaviour which attracts negative comment tends to disappear only temporarily. Just looking for something positive to say to a child who always seems to be doing the wrong thing can sometimes be productive. Here again it is useful to makes checks on the comments you make from time to time.

A major problem for teachers is finding enough time to make assessments. A number of the suggestions above may be relevant in helping to create more time for this, which is a part of both the literacy and numeracy strategies. You also need to have some types of work which you know children can be left to do without interrupting you when you want to check on an individual child's learning. Reading is an obvious task with older children and various forms of play may occupy younger children, although play is less useful if no adult is involved. It may be possible to give children more than one task to do at a time so that they can go on to another task if they find difficulties with the first one. It will also be helpful if you have other adults helping you in the classroom who can help to deal with problems while you are dealing with an individual child.

The use of space and resources

Children learn from everything that happens to them and the classroom environment is a tool for the teacher which can affect children in the following ways:

It can set aesthetic standards for children
Children should be able to get pleasure from what is around them. This has several benefits. What we know about learning suggests that attitudes towards school and towards learning are formed early. A pleasant environment is likely to contribute to the formation of good attitudes.

We set standards by the environment we offer to children. We need to provide things of quality and give children a chance to enjoy them. Plants and reproductions of paintings are comparatively inexpensive and objects which can be handled may be included along with examples of good work from children. This is how standards are formed and maintained, and the less likely children are to get such experience at home the more important it is for the school to offer it.

The classroom displays can set standards of presentation
The teacher sets a standard of displaying work and teaching materials which will be reflected in the children's own work. This should lead gradually to children putting up displays themselves and learning about how to display material effectively.

Primary teachers often feel that they could do with more display space than they actually have. Pinboard is a very desirable wall covering but if you have only a small amount you can add to it in various ways.

Hessian wallpaper which takes pins is a very attractive surface which can be stuck directly onto plaster or over pinboard which has become unsightly. Corrugated card can be used in many ways and lengths of it can be pinned to a small amount of pinboard and so provide extra display space. Carpet tiles of the cheapest kind make a good pin-up surface and have the advantage that they absorb noise. They are more expensive than pinboard but provide a more attractive background for display and can be bought a few at a time.

The classroom should be easy to maintain
You need good arrangements for getting things out and putting them away and with a new class you need to spend time training children to do this. One simple approach is to make every child responsible for the tidiness of a small area of the classroom. The child's name is stuck to the section together with a list of what should be there. There should be a definite place for everything and each place should be labelled appropriately so that it is easy to see where things go. At the end of each session each child checks the list and tidies his or her area. It is easy for the teacher to see whether the work has been done and who should be doing it. This enables you to clear up very quickly and ensures that everyone takes a fair share of the work.

The classroom should stimulate children

This means that you display some material designed to start children thinking and asking questions and sometimes to start them working. It also means that you need to change the display fairly frequently and check that what is on show is really looked at and used. It is not unusual to find a classroom with a considerable amount of attractive material displayed but having no impact because the teacher has not stimulated the children to look at what is there. You need to train children to look at displays and to see what is there and provide opportunities for discussion about what they see. It is sometimes better to display less, use it more and change it more frequently.

You can also stimulate children in the way you set out materials for their use. A good collection of scrap papers and fabrics for collage may spark off interesting pictures. Other scrap materials may stimulate development in technology.

Organising the use of space and resources

The classroom should provide for the work you want to do. This means careful thought about storage and the way in which the grouping of children and the pattern of work relate to the environment and the resources available. Are you getting the best use of the resources you have at your disposal? Are the computers in your classroom used for as much of the time as possible? Could you make more use of this resource if you organised differently? Are you sure you are using everything that is available? It is surprising how often a teacher who is clear about what is needed finds ways round limited funding. There is very often equipment and material lying unused in someone else's cupboard and schools need to make sure they are sharing what is there, perhaps keeping a list of what is available which states where things are so that teachers can borrow them when needed.

Managing the space

In most primary classrooms the vast majority of the week's work has to take place in the same space, with only a small amount of specialist space available, if any. The classroom has to be used for many different activities, some of which don't go too well together. It is never very satisfactory to have to use such materials as paint and clay in the same space as clean work, however carefully you clean up.

You may find it helpful in thinking how best to use your room to work through the following questions:

- *What space is actually available?*
  Is there space outside the classroom which could be used for some of the time? This might be corridor or cloakroom or shared space. Draw a plan of all the space you have available for use in planning.
- *What activities will need to take place in the space you have available in the course of the day or week?*
  Most teachers will have a list which includes reading, writing, mathematics, science, technology, discussion, drawing and painting and working with materials (both clean materials such as fabric and messy materials such as clay and foodstuffs). The list may also include music-making and drama. You need to think too about the balance of whole-class teaching, group and individual work and plan the use of space with the demands of these organisations in mind. With very young children you will need to think about the play opportunities you want to offer. You also need to think about the storage you need. Each child will need somewhere to keep his or her things and you will need places for the equipment for each area of curriculum.
- *What does each of the activities you plan require in terms of space, equipment and storage? How can the space available best be used to provide for all these activities?*
  Inevitably you must compromise to some extent. If you have drawn a plan of the space available roughly to scale, you can go on to make cut-outs of the base of each piece of furniture. This allows you to find different ways of arranging them. You may want to designate particular areas of the classroom for particular activities, even if this is just a matter of arranging the storage for particular materials and equipment.

  When you have arrived at an arrangement of furniture which seems to meet your needs, try to find time to check how it is working out and whether there are modifications needed.

The seating of children

As teacher you decide the way children are seated. Children in primary school classes are often seated in groups, but research suggests that comparatively little use is made of this form of seating for co-operative work.

Wheldall and Glynn (1989) studied two year 3 classes, one of twenty-eight and one of twenty-five children. The classes were observed for two weeks seated round tables looking at the amount of on-task behaviour which took place which was defined as doing what the teacher had instructed. Tables were then moved into rows and the children were observed for another two weeks. Finally, tables were moved back to their original position for a further two weeks. The researchers found that:

> The on-task behaviour of the first class rose from an average of 72 per cent to 85 per cent in rows and fell back to 73 per cent when tables seating was resumed. Similarly the performance of the second class rose from averaging 68 per cent on-task behaviour during baseline (tables) to 92 per cent during rows, and fell to 73 per cent for the final tables phase.
>
> (Wheldall and Glynn, 1989: 89)

They found that the seating arrangements had the most noticeable effect on children whose on-task behaviour was low. In some cases there was an improvement of 30 per cent. The children themselves said they preferred to be seated in rows.

Bennett and Blundell (1983) also studied seating patterns and had similar findings. The children's involvement in their work and the quantity of work completed rose significantly when the children were seated in rows rather than in groups.

These findings suggest that children might get more work done if they were seated in rows rather than in groups. However, this is less convenient for co-operative work, although it is fairly easy to form groups of four by turning chairs round. Seating in rows is also less convenient for class discussion, because children cannot see each other. One alternative which may be better is to sit children in a horseshoe. This is good for discussion and is not difficult to rearrange into groups for co-operative work.

Wheldall and Glynn also studied the effect of mixed-gender seating. In a year 4 class the level of on-task behaviour was 90 per cent during mixed-gender seating and fell to 76 per cent when children sat with same-gender partners. It rose again to 89 per cent when mixed-gender seating was resumed. There was also less disruptive behaviour. They point out, however, that more on-task behaviour does not necessarily mean that the work is of higher quality. They also found that children thought they concentrated less when they were in same-gender pairs and worked harder in the mixed groups.

These findings are thought-provoking. Mixed-gender seating would undoubtedly be unpopular with children but you might try experimenting to see whether you have similar findings to the researchers.

Whatever your seating arrangement you need to think about sight lines. It is easy to miss children who are at the extreme right and left of you towards the front of the classroom. A check on who answers questions will help to ensure that this doesn't happen.

Storage

It is rare for a teacher to get exactly the furniture he or she would like and rarer still to get a sufficient amount of storage. Most teachers have to make the best of what they have and do a good deal of improvising and arranging things to meet the needs of their children's work.

Storage is a problem in most classrooms. You need to store things in such a way that they are easy to find, placed so that children do not have to wander about the room to collect things to do one job, easy to return and keep tidy as well as using space as economically as possible. Start thinking about storage by considering what you need to store for each aspect of your work and then see how this matches up with the space available. Look for spaces which could take additional shelves, including some high shelving for things not often needed. Look also for existing shelving which uses space uneconomically which might be adapted for better use.

Cupboards are often more useful without their doors, or you can plan that when the doors are open your storage is carefully set out and the doors used for pinning up information or suspending material in pockets. It is a good idea to mark shelves with outlines or labels of what should be stored there so that everyone can see the space to which it should be returned.

Flat materials can be suspended in bags which can be hung from wire coat hangers which in turn can be hung on a rail.

Trolleys are always useful, particularly for materials such as paint, where you need to clean the surfaces where they are stored fairly frequently. A deep box trolley is very useful for various kinds of scrap material and for clay, providing it has a lid.

Pegboard is useful for storing tools and each tool can be outlined on the pegboard so that it is easy to see where it should go and whether it has been returned.

You may analyse your use of time, space and resources in the classroom using the questions set out in Analysis 13.4.

Analysis 13.4 The use of time, space and resources

1	Could I improve the way I am using time?
2	How much time are the children on-task? Could I improve the way they are using time?
3	How much time do children spend waiting to see me?
4	Am I using space to the best advantage?
5	Is the seating arrangement I have for children the most conducive to on-task work?
6	Does what I have displayed at the moment include both children's work and material to stimulate? How long has it been in place?
7	Does everything in the classroom have its proper place? Are all the places labelled?
8	Are resources easily accessible and close to the places where they are to be used?
9	Have I a good scheme for getting everything returned to its proper place after use?

14 Individual children

Catering for individuals within a class is never easy. In every class there will be some children who not only need individual help with some of the work but also, for some of the time at least, an Individual Education Programme (IEP). You may have children in your class who would formerly have been in a special school and who make considerable demands on your time and attention. There will also be others who have special educational needs of one kind or another. Your school should have a teacher who co-ordinates work with children with special educational needs who should be in a position to help you to provide for such children in your class. This group is likely to include children with:

- low ability;
- specific learning problems;
- emotional/behavioural difficulties;
- problems of sight or hearing;
- other physical disabilities;
- gaps in schooling;
- language problems, including non-English-speaking home background;
- outstanding ability of some kind.

Your first task is one of diagnosis. You will have discovered from the records which children have major problems. Some of these, such as the child with a physical disability or a lack of English, are easy to identify and it is easy to see the reasons for the difficulties; other problems, such as the child who is nine but whose reading age is six, are comparatively easy to identify but it may be difficult to discover the reasons for the problem and still more difficult to know what to do about it. Yet other problems may pass unnoticed for a time, such as the child with an undiagnosed hearing problem. This is especially true where the child is quiet and well behaved.

It may be helpful at this stage to look briefly at each of the groups listed and decide which of the categories above fit each of the children you have identified, remembering that a child may come into more than one category.

Children with low ability

Children with low ability are likely to need a certain amount of special attention at every stage of schooling and this needs to be accepted and planned for. They are likely to be at an earlier stage than other children in the class and you will need to do a great deal to encourage them and reward their progress so that they are not too depressed by this.

The extent of the special attention they will need will depend upon the class they are with. If they are in a class where the average IQ is well below 100 the work is likely to be nearer their needs than would be the case if they were in a class with an average ability range. A child with a much higher IQ may need special help if he or she is with a group of high flyers. This makes it difficult to talk about children with high or low ability in the abstract. Although the terms are defined by national norms of ability, the extent to which the level of ability of a particular individual affects the work of the school or class is a matter of the norms within it as well as the ways in which the child's ability differs from the norm.

It is particularly important to look at what motivates these children and to use this to help them to learn in appropriate areas. You also need to look at what they know and do not know within the core subjects and plan work to fill the gaps you discover. Teachers sometimes take the view that, since children who are slow learners are poor at reasoning, they should learn by heart. This is unlikely to be a successful ploy as they probably have a poorer memory than the majority anyway and you need to think of ways to help them fix learning in their minds. What is needed is work designed to help them to learn to reason and develop appropriate strategies for learning, so that they become more capable learners. All children need this teaching, but in some ways the need to provide this for slow learners is greater than it is for others because of the limited amount of time you have available to work with them. It also helps to get them to use sight, hearing and movement to remember. In learning to spell, for example, it helps to say the word and write it. It may also help to draw it in the air. In number, they will need more use of apparatus than the majority.

Children with low ability tend to need short-term goals which they can enjoy achieving. You are more likely to be successful in teaching such a child if you identify clear objectives which you share with the child, which can achieved within one lesson, or even within a shorter period. You then give praise when the objectives are achieved and perhaps record the achievement somewhere for the child to see.

It is likely that there will always be children of low ability in your class. It is therefore worthwhile making or buying specific materials for them, firstly for developing work in the core subjects and secondly to provide for them to develop their work in other aspects of the curriculum. Material of this kind can then be used many times. If you add to this collection a little at a time and start with material you know you will need time after time, you can gradually build a collection and this makes it easy to provide for children at the right level. A similar approach is needed for very able children.

Children with specific learning difficulties

These children form a very varied group. There will be some who are apparently of average or above average intelligence but who are not achieving at their proper level. There will be others who appear to have difficulty in one particular aspect of their work while managing the rest quite well. There may be children with minimal brain damage which creates problems for them and there may also be children whose school work seems to be well below average who have problems which have not yet been diagnosed.

Children in this group may need special attention for a period and may then be able to cope normally. It is particularly important to spend time analysing what they know and do not know and what they can do and not do, so that work can be directed appropriately and time is not wasted. Some of these children may have the services of a support assistant if their problems are serious and you will need to give careful thought to the way this help is used in the classroom.

Children with emotional/behavioural problems

Most teachers find this group the most difficult to deal with and most demanding professionally. Evans and Wilson (1980) list teachers' views of the type of school situation most likely to cope well with these children and found the most important characteristics to be as follows:

*   warm, caring attitudes in adult–child relationships;

- improvement of the child's self-image through success;
- individual counselling and discussion;
- a varied and stimulating educational programme;
- continuity in adult–child relationships;
- firm, consistent discipline.

Successful specialist teachers of these children tend to use one or both of two main ways of working with them. They make considerable effort to know the children well and this leads into counselling about work and behaviour. It sometimes involves teaching a child how to behave in a given social situation because sometimes children behave badly through ignorance of the acceptable thing to do.

The second approach is that of behaviour modification. This involves setting very specific goals which appear to be within the child's capacity to attain. For example, you might agree with a child that he or she will work quietly for ten minutes by the clock without getting up or speaking to anyone else. If the child achieves this goal, you reward him or her with praise and perhaps a mark on a personal chart. You then go on to set further goals. If the child is unable to achieve the goal set then you make it easier – working for five minutes, for example. A detailed account of this way of working can be found in *Positive Teaching: The Behavioural Approach* by Wheldall and Merritt (1984).

In some cases you may find that a child who is easily distracted is helped if you arrange for him to work in a carrel or booth. You can create areas for individual learning of this kind by placing hardboard between two tables or placing a cupboard at right angles to the wall. The child sits facing the wall. Working there should be treated as a privilege rather than a punishment, since a distractible child may wish as fervently as you do that he or she could behave like other children. You may find that other children like working in this situation.

From time to time you may experience a child who creates a situation which challenges your authority as a teacher and perhaps demonstrates to the group that he or she is managing you. The child swears at you, defies you, deliberately does something you have forbidden and creates a dramatic situation where all the children are waiting, breathless, to see what will happen. When this kind of situation occurs you usually have little time to think. The first thing to do is to retain a professional calm, acting the part of someone calm even if you are boiling inside. You can then take one of several courses of action:

- *You can separate the child from the others*
  You may do this in various ways. You may perhaps take him or

her out of the room or at least out of earshot, if not out of sight, of other children in order to talk without an audience. This is probably the best solution and has the advantage of ending the drama. How you deal with the child then will depend upon your knowledge of the particular child and the situation, but you have a better chance of making an impression when the child is not playing to the gallery.

- *You can assert your authority*
  You may do this in any way you think may be effective. Some teachers demonstrate blank astonishment that anyone could do such a thing; others produce a show of anger, looking directly at the child and maintaining eye contact while moving towards him or her. Both of these tactics can work, but you have to feel reasonably confident that this kind of action won't lead to further defiance. It is also easier to stay in control of the situation if you are acting as if you are astonished or angry and not really feeling it. This is often difficult to do.

- *You can pass it off lightly*
  You can imply that it is not important or treat it as a joke or by saying something like 'I'm sure you didn't really mean that. How about starting again?' Then you take a later opportunity to talk to the child in question and try to find out the reason for the outburst.

- *You can behave as if nothing has happened*
  You can more or less ignore the behaviour at the time and discuss it later. If you are dealing with a child whose behaviour is known to be abnormal and recognised by the other children to be so, this is not an unreasonable thing to do, especially if you can couple it with an opportunity to retract or rephrase what was said. A comment like 'I didn't quite hear that. Would you mind repeating it?' very frequently produces something more moderate.

It is useful to keep a note of situations where a child or a group of children have been particularly difficult, noting what led up to the situation. If you do this over a period, you may be able to see a pattern in what triggers unacceptable behaviour and this may enable you to avoid situations which create problems. You can also discuss with an individual child what makes him or her angry and badly behaved and use the techniques of behaviour modification to help the child overcome the problem.

Problems of sight or hearing

You may have within your class children with problems of sight or hearing. They may be with you for only part of the time and in a school-based unit for the rest of the time, but you need to be aware of the problems they have and the implications of those problems for you as teacher. You may also have children whose problems have not yet been diagnosed, particularly if you teach very young children and you need to be alert for children who appear to be having difficulty in seeing the board or children who hold their heads in an unusual position who may have hearing problems. You can check sight by asking a child for details of what he or she can see close to and at a distance and you can check hearing by standing behind a child and saying something in a normal voice and asking him or her to repeat it. Children who appear to have reading difficulties should be checked for sight and hearing problems.

Children with poor vision need very good light for their work. They certainly need to sit near a window and if their problems are serious they may need a reading lamp. They also need to sit near the board and some will need someone to read what is on it for them. Whiteboards are easier to read than blackboards. Worksheets also need to be in black and white and may need large print.

If you have a child with serious sight problems you may need to familiarise him or her with the classroom layout when the child first joins you. It is useful to use clock face directions in describing where something is if the child is old enough to understand them.

If a child has had poor sight from birth, he or she will have developed a rather different picture of the world from a normally sighted child and this will affect the way concepts have been formed.

One very common sight defect which is not sufficiently noticed in schools is colour blindness. You are likely to have at least one child in your class at some time who has a degree of colour blindness. This creates problems for the child when things are colour-coded as well as problems in art and craft and in daily life. This is a defect which cannot be remedied, but if you know about it you can help the child in question by giving other references as well as colour.

It is easy to check whether you have any colour-blind children in your class by asking everyone to draw a flag with diagonals on it. You then ask them to colour in each section as you do and you show them a flag coloured with some sections red and some green. Colour-blind children will have difficulty doing this because red/green colour blindness is the most common. They will, however, have learned to make up for their deficiency and will identify red and green crayons, perhaps by reading their labels or by some marking on them. They will also look to see what other children are doing. It may therefore be best to divide the class in half. One lot of children might be asked to colour their flags blue and orange, which are other colours often confused, and the others red and green and then they could change over. Look out for children looking around to see what others are doing. They are quite likely to be colour blind.

Children with hearing problems also need to sit near the board and they will need to see your face as you speak if they are to understand what you are saying. Try to avoid talking while you are writing on the board or asking children to look at something on their tables while you talk about it. A child with hearing problems will find this very difficult.

A child who has had serious hearing problems from birth will almost certainly have more limited speech than his or her contemporaries and will therefore have more difficulty in understanding. Speech problems will include not only pronunciation but also limitations in vocabulary and language structure and this may need explaining to other children who may find such a child odd because of the peculiar speech. It is obviously best to do this at some time when the child in question is not there.

In both the cases of visually and hearing impaired children it is important to see that they have with them and are using the aids they need. Glasses and hearing aids are essential to them but they do not always want to use them. The teacher can do much to help the child to find these aids more acceptable.

The child with physical disabilities

You may have in your class a child with physical problems of one kind or another. It is very easy to assume that such children will make slower progress than children without such problems, but this is not necessarily the case. Children with physical disabilities probably represent the same range of ability as that in the normal population and their needs need to be assessed in much the same way.

The major problem you have to tackle with such children is what they can do physically. There will normally be advice available to you about what the problems are and how best to tackle them. Such children may have considerable difficulty with subjects such as science and technology if their hands are affected by their disability and you may need to seek out ways in which they can be enabled to do the work that others do, perhaps by working with a partner or by supporting them in some way. They may be able to do some things in physical education and generally should be encouraged to join in as much as possible, providing the medical advice allows this.

You may also have children with a variety of medical conditions, including such problems as asthma, epilepsy and possibly acquired immunodeficiency syndrome (AIDS). Each needs to be dealt with according to the advice offered by doctors and parents, but you would be wise to find out all you can about any disability suffered by a child in your class. Your task is to help him or her to learn and if your knowledge is good you can make provision with more confidence.

Children with gaps in schooling

A child may have missed a period at school through illness or for other reasons. He or she may have been taught badly or missed something by changing schools. Careful analysis will be needed especially for initial reading and number. If you have new children fairly frequently in your school it is a good idea to have some appropriate test material on tape or on paper so that you can find out, for example, whether a child has all the phonic knowledge needed at the stage that most of the rest of the class have reached, or whether a child has sufficient knowledge of spelling rules, what his or her knowledge of the four rules of number actually is and so on.

It is not sufficient to find out what is missing, however. You also need teaching material you can use with such a child on an individual basis. Once again the best way to build an appropriate stock of such material is to make or buy a little at a time to meet the needs of a particular child and then to file this for future use.

Children with language problems

Language problems can range from the child who comes into school with virtually no English because this is not the language used in the home to the child whose language is so far from standard English that he or she has difficulty in understanding and being understood. Problems also include children who have some impediment in their speech or difficulty in using and understanding normal language. Where there is a group of such children with similar problems who can be helped together, perhaps by a specialist teacher, this is less of a problem than where the situation is one of a single individual who has problems which make demands on the single classroom teacher with everything else to do. On the other hand, if the problem is one of learning to speak English, the lone individual may make more progress than the child in a group where there are other children speaking the child's home language.

Almost all language problems involve some work on a one-to-one basis and it is clearly impossible for a teacher with a normal class to provide this on any scale. You therefore need to consider what other help you can muster and, if you can find it, how you can organise the work so that the time is well used. You may be fortunate enough to have a support assistant for a child with language difficulties or a general classroom assistant. You may also have the help of parents who may be willing to come in and talk to children who need practice in English. It may also be helpful to invite in parents who are bilingual in the child's home language who can read or tell stories in that language and then translate them into English.

In dealing with children with a limited knowledge of English it is important to use the same phrases many times in the same contexts. In managing the day-to-day work of the classroom there are many occasions for this. Phrases such as 'put your things away', 'put your coats on', 'wash your hands for lunch' and so on will soon be picked up by children learning English, who will be able to see what the phrases mean from the actions of the other children. You can then get different children to say the phrases so that those learning English get practice in speaking.

Individual work with such children might involve work with tapes and pictures or slides designed to teach the names of everyday objects and actions.

Work with children with language disabilities should involve advice from a speech therapist. This is likely to vary from one child to another according to individual need.

The child with outstanding ability

In any class there will be some children who are more able than the majority in some or all of the work of the class, who will need individual programmes for some work. From time to time you may encounter a child who is so far ahead of the group that he or she needs an individual programme for almost everything or at least a variation of the class or group programme.

It is tempting to believe that such children are easy to identify and don't need any extra help because they can get on by themselves. The evidence from a number of studies suggests that this is not the case; some gifted children use their ability to hide their gifts so that they are like their peers and not all of their gifts are known to their teachers, particularly if they are disinclined to conform and do as they are told.

If you want to be sure that you are catering for such children you need to do the following:

- *Develop your skill in identifying children of outstanding ability*
  Look particularly for the child who is unusual in some way, who asks unusual questions or has original ways of looking at things. Where you have queries about such a child, ask if he or she can be seen by an educational psychologist.

- *Make sure your overall programme is rich and varied enough for latent gifts to emerge*
  Some people reveal their gifts only if the circumstances are right and when something strikes a chord for them.

- *Consider possible teaching approaches for a child of outstanding ability*
  Try to ensure that you ask questions and present material at a variety of levels and that you include open-ended questions in any questioning session.

- *Assess carefully the levels of ability and stages of development within the class*
  Examine the ways in which you check on the abilities and stages of development of your children. Is it possible that you have a child who could do much more demanding work than you are giving him or her? It may be a good idea to go through the register asking yourself this question and then check up on any children you think may have more ability than is apparent, by talking further with them and looking at their work.

- *Organise work at different levels*
  With any topic work you plan to do with the whole class, see that there are, within the plan, opportunities for doing more or doing work which is more demanding. Very able children don't necessarily need the next stage of the work which is in hand, although it may sometimes be appropriate to go on to the next level of the National Curriculum. They are often able to do more than their peers and can enjoy a richer programme involving their own investigations or ideas which you or they suggest. It is a waste of any child's time to do more of work already mastered, although it can sometimes be difficult to avoid this. Bennett *et al.* (1984) found that teachers tended to underestimate the most able children and they were often given tasks which were practice of what they already knew rather than consolidation of new learning.

- *Consider the basic curriculum in relation to such a child*
  Since able children are able to learn quickly, their basic learning can be more concentrated than that for other children. It may be a good idea to look through the books and materials you are using to see whether there are short cuts or ways in which a child who

grasps things easily can get through the essential work more quickly than the majority. Try building a collection of material for the faster workers. It multiplies the material if a group of teachers collaborate in making and collecting such material and share it.

A child who works quickly has time for other work. Try to find some genuine problems which are within the capacity of such a child and if possible enlist help from parents, students and others who may be interested. For example, the production of a school or local guide book for new children and their parents in the area is a project which requires a good deal of research and needs to be written with a particular readership in mind. Such project material must actually be used, however, and the child or children must be aware of this from the outset; otherwise the discipline of working in a real situation will be lost. A further project might be to evaluate the effect of this work.

Children of high ability have a particular need to acquire study skills so that they are able to work independently and are not too dependent on a busy teacher.

Successful work with children with learning problems

It may be helpful to look at the factors associated with successful work with children with learning problems. Many of these factors also apply to children with outstanding ability. You are most likely to be successful in teaching such children if you:

- Study them as individuals with interests and a preferred style of working and make a careful diagnosis of the nature of their problems.
- Devise a programme for each child to meet the needs revealed by the diagnosis and involve the child in setting and achieving realistic short-term goals.
- Break down the necessary learning into steps which are small enough for the child to take successfully, but which also have purpose in his or her eyes and involve decision-making and thinking and are not overdependent on memory.
- Enable each child to see his or her own progress and reinforce learning, including the behaviour you want, by specific praise and encouragement and perhaps by charting progress in some way so that the child can see how he or she is doing.
- Provide opportunities for each child to take responsibility and become independent.

- Provide genuine opportunities for these children to contribute to the life and work of the class.
- Gain the co-operation of the child's family and work with the parents to help them to find specific ways of helping their child.
- Keep careful records and review progress regularly, often involving the children themselves.
- Maintain a positive attitude in all circumstances and provide many opportunities that are more likely to lead to success than failure.

It is possible to take a positive approach even in the areas in which a child is weak. Most children at the primary stage are anxious to do well, and if you can get a child to join you in setting targets and achieving them in a given time you enable that child to work positively to improve and add to achievement.

For example, suppose you want a child to improve his or her knowledge of multiplication facts. One way forward would be to agree a target day by which he or she would try to learn a specific range of facts and then discuss all the possible ways of working to achieve this. Children might, for example, dictate tests onto tape and then play them back when they think they know them, writing the answers. Another possibility would be to work with another child playing games designed to teach the learning needed and so on.

Schools are now likely to contain many more children with disabilities than formerly. This has advantages for the children concerned and it is valuable for other children to learn alongside children with disabilities but it also poses problems because children with serious disabilities will be expected to cope with as much of the normal school programme as possible and to follow the National Curriculum.

It is probably true to say that many people with disabilities can, if motivated, do more than other people often think they can and this should be encouraged. Older children, in particular, need to be encouraged to be helpful to, but not make pets of, children with physical disabilities and to treat them as they would other children except where their disability requires particular attention. In the main, the way children with special needs are treated by other children will come from the example set them by the staff. It is important that you demonstrate that you hold high expectations for such children.

Children with and without disabilities may pose problems in school. Difficulties such as poor sight or motor control problems, hyperactivity and others may make the normal programme of work inappropriate or lead to problems of understanding which result in disruptive behaviour. Maladjusted children may create a range of disturbances and may have difficulty in relating to others. You may have to teach specific interpersonal skills and discuss ways of relating to others with such children. Personal problems from home may also occupy a child's mind to the exclusion of everything else.

From your point of view, while it is valuable to know what causes a particular difficulty, the more important question is how to deal with it. Part of knowing how to deal with it is knowing enough about it to know what is possible and what is impossible. It is easy to be so concerned by what you discover about a child's background and so sympathetic towards him or her that you give too little attention to learning needs. The fact that Jackie lives daily with violence and family rows may make you sympathetic when she finds it difficult to concentrate, but it may be that the most helpful thing you can do is to help her succeed in learning to read. Every teacher needs to be a sympathetic human being, but no teacher has time to be a psychologist as well. It is generally better to concentrate on the professional task of the teacher, showing human understanding as part of your everyday relationship with children.

Your work with individual children may be reviewed using Analysis 14.1.

Analysis 14.1 Individual children

1	Which children in my class need to be treated individually for some of the time because of their special needs?
2	Have I diagnosed the problems of each of them?
3	Have I provided suitable programmes for each of them designed to meet their particular needs?
4	Have I any children of outstanding ability? Can I recognise the signs of outstanding ability when the child in question tries to disguise it?
5	Am I aware of all the children who have problems of sight or hearing? Could there be some children with these problems which have not been diagnosed?
6	Have I any children who are colour blind? If so, what am I doing to help them?
7	How well am I coping with children who have behaviour problems? Have I strategies for dealing with the problems they create?
8	Am I creating situations in which children with special needs experience success?
9	Does my organisation enable me to spend time with these children? Have I organised their work so that they do not waste time?

15 Working with parents

Many schools have developed excellent work with parents but research suggests that there is still quite a way to go if schools are to create the kind of co-operation with parents which will truly support their children's learning. Atkin *et al.* (1988) suggest that when parents understand what the school is trying to do, identify with its goals and support its efforts, understand something of their role as educators and take an interest in and provide support for their children's school work then the effects can be dramatic and long-lasting. It must also be remembered that parents are each child's first educators and that children spend more time with their parents than they do with their teachers. Parents are a valuable resource and have unique opportunities to contribute to their children's education. The school needs to harness this resource for children's learning.

Both parents and teachers tend to have stereotypes of each other, and the parents' views of teachers will have been largely formed by their own experience and level of education. This has left some people very hesitant about entering a school and talking with their children's teachers. Parents may see teachers as the fount of all knowledge and wisdom, as intimidating figures or as rather underpaid employees. Teachers, for their part, often blame parents for the problems that their children create in school and frequently comment that it is the parents who do not come to school whom they would most like to see. Teachers may also hold the view that working-class parents are not particularly interested in their children's progress at school.

Tizard *et al.* (1988) noted that 70 per cent of teachers in their study made negative comments about Black parents – mainly that they were 'over-concerned with their children's education', 'had too high expectations', 'lacked understanding of British education' and so on. A more recent study of inequalities in education of race, class and gender (Gillborn and Mirza, 2000) found that although Black

Caribbean children started school with some of the highest attainment levels of any group they left school with the lowest attainment. This suggests that the parents' high expectations may have had some justification.

Tizard *et al.* (1988) in their study found that virtually all parents said they gave their children help with school work and more Black than White parents started to teach their children to read before they started school. It would seem that there are really very few parents who are not interested in their children's education but some are hesitant about coming to the school.

Atkin *et al.* (1988) suggest that schools do not give parents sufficient of the right sort of information. Parents get their ideas of what the school is doing mainly from what their children say about it and from looking at the work their children are doing. They will probably not be aware of the educational philosophy of the school, its policies and teaching strategies. Teachers too rarely explain what the term's work will consist of and suggest ways in which parents might help. Nor do they always explain the processes by which they are helping children to learn. In general parents tend to get the message that teachers would rather they left the business of educating children to them. In practice most parents try to help and this is a resource which should be harnessed.

Tizard *et al.* (1988) found that teachers did not give a great deal of feedback on children's progress. In the reception classes they studied, 41 per cent of White parents and 16 per cent of Black had been told how their child's reading compared with that of other children. In the middle infants these figures were 44 per cent and 23 per cent. They were concerned to find that only 20 per cent of parents had been told that their child was having difficulties when testing suggested that the overall figure was considerably higher. Only 12 per cent of parents had been told that their child posed behaviour problems although the teachers said that 26 per cent of children posed such problems. There was also a feeling on the part of some parents that teachers tended to be defensive about problems rather than being prepared to discuss them openly. While this study is now some years old there is little evidence to suggest that the situation has changed to a substantial degree.

Parents as partners

Research suggests that there is much to be gained by treating parents as partners in the education of their children. If, as studies suggest, the large majority of parents are keen to help their children, this is a resource which teachers would do well to use. Atkin *et al.* (1988: 59) note that evidence suggests that parental familiarity with the school tends to:

• sharpen their sense of parenting, rather than blurring its distinctions from teaching;
• promote a positive view of school life which is nevertheless sanguine about its weaknesses and limitations;
• serve as a stimulus to the development of home-made, compensatory strategies to tackle perceived difficulties, as they affect their children.

There have been a number of studies of parents hearing their children read on a regular basis and in all cases this has been found to be beneficial. Children's interest in reading has been found to increase and they become more motivated towards school learning. There are also gains in that there are closer relationships between teachers and parents. Topping and Wolfendale (1985: 12) describe the contributions teachers and parents make to children's developing skill in reading as follows:

> Teachers bring knowledge of child development and theories of learning and teaching and have the advantage of an accumulating store of professional wisdom as the backcloth to their practice. They can appreciate differences in learning receptivity, rate of learning etc. and can match each child's learning needs to the provision on offer.
> Parents contribute life experience as well as accumulating knowledge of their own child's (or children's) development and individual characteristics and have the advantage of experiencing minute-by-minute child contact in a variety of situations. They too can appraise their child's responsiveness; they can make predictions as to outcomes and make a match between what the child needs ... with whatever resources and support the home has to offer.

The success of programmes for parents reading with their children suggests that there is scope for similar programmes in mathematics. There are many opportunities available to parents for helping children to learn basic mathematical skills in practical situations. Parents may also help by playing games with their children which involve knowledge of number facts. This is a resource which schools would do well to include.

Nursery and reception class teachers are well aware that children's home backgrounds make a difference to the way children settle into school. Wells (1985) found that the strongest association with reading attainment at age seven was the child's knowledge of written language at entry to school. Tizard *et al.* (1988) found that letter identification at nursery stage was a stronger predictor of reading ability at top infant level than concepts about print or word-matching. They also found that the children of parents who tried to teach them to read and used books scored higher at later stages. The number of books a child had access to was also a predictor of good performance.

Tizard *et al.* (1998) also found that families with high incomes did no more than other families to help their children, but gave them more experience with books. They were also likely to have greater knowledge of schools and believe that success was due to family influence. Mothers with higher educational qualifications were more likely to have positive attitudes towards helping their children but did not give their children significantly more help. Progress in reading and writing through the infant school was significantly related to parental contact with the school.

Hughes (1986) investigated the mathematical knowledge possessed by preschool children and found that when children were asked to work in practical situations their knowledge was considerably greater than might be expected. He found that, even at this early stage, there was about a year's difference in performance between children from working-class and those from middle-class homes. This suggests that schools need to do all they can to help parents to prepare their children for school. A number of schools have developed packs of material which parents of preschool children can use at home with their children in preparation for school. These encourage parents to use opportunities for children's learning and help them to understand what the school may want later.

There are a number of ways in which a school can facilitate home–school links, including the obvious ones like establishing a parents', teachers' and friends' association and making use of the home–school agreement. Schools can also:

- provide social functions where parents, teachers and other interested parties can mix on an informal basis;
- organise parents' meetings in a flexible way so that everyone has a chance to come;

- provide opportunities for parents in small groups to discuss common problems with teachers. This requires skill on the teacher's part but could be helpful to parents and also to teachers in understanding how parents view things;
- establish a parents' room where parents can meet, make coffee, look at books and undertake work for the school's benefit;
- develop a plan in which a parent is responsible for involving other parents in each particular road in the catchment area, welcoming new parents and visiting parents who don't come to meetings;
- develop shared reading plans where the parents agree to hear the child read at home and note what has been read;
- involve parents in work in mathematics, suggesting ways in which they could help their children practise necessary skills;
- involve parents in topic work or work in history and geography, perhaps asking for stories about their youth or inviting them to help with an outing or with collecting material and information;
- ask parents to help with recording stories on tape for children to follow with text;
- ask parents who can do so to type stories by children at their dictation; these stories can then become reading material for the child who has written them and others.

Communication with parents

Parents have a unique view of their children which is much more comprehensive than a teacher's can possibly be. Teachers have therefore a good deal to learn from parents about the children they teach, but little opportunity is usually provided for this. What is needed is a regular meeting where both teachers and parents inform each other. The parents inform the teacher about the child and how they view what seems to be happening in school and the teacher informs the parents about the work the child's class will be doing and how they can help. Both teacher and parents also discuss frankly the problems they are encountering and discuss how they can work together to overcome them. This is an ideal to be aimed at which would be rather difficult to achieve in practice. What you need to remember as teacher is that there is much to be learned from parents about the children in your class so that you use any opportunity which occurs to find out more about them.

The studies suggest that there are two further ways in which teachers are not always effective in communicating with parents. In talking about how parents can help they tend to dwell on what not to do, rather than on what to do. They are also inclined to use what parents see as educational jargon. The problem about jargon is that one person's jargon is another person's technical language. Teachers quite properly have ways of talking about what they do which are particular to the education profession but are confusing to other people. It is a good idea for a group of teachers to try to think of all the words and phrases they use which may be seen by others as jargon. For example, core subjects, Key Stages, SATs, attainment levels and many other words and phrases are unfamiliar to parents because they have come in since the parents were at school themselves. You need to either avoid them or explain them.

The appearance of communications to parents is also important and with the present use of computers it is possible for anyone to produce good-looking material. General communications to parents should be short and arranged so that they are easy and quick to read, perhaps with large headlines which stand out. The language needs to be friendly and lacking in jargon and complicated sentences should be avoided. Parents have usually a good deal to distract their attention and anything complicated or long will probably not be read. Where appropriate, communications will need to be in more than one language so that they are intelligible to all parents. Parents themselves may be able to help with the problem of translating and rewriting documents in other languages.

If parents are really going to be partners in their children's education they need to be taken into the confidence of the school to a large extent. Many of the plans for learning should be discussed with parents. School policies should also be discussed and be made available on request. At the level of the individual class the teacher needs to inform parents about the work being planned. There is much to be said for holding class meetings at which the teacher talks to parents about the work that the children will be doing in the coming term and suggests ways in which they can help. Methods need to be explained as well as outcomes so that parents learn how to work with their children in ways which complement the work the teacher is doing.

You may also like to consider a class newsletter which informs parents about the work in hand and suggests ways in which they can help. This might also include information about school journeys and visits and what is needed for them as well as what may be needed for different aspects of other work. A newsletter may be a good place to ask for specific help with particular activities, such as helping with a school trip or making costumes for a play. It will, of course, be important not to cover the same ground as any school newsletter and again it may be necessary to enlist the help of certain parents to translate the letter into other languages.

Most teachers will regard it as important that children see their progress as improving on their own performance and will want to limit the extent to which children are discouraged by comparison with the progress of other children, particularly where less able children are concerned. However, parents will certainly want to know not only where their child stands currently but also how he or she compares with other children of the same age. In most cases this will be a fairly complex picture with children being well up with the age group or beyond it for some work and doing less well in others. You will need to explain to parents the way in which the Standard Assessment Tasks give the results in different levels for children at the appropriate stages. Discussion about the stage a child is at needs to be followed up by discussion of what the teacher and the parents can do to help a child in the areas where he or she is at the lower levels. Try to have some really positive suggestions about ways in which the parents can help and give them a clear idea of what you are planning to do.

It is important in these discussions to keep a positive view of all that is being said. Try to emphasise the areas in which the child is doing well and be positive about the action to be taken where he or she is doing less well. Try also to avoid stressing what not to do and concentrate instead on what the parents can do.

Discussion with each child's parents needs to go further than discussion about the core subjects. Progress in other areas needs to be discussed and any problems of behaviour. Teachers, not unnaturally, feel that this is a very delicate area which could imply they are not doing their job or that the parents are not doing their job. Tizard *et al.* (1988) report that, in the one in four cases in their study where teachers actually discussed behaviour with parents, about one-third of parents responded positively, another third agreed with the teacher, about one-quarter responded negatively and the remainder couldn't see the problem. This suggests that children often differ in their behaviour between home and school and that there is everything to be gained from parents and teachers each knowing about the problems the other finds and working together to overcome them. Parents are also often grateful for the opportunity to discuss the problems they encounter with someone else.

It has been customary for most discussion about children to take place on the school premises. However, there is a great deal to be said for visiting the children's homes to discuss them with their parents. Parents feel more confident on their own ground and usually appreciate that a teacher has taken the trouble to come and see them. This kind of meeting can be more relaxed than a meeting in school, where there may be others waiting to see you, and it gives the opportunity for you to learn about the parents' view of the child. You can also learn a great deal about a child by seeing his or her home setting and the discussion tends to go better than it sometimes does at school. This takes time but is very rewarding. It is important to develop techniques for finishing a meeting so that you do not spend too long in any one home. Usually putting papers together and making summarising statements give an indication that the meeting is ending. These are also useful techniques for concluding meetings in school.

All schools must now send parents a written report on their child's progress, stating where the child has reached in the National Curriculum and giving information about skill development, behaviour, attitudes and any problems as well as information about the average class performance. It is important to be positive as well as honest and there is much to be said for a form of report which allows the parents and possibly older children to comment.

Parents in the classroom

It is fairly common practice in primary schools to invite parents to help in the classroom or about the school. This has a lot of advantages in that parents begin to see how teaching takes place and this not only helps them to support their own children but may well also make them good advocates for the school. The teacher is also helped in many of the tasks which take time from the more professional aspects of teaching.

There are also problems. The first and most difficult problem is that of whether you select the parents who come in to help or take all comers. Where parents are selected this can lead to a good deal of bitterness and upset, but avoids the problem of the parent who wants to take over or the parent who is not very literate. On the other hand, the kinds of parents who are not selected may be just those who would benefit most from being in the school and working with teachers. The problem of the parent who wants to take over may disappear if you are clear what you want and the problem of literacy may be largely a matter of allocating the right tasks to the right people. However, this too may be a problem because inferences can be made from the tasks allocated to parents. It is also important to stress to parents the need for confidentiality about the work of children other than their own.

Another problem arises from the fact that there are now more paid assistants in many schools and parents may find it difficult to accept that one person is paid for supporting the teacher in the classroom

Analysis 15.1 Working with parents

---

1   Do I know all the parents of the children in my class by sight and by name?

2   When I discuss each child with his or her parents do I discuss behaviour as well as academic and other progress?

3   Do I listen to what parents can tell me about their children as well as telling them what I have discovered?

4   Do I try to avoid jargon and explain the terms we are using in school?

5   Am I ever too defensive about what I am doing?

6   Do I keep parents informed about the work we are doing in class?

7   Do I explain to parents the way I am trying to teach their children?

8   Do I make positive suggestions about ways in which parents can help their children in different aspects of the curriculum?

9   Am I making use of any particular skills and knowledge among my parents?

10   Am I making use of parents in the classroom?

11   Do I plan what they will do each day, so that they reinforce my work?

---

and another expected to be a volunteer. This can be partly dealt with by the tasks each group is asked to do.

In inviting parents to work in the school, you will need to discover what any individual parent has to offer. A parent may have special knowledge and skills which could be widely used in the school. It is also important to plan the work of parents and any other ancillary staff in considerable detail. Bennett and Kell (1989), studying the work of infant classes, make the point that in many of the classes they observed ancillary workers and parents were left to their own devices and in some cases were not supporting the teacher in a very satisfactory way because the teacher had not thought out how to use their services in sufficient detail.

If you have parents or assistants hearing reading, for example, you should make it clear what the listener should do if a child is stuck for a word or makes a mistake. If parents are supervising children working with sand and water, or working at cooking, they need to know how they can introduce appropriate language and encourage children to experiment and discover. Play is more effective for learning when an adult takes part, but the adult needs to know what he or she is doing. Some parents will do these things instinctively. Others will need help, but in helping them to see what is needed in the classroom you will also be helping them to see what it is important to do in the home. This all suggests that teachers need tactfully to give parents some training in some aspects of helping in the classroom. It may be best to start with asking them to undertake tasks such as preparing materials in the first instance and gradually involving them with the children.

A summary of working with parents is given in Analysis 15.1.

16 Evaluation and assessment

Evaluation and assessment have become more important aspects of teachers' work in recent years, especially as a result of the requirement to assess children at the end of each Key Stage. It would be easy to forget that we are continually evaluating all kinds of things in our everyday lives and that teachers have always evaluated the work of their children. The change we have experienced is towards a more systematic and regular evaluation with outcomes made public.

Normal living involves us all in the process of making judgements about people and events in order to predict what may happen and decide what to do next. We do this from a very early age and it becomes our response to many situations. This is evident when you go to a course or if you are on holiday and meet new people. You listen to them, look at them and ask questions to discover ways in which they are like you and the ways in which they differ and what their interests are and so on. The judgements you make may not always be accurate, but this may not matter in such circumstances, particularly if you are aware that you are making judgements on inadequate evidence.

As a professional teacher, however, you need to be much more sure of your evidence because much depends upon the outcome of your judgements. You therefore need to extend the everyday practice of making judgements in order to be sure that the judgements you make are as valid as possible.

As a teacher, irrespective of external tests, you need to check and test and observe children, question them and explore their thinking about what they are doing, so that you can lead them on from the point they have reached. Assessment is one of the most powerful factors for improving learning. The following are important aspects of classroom assessment:

- effective feedback to children on their performance;

- their active involvement in their own learning;
- using the results of assessment to plan teaching;
- recognising that assessment has an important influence on children's motivation and self-esteem;
- the need to train children to assess themselves.

The report of the Task Group on Assessment and Testing (Department of Education and Science, 1988: 2), which set out the ideas on which the present systems of national testing are based, gave four criteria which it felt that any system of assessment should satisfy:

- The assessment should give direct information about pupils' attainment in relation to objectives: they should be criterion referenced.
- The results should provide a basis for decisions about pupils' learning needs.
- The scales or grades should be capable of comparison across classes and schools if teachers, pupils and parents are to share a common language and common standards: so the results should be calibrated or moderated.
- The ways in which the criteria or scales are set up and used should relate to expected routes of educational development, giving some continuity to a pupil's assessment at different ages: the assessment should relate to progression.

Ofsted (1998: 5) lists the following main findings about schools where teacher assessment was used effectively to raise standards:

- Teachers decide how and when they will assess pupils' attainment at the same time as they plan the work.
- Teachers are proficient in using a range of assessment techniques in the classroom, such as asking questions, observing pupils and setting tasks or tests at the end of a series of lessons.
- Manageable written recording systems are used alongside the sensible retention of evidence.
- Teachers make accurate judgements about the standard of pupils' work based on reliable sources of evidence.
- There are effective arrangements for moderating teachers' judgements about pupils' work.
- There are effective procedures for reporting on pupils' progress and attainment.

In schools where teacher assessment was unsatisfactory, Ofsted found the following:

- Teachers fail to share the findings of assessment with pupils as a means of helping them to improve.
- Records of attainment continue to be based on unmanageable tick lists.
- Teachers' judgements are neither accurate nor secured through effective moderation arrangements.
- Teachers lack confidence in assigning a 'best fit' National Curriculum level to each pupil.
- The links between planning, teaching and assessment are weak;
- Pupils' reports are written on inadequate records.

They found that the best systems involved teachers selecting a piece of work from each child each term, annotating it with a note of the level reached and noting future targets which had been discussed with the pupil. They found that teachers were generally accurate in their judgements about pupils' standards of attainment and regular moderation of work with other teachers contributed to this. There was often sampling of pupils' work by year group co-ordinators and subject co-ordinators. They were critical of the fact that teachers seldom shared attainment objectives with their pupils and the pupils were not generally aware of the criteria by which they were being assessed.

The process of evaluation and assessment is continuous. It starts before the children come to you and must be there at every stage in between, sometimes as part of a formal process, but more often as part of your day-to-day observation of children at work. It is important that you are on the look out for children who are underachieving and that you note pupil attitudes and the effect of these on how they learn. The way you mark work is also important. Children should be made aware of the criteria you are using to make judgements and be encouraged to use these criteria to judge their own work and sometimes that of their peers. A number of studies suggest that this doesn't happen very often and that children tend to think that the presentation of their work is more important than the content. It is also important in marking work to comment on those aspects of the work where you think the child has done well and to suggest ways in which the work could be improved.

Many schools have built up assessment materials for use at various stages in the school. These complement the Standard Assessment Tasks and may include standardised tests of various kinds as well as teacher-developed materials. There is also value in noting incidental occurrences in the classroom as they occur.

You also need to evaluate your own performance, skills and abilities as well as those of the children and appraisal should help with this. Many of the chapters in this book suggest questions you might ask yourself and provide tools for assessing yourself.

The language of assessment

The words *assessment* and *evaluation* are frequently used as if they were interchangeable. They are not really quite the same. There have been many definitions of these two words and they tend to mean slightly different things in different contexts. For the purposes of this book *assessment* refers to the process of gathering and collating evidence; *evaluation* occurs when you make judgements based on that evidence.

If you are to decide what evidence to look for in making an assessment, it is important that you have in mind criteria against which you will weigh the evidence you find. This means that if, for example, you are checking to see whether a child can add numbers to ten, you are clear on what evidence you will base your judgement. Are you looking for this ability as mental arithmetic? Are you prepared for the child to use apparatus of some kind to help in the calculation? What about counting on the fingers? It will depend upon the age of the child which of these is acceptable, but you need to know what you are looking for before you set out to check in each situation.

There are a number of other words used in the process of evaluation which it may be helpful to define:

Formative evaluation:	Assessment of work while it is in the process of being carried out.
Summative evaluation:	Assessment carried out when a piece of work is completed.
Process/product:	In any evaluation you can look at what children are getting out of doing something (process) or at what they finally achieve (product).
Validity:	A test or assessment is said to be valid if it can be shown to test what it sets out to test. Thus a written intelligence test given to a child who is unable to read might be said to be an invalid test of his or her reasoning ability.

Reliability: To be reliable, a test needs to give similar results when given to the same person on different occasions.

Criterion-referencing: A criterion-referenced test is one in which the results are compared with previously defined criteria or objectives.

Norm-referencing: A norm-referenced test is one in which the results are compared with norms for children of a particular age. Norms are usually established by extensive testing on large samples of the population.

Sampling: We can never know everything that is in a child's mind. Any test is a sample of what he or she knows, understands and can do and may not be a true representation of that child's ability or achievement. It is no more than the best information we can obtain.

Methods of assessment

Observation

The basic method of assessing children is that of observation. This may be observation of the child's performance or of his or her work. Observations may be extended by testing.

There is a sense in which all forms of assessment are a kind of observation. Tests and examinations, records and check-lists are devices to make observation more systematic and therefore more likely to be accurate. But you can only assess what is evident. A child may know and be able to do more than he or she can demonstrate in a test situation. You need to be continually asking yourself whether a child's performance is representative of what he or she knows and whether the sample piece of work or behaviour you are considering is typical and whether the result would be the same on another occasion.

The same is true when you want to make assessments of the class as a whole. One reason why a teacher's assessment may sometimes be more accurate than a test is because the teacher helps the child to demonstrate what he or she knows and can do in all sorts of situations, whereas a test only reveals the child's performance in one situation. The sample of the child's performance which the teacher sees is thus more likely to be a valid one and to reflect his or her potential.

Observation in the normal sense has the advantage that you can take into account at the same time many features acknowledged to be important but not easy to test. For example, in hearing a child read, you may note the words he or she is able to recognise, the ability to put them together into sentences, the child's understanding of what he or she is reading, his or her ability to make inferences from the text and the mistakes made and their possible significance. It would be difficult to find a test which could do all those things at once with any validity, and while you may be mistaken in your judgements you are in a position to follow up your findings and check them further.

One disadvantage of this kind of assessment is that you will only see what your experience, background and frame of reference will allow. You may miss things which an observer with different background experience would see because you have not experienced them before. For example, if, in hearing a child read, you have had no experience of considering the significance of the types of errors made by children, you will probably miss some of the particular clues being offered.

Perhaps the really significant point to note here is that the skill of observation is one of the most important skills a teacher can have and it is one that you need to work to improve all the time. One way of improving your own skill in observation is to look at children and their work with other teachers, who, because they are different people who bring different experience to bear on the situation, will see differently from you and may thus enlarge your seeing. This is particularly important at the beginning of your teaching career when you are learning what to expect from children at a particular stage of schooling, although experience can sometimes make a teacher look at situations less sensitively if teaching becomes a matter of habit. Many schools use forms of moderation to make judgements about their children and this benefits everyone.

It should also be noted that observation is not confined to what one can see. It involves checking by questioning and discussion and exploring how children see things. Observation is also the main way in which we assess children's progress in more nebulous areas such as personal and social development. Such areas need as much thought and care in assessing them as in making assessments of academic work. Teachers are sometimes reluctant to make formal judgements about more personal aspects of a child's development, but actually do it informally all the time. While it is natural to be hesitant about putting statements about such matters as a child's ability to relate to others on a child's record, it should be remembered that personal development happens and teachers affect it whether it is recorded or not and it may be better to give it careful consideration, thinking about the needs and problems of each child, rather than leaving it to chance. You don't avoid making assessments by not discussing or considering them.

You can assess by observation formally or informally. In the course of your everyday work there will be points which arise which you need to note. A child will give an answer which makes it clear that he or she has understood something important and made a major step forward. There will be other situations where the opposite happens and a child whom you thought had grasped something demonstrates a lack of understanding. There will be situations where you discover that you have over- or underestimated a child's ability in the work you have allocated and it will be important to remember this and make a change for the next piece of work. There may also be critical incidents in the classroom when you learn something about the way particular children react to particular situations or discover that your organisation or planning was less good than you thought.

It is not easy to find time to note such incidents, yet they may offer you valuable information. It may be that you reserve time at lunch time and at the end of the day to note down anything of the kind which you have noticed in the course of the day. There may be some opportunities during class time when you can enter a note. It is important that these notes are made in places where you will link them with the notes you make when you are checking on particular children's learning. Having a page for each child for odd notes is valuable and this can be filed when completed alongside notes for each child about other progress.

Observation can also be carried out more formally to check specific aspects of learning. This may be the observation of a group or an individual. Here you need to decide in advance exactly what you are looking for and the way you are going to check it or whether you are simply going to observe or enter into conversation with the child or children to see what their thinking may be. You may also need to decide in advance whether you are going to use the opportunity to extend thinking or whether you are simply observing. Then you need to decide after the observation whether the children in question have grasped the work or whether you need to observe and teach further.

You may be assessing not only the actual learning that has taken place but also the children's learning ability. When you are observing a group, you may be looking at how the children share group tasks, the kind of discussion that takes place, the involvement of the group members, the emergence of leaders within the group, time spent off-task and so on.

It is worth trying to reserve some time for this kind of observation each week. If you plan to observe a small number of children in detail each day you can gradually work round the class and spend time observing every child.

Testing

A test might be regarded as one way of making observation rather more objective. Teachers need to give tests for a variety of reasons and there is certainly a place for both teacher-made and standardised tests as well as SATs.

Teachers often feel that there is something special about standardised tests which makes the results of a child's performance in such a test much more reliable than a teacher's judgement. While it is certainly true that occasionally a test result will make a teacher think again about a child, the judgement of an experienced teacher is also a very good guide, as was noted in the Ofsted (1998) survey of teacher assessment at Key Stage 2.

One of the reasons for feeling that standardised tests give special information is that they are the nearest thing we have to an objective assessment and subjective judgement is often doubted. There is a sense, however, in which all assessment must be subjective. In the first instance there are subjective views involved somewhere in the choice of test, whether chosen by the DFES, an LEA, the head or the teacher. There is also an element of subjective judgement in interpreting the results.

A particular point to note about testing is that there is a difference between testing for mastery and testing for other purposes. When you give children a test on something they have learned in order to see how well they know it, you should expect a high proportion of good answers from everyone if the learning has been adequate. If you are testing to discover how each child stands relative to his or her peers or to help you make decisions about grouping children, you need a spread of scores, with some children getting very high scores and others very low scores, because the purpose of the exercise is to differentiate among the children. A diagnostic test which is planned to discover problems may have any kind of score for any child because it is designed to discover difficulties. The SATs are mainly designed as mastery tests, although it will obviously be possible to identify children who have problems which need to be explored further.

It is important to distinguish between testing for mastery and testing for discrimination since the overuse of discriminatory tests is very discouraging to children who do badly. Generally speaking success leads to success and the teacher's task is to organise so that every child is able to succeed at some level.

Teachers normally use tests and observations to find answers to the following questions:

1   *Is this child or are these children ready for the next stage or for a particular form of learning or teaching?*
    In this context you might test to discover what a child can do and what he or she already knows. You might be interested in how the child sets about the task. Intelligence tests of various kinds might be said to come into this category, which may include some diagnostic tests. The SATs are intended to serve this purpose among others.

2   *Has this child or have these children learned what I wanted them to learn?*
    This is probably the most common reason for testing in school and teachers usually make their own tests for this purpose. It may be a good idea gradually to develop a set of test materials for work in specific areas of curriculum, which can be given to individuals or groups when you feel they are ready to have their work checked. If you regard each test you give as feeding into a test system over a period and code and store it carefully, you will in due course build up a body of material to use in this way. This also means that the time spent on devising tests is used to full advantage. Some schools do this on a year-group or school basis.

3   *How does this child perform relative to others of his or her age?*
    Most primary teachers like to encourage children to work to improve their own performance and discourage too much rivalry. There is, nevertheless, a need to know how a child is doing relative to norms of some kind and you may want to make this clear to parents in a tactful way. This will emerge clearly from National Curriculum testing, but you need to explain to parents and others that the relationship is a complex one, perhaps with a child doing well in one aspect and less well in another. This should also make it clear to both children and parents in which areas there is a need for improvement.

    There may be a case for occasional use of a standardised test which gives national norms to check whether there are children who are underachieving. It is very easy to regard the group you teach as the norm and accept some underachievement without realising it.

4   *What particular difficulties is this child experiencing?*
    When a child fails to make normal progress, you need to discover
    why. You also need to discover just what it is the child doesn't
    understand or can't do. You may therefore need diagnostic material
    as well as your own observation. There is some published
    diagnostic material, but you really need to develop your own
    alongside this. You need spelling tests which identify gaps in phonic
    knowledge and lack of knowledge of spelling rules. You also need
    tests of mathematics which include knowledge of number bonds
    and tables and identify difficulties with particular operations. Such
    tests may be on paper or on tape and can be used by individuals,
    groups or the whole class and can be especially useful at the
    beginning of the year when you are finding out what children know
    and can do. Here again, if you work over a period developing test
    material, you gradually build up a kit of diagnostic tests. It is also
    helpful not only to collect test material but also material for
    teaching and practising the learning which the diagnosis identifies
    as being necessary.

Record-keeping

Record-keeping has always been an important part of the teacher's
work but the assessment required by the National Curriculum has
made even greater demands. Teachers now need evidence of children's
work which enables them to decide the level each child has reached in
the core subjects. There is also a need for long-term records which
follow a child through the school and for records of your own input to
work and the corresponding output from the children.

Purposes of record-keeping

There are many reasons for record-keeping besides those of recording
progress in the National Curriculum. An important reason for record-
keeping is continuity. If you should happen to have a long illness or
leave your present school in mid-year, all that you have learned about
your children may be lost if you do not leave appropriate records so
that someone else can take up where you left off.

Records may help you to match work to individual children and
help them to overcome learning problems. Something a child does
once may not appear to be significant, but if it happens several times it
may give you important clues to the nature of a difficulty. You may
not notice this if you do not keep appropriate records. It would be

difficult to keep this kind of record for all the children all the time but you can do it for a small number who have difficulties.

Important items from a child's background over a period may help you to understand his or her difficulties and put you in a better position to help. For example, a child who has changed schools a number of times may be insecure and need help in filling gaps in learning. A child who has a handicapped sibling may find it difficult to cope with the extra attention that the sibling needs from his or her parents. Background information of this kind is sensitive and you or your headteacher may need to ask the parents concerned if they mind having it recorded so that teachers are aware of any difficulties the child may have. There is much to be said for involving parents in compiling background records of children.

You also need to keep records which show what worked and what didn't work with individuals and with the group. This means keeping records of what you have tried and with what success. Such information is important for your development as a teacher as well as that of the children.

Your records are also important information for the teacher who takes your class after you and for your headteacher and possibly for a year-leader or co-ordinator who may be relying on you for information about children and the success of the programme planned. You may also need to provide information for other services from time to time such as the school psychological service, the health service or social services.

Assessing the National Curriculum (SEAC, 1990) makes the following points about the records of children's progress. They should:

- be simple to complete so that they do not cause too much interference in classroom activities and practice;
- include all the relevant information so that they may readily inform decisions about future action;
- be meaningful to others who may have access to them;
- be accessible to pupils so that they can enhance pupils' understanding of the teaching, learning and assessment process.

What needs to be recorded

Every school should keep long-term records giving relevant information about each child's background and you should be able to turn to such records to discover what you need to know about your children. Background records ought to give some health information. You need to know about disabilities and defects, particularly when they are not very obvious. You need to be aware of children who should wear glasses, children with inadequate hearing, children who are colour blind and so on. You also need to know of any children with problems, such as a weak heart, or asthma or epilepsy, which could affect what you do with them in school or any children who have had long absences through illness. You also need the kind of background information about the child's family which was mentioned above.

If you are to take on where a previous teacher left off, you need to know the facts about work covered in the previous year. The National Curriculum makes this easier in some ways even though it demands a great deal from teachers by way of recording. It should be possible to review a child's progress right the way through schooling.

School records or records to be passed on need to contain only what might be described as *considered records*. Your own day-to-day notes may contain comments about individual children and the success or otherwise of particular pieces of work, recorded for your benefit alone. These notes will inform your final records but be different from them.

We have already noted that it is helpful to keep a loose-leaf file with a page for each child. You can then add material and put the page into a longer term record when it is full. You need to find time for talking with each child about his or her individual progress and agree targets for future work. The loose-leaf file will provide useful material for discussion.

Types of record

Recording is a time-consuming process and it is therefore important to find forms of recording which can be completed easily. Records can be classified as follows:

Notes of observations

These can be notes of things that occur which you feel are of interest and can be made day by day as things happen. You can make this kind of observation more systematic by observing and talking with a few children each week and recording these observations in greater detail. Notes of this kind, kept over a period, provide insight into a child's development.

Records of achievement

Primary schools are expected to keep records of achievement for children. SEAC (1990) describes them as follows:

A record of achievement is:

- a cumulative record of an individual child's achievements in school;
- compiled by the pupils, the teacher and others who are involved in the learning process;
- usually confined to positive achievement;
- the place to note personal and social attributes and a wider range of activities and experiences.

SEAC goes on to state the purposes which records of achievement might serve:

- to involve the child and parents more closely in planning and reviewing the child's progress;
- to enable teachers and parents to help pupils to develop as individuals;
- to ensure planned continuity and learning development across points of transition in the child's school career;
- to identify with parental help a child's strengths and weaknesses.

It is easy to see the benefits that might result from this kind of record. It encourages the child to develop the habit of self-assessment and involves parents and child in considering development. Parents thus become involved in what is happening to the child in school and aware also of the value of some of the child's out-of-school activities. It also involves teachers in considering how best to carry out this work, which will add to their understanding of the individual child.

Collection of specific information about each child's work and behaviour

You may make observations against a check-list of specific items such as the ability to work with others towards a particular goal or the ability to use the class library to find particular information. It is useful to identify a series of items and look for different things weekly, monthly or termly.

Part of this record might be some form of profile. A profile has been described as a competency map which shows areas of weakness or strength, as can be seen from Figure 16.1. Profile recording is

Name .... Date						
	+ +	+	Av	−	− −	
Imaginative						Lacks imagination
Persevering						Gives up easily
Well organised						Disorganised
Confident						Lacks confidence
Persistent						Distractible
Co-operative						Uncooperative

Figure 16.1 Profile record

particularly useful for non-measurable aspects of development. When a profile is used for personal characteristics it is important to see it as a starting point for improvement rather than a description of inborn characteristics. The example in Figure 16.1 would be useful to discuss with a child and consider his or her view of how it should be completed.

Check-lists

It can be helpful to use check-lists of such things as phonic knowledge and knowledge of number facts, ticking off the items as you check them.

Collection of errors made by an individual

Errors in reading, writing and number work provide a teacher with important clues to a child's thinking. These clues become increasingly informative if lists of errors are kept over a period. Children can help by doing some of this for themselves.

Tests and assessments

Test scores and assessments are part of the process of implementing the National Curriculum and over a period they will show patterns which will be of interest. You need to be systematic in reviewing this kind of information about children. One way of doing this is to look particularly at the records of a small group of children each week so that over the term you look carefully at all the children's work. This can link up with individual discussions with children about their progress and targets.

A collection of samples of children's work over a period

Most schools now collect samples of work in order to assess the levels each child is achieving, and if these are collected over a period they can give a good picture of a child's progress. While the collection of samples is not very time-consuming it is easy to collect more material than you really need and have difficulty in keeping it sorted. It can be useful to involve children in selecting work for their record folder. It is also useful to mark each item with the level you think it has achieved.

A record of progress through schemes with clear stages

A scheme which has clear stages, whether a published scheme or the teacher's own, provides a record of the stage each child has reached in the particular work concerned. This may be simply a matter of noting the page or chapter that a child has reached or the books he or she has read and children can very often keep this kind of record for themselves.

Lists of work covered or attempted

This is another record which children can keep for themselves. It may also be useful to make a duplicated sheet for each child of work done by the class over a term or year and then add a note of individual variations. These lists can then go into the children's record folders.

Organisation statements for daily work

If you give children some work in writing, the statements you make can form part of your record of work if you think out carefully the best way to do this.

Notes made by children of work done

It will depend to some extent on the way you work and the age of your children how you use this kind of record. It is helpful, on completing a project, for each child to note down the things he or she did as part of the work. It can also be useful to ask children to record what they did at the end of each session in a notebook kept for this purpose. If you review these notes they can give you some idea of how much work individuals are actually doing and the notebooks may suggest targets which individuals should try to achieve.

Notes of discussions held with children and their parents

We have already noted that it is valuable to have regular meetings with each child at which work is discussed and targets set. The information from these meetings then feeds into the meetings with parents. It is important to make notes of what is said at both these meetings for future reference.

It can also be valuable to review each child's work with another teacher in order to check on your own conclusions.

Reports to parents

Schools are required to provide reports to parents on their children's attainment and progress at all stages including reception. The Qualifications and Curriculum Authority (1999: 32) suggests that these should contain the following information:

- brief comments on the child's progress in each subject and activity studied as part of the school curriculum – these should highlight strengths and development needs;
- the child's general progress;
- arrangements for parents to discuss the report with a teacher at the school;
- total number of sessions (half-days) since the child's last report or since the child entered the school, whichever is the later, and the percentage missed through unauthorised absence.

There should also be comparative data about children in the same age group, the same school and nationally. The Qualifications and Curriculum Authority (QCA) paper suggests that parents want to know how their child's performance compares with previous performance, the strengths and weaknesses, areas for development and improvement, how they can help and whether the child appears to be happy, settled and behaving well. They also suggest that it is important not to obscure low achievement or underachievement by the use of faint praise or by avoiding any mention of the problem.

Records to be passed on to the next school

Whether a child is transferring to a new school at the normal transfer age or transferring because the parents are moving him or her, the sending school has a responsibility to send on records. These should include:

- personal information about the child;
- the primary school record of achievement;
- National Curriculum assessment test records and teacher assessment;
- a folder of written work which represents the best the child can do;
- information about special educational needs where this is applicable.

General points

In deciding what records to keep, bear in mind that you want records that are not only easy to maintain but also easy to use. Records which give you information at a glance are more likely to be used than long pieces of writing. Look, too, to see how much recording the children might do themselves. Any factual record can be kept by children in some simple form from the earliest stages. Even five-year-olds can make a mark in a box when they finish something.

A school has to decide who has access to the records of an individual teacher. Ideally, records should be kept in a form that can be shared with children, parents and other teachers. This avoids having to make additional records for discussion with others or for passing on to the next teacher or school. However, it may be necessary to summarise records for passing on and there will need to be agreement about how much should be passed on to the next school.

There must also be agreement about for how long records which are not passed on should be kept. There may be queries long after a child has left the school and this suggests that the records of an individual child should probably be kept until he or she reaches school-leaving age.

Evaluation of the work of the teacher

Schools are now required to manage the performance of staff through monitoring, regular appraisal and target-setting. All teachers need to reflect on and review their own performance and appraisal should help with this. Targets will reflect those the school has agreed with the LEA and the school's own target-setting. Monitoring will include observation of classroom teaching by team leaders, or, in small schools, the headteacher or deputy, giving feedback on previously agreed issues. It is also valuable, if it can be arranged, for teachers to observe each other. Arrangements for classroom observation should always be discussed beforehand, with the teacher whose work is being observed explaining the plans for the lesson and what he or she hopes the children will learn and the aspects of the lesson on which it would be helpful to have feedback. There should also be discussion as soon afterwards as possible.

Preparation for the appraisal interview should involve you in self-evaluation, trying to identify the areas in which work seems to be successful and other areas in which there are problems which might benefit from discussion. The interview itself should be supportive and identify any training needs you may have and should conclude with a small number of agreed objectives for the coming period. Advice on target-setting suggests that targets should be SMART – specific, measurable, achievable, relevant and time-related. There should be follow-up discussions later to discuss how things are going and whether there is a need to modify any of the targets agreed. Where appropriate there should be coaching to help develop any new approaches being considered. You may also need to update your job description.

When you have reached the top of the main salary scale, you may apply to cross the threshold in order to gain a higher salary. This involves demonstrating that you meet certain standards. The first of these is for knowledge and understanding for which you must demonstrate that you have a thorough and up-to-date knowledge of the material you are teaching. You will need to show that you are using the literacy and numeracy strategies well and are keeping up to date through in-service training with other aspects of the curriculum, particularly any for which you have a school-wide responsibility.

Next you will need to show evidence of the quality of your teaching and assessment, describing the strategies you use and how you use the range of whole-class teaching, group and individual work. You will need to describe your methods of assessment, marking, recording and reporting.

Pupil progress is the next area in which you need to demonstrate effectiveness. You may have evidence from baseline assessments, SATs or internal and standardised tests to show that your pupils are making good progress.

Wider professional effectiveness is concerned with professional development and making an active contribution to achieving the aims of the school. You may be able to list here the courses you have attended and any work you have done to develop work in the school more generally. Finally, you will be judged on professional characteristics, such as motivating pupils, analysing and reflecting on work, team work and so on. Your headteacher will make an initial judgement on your application and it will be checked by an external adviser. You may make your own initial self-evaluation and self-assessment using Analysis 16.1.

Teacher self-evaluation

This book has included a number of analyses to help you to determine your style and preferences and to assess your own performance. The analysis charts are listed on p. vii.

Problems about assessment

Time

Every primary school teacher will be aware that the major problem about assessment is finding sufficient time to do it. You need to seek out ways of assessing which are part of your normal work and do not require any special activity. The time problem looms less large when one breaks it down into a small number of children to check each day and each week so that, in time, you get round the entire class. It also helps, particularly with older children, if you explain what you are doing and invite children's co-operation in not interrupting you when you are making checks on other children's progress.

Provision for children with special educational needs

Children with special needs, in particular, will need work broken down into smaller steps than most children. Statements in the National Curriculum about what children should be able to do will need to be broken down to meet the needs of individuals and your evaluation of their work should be against targets which they are able to meet.

You should also consider the needs of the very able and the kinds of targets you might set for them and how you will assess their progress.

Children whose home language is not English

It will obviously depend a good deal on how good a child's English is whether this poses a problem or not. There are likely to be some problems of understanding, even with older children. It may be possible to reword what is being asked in such a way that the child understands. Bilingual adults may be ready to help and it may be necessary to enlist the help of a bilingual parent to translate questions from time to time. Other children may also be able to help in translating. In addition, it may be possible to make judgements from what the child does rather than what he or she says.

Children may be upset by not attaining as well as others

This is undoubtedly a danger but may to some extent be met by giving each child targets within his or her reach. Your attitude of expectancy that a child will achieve at a given level is also important – you need to convey to children that you believe in their ability to achieve.

Analysis 16.1 Evaluation and assessment

1	Do I plan assessment and evaluation at the same time as I plan programmes of work?
2	Do I use a range of assessment techniques to evaluate children's learning?
3	What evidence do I use to make judgements about each child's performance? Is this adequate?
4	Do the records I keep give a fair picture of each child in my class?
5	Do I discuss my assessments of children with other teachers?
6	Do I share with children the purposes of my teaching and the criteria by which I assess their work?
7	Do I train my children to assess their own work against these criteria?
8	Are my records manageable?
9	Do I give parents a full picture of their child's progress and behaviour? Do I suggest ways in which they might help?
10	Could another teacher take my class on from where they are now using my records?

17 Conclusion

We have now looked at all the main aspects of teaching and learning which are part of the difficult professional task of educating children. We have discussed all the factors involved in teaching a group of children and you should now be in a position to make decisions about all the issues involved in organisation. You may like to turn back to Analysis 1.1 on p. 4 and look again at your answers to see if they would still be the same in the light of your consideration of the issues involved.

Each decision you make has implications for how you set about your task and for your long-term plans. You will also need to consider how you will work towards the organisation you want and what you will do to train your children to work in the way you choose. If this is very different from their previous experience it may take time and you would be wise to introduce changes very gradually and one at a time. If the change you envisage is considerable, it may take half a term or more before you begin to see results. Be prepared for this and be prepared also to stop and consolidate or even go back if something isn't working.

A particular picture of the well-organised classroom has been implicit in much that has been said in this book. It would therefore seem appropriate to conclude with a description of what such a classroom might look like.

The well-organised classroom is attractive and welcoming. There is colour and interest and it makes a visual impact on the visitor. At the same time, it is clear that it is a workshop in which many activities take place. It is therefore functional with materials and tools carefully arranged so that they are easy to find, use and keep in good order.

Children are comfortable and at home in this classroom and it is easy to see that it is as much their base as the teacher's. Their work is much in evidence. It is carefully and attractively displayed, often by the children themselves, who are encouraged to think about the way things can be mounted and shown. There is never too much display at the same time, however, and there is discussion of what is shown and it is frequently changed. Display is also used by the teacher as a starting point and stimulus for work.

Children in this classroom feel secure in knowing what they may and may not do and this means that the day runs easily with children moving from one task to the next. They start work as soon as they come into the classroom and it is unusual to see a long queue of children waiting for attention from the teacher. There are very few enquiries to the teacher about minor matters of organisation because they are largely taken care of by arrangements about the classroom. Children talk sensibly about what they are doing and learn from one another.

There is a sense of purpose in this classroom. The teacher has discussed with each child what he or she should be aiming to achieve and children have been trained to do a good deal of planning and organising of their own work and are well on the way to becoming independent learners. Many children become so absorbed in what they are doing that they are prepared to continue with it at home and would choose to work through breaks in the day. They are confident in their ability to learn and do things and have many ideas which they are well able to follow up. The teacher suggests ideas for homework and also involves children in suggesting ideas. The children have also become self-critical in a way which helps them to further their own learning. In consequence the standards of work achieved by all the children are extremely high.

The curriculum followed by the class is broad. The literacy and numeracy hours give rise to much interesting work and there are many opportunities for using the core subjects in other work. The differing needs of children have been carefully considered, with good provision made for children with special educational needs and for the very able. The teacher is very conscious of the need for first-hand experience and frequently takes the children out of school and brings objects, materials and people into school to extend the children's experience. The teacher also listens to children and encourages discussion, using questions which extend the children's thinking, and considers carefully how best to develop skills of all kinds, seeking out situations in which the children can communicate for a genuine purpose rather than as an exercise.

The teacher is very clear about the objectives of any given piece of work and shares this information with the children so that they are clear what is the expected outcome. The teacher also shares with the children the criteria by which each piece of work will be assessed and encourages them to assess their own performance.

The work of the classroom is planned to include class work, group work and individual work and these approaches are chosen very carefully to match the teacher's intentions and the needs of the children. The teacher is skilled at holding the interest of the whole class and uses whole-class teaching very effectively.

Work in groups is well-used. This is sometimes a matter of children of similar ability being taught as a group or given similar work and sometimes a group working co-operatively to agreed ends. The ability to work as a group has been carefully nurtured by the teacher and many children are now competent group leaders as well as being able to contribute to the work in hand, sharing and taking turns and trying hard to further agreed goals. There is also work in pairs with children helping each other and checking each other's work.

The teacher is also well-organised with work that is carefully planned, but at the same time provides flexibility and the opportunity to pick up children's questions or interests if they look as if they would be valuable to follow up. The teacher has clear aims and regularly reviews work in the light of them, demonstrating an enjoyment of learning which is communicated to the children in many areas of work.

It is evident that the teacher likes children and enjoys their company, respecting them as individuals without dominating them. The ideas and suggestions they offer are received in a positive and encouraging way because the teacher has the ability to see things from the point of view of each individual child and is thus able to motivate children and match work to each one. Each child has the opportunity to enjoy the challenge of work which is just within his or her capacity but at the same time is able to succeed.

The teacher in this classroom uses time to good advantage and is relaxed. As the children have become more independent it has become possible to turn attention to longer discussion and work with individuals and small groups, making them think through ideas and helping them to plan work and evaluate. There is also time to discuss how children feel about things and to consider the development of their emotions.

Parents are welcomed to this classroom and the teacher takes time to talk with them and find out about their children. They are given positive suggestions about ways in which they can help their children with the work in hand and their contributions are welcomed.

The teacher is involved in the wider professional setting of the school and also more generally as a professional educator. This means working to keep up with what is happening in education and seeing whether research findings and knowledge of how children develop and learn have any relevance to the classroom situation.

The relationships between the teacher and the children are reflected in the relationships of the children with one another. There is always a sense of caring in this class and it is evident in many of the day-to-day activities.

Few of us may feel that we can aspire to this picture, yet it is greatly to the credit of teachers in British primary schools that so many achieve something like it.

References

Alexander, R. (1992) *Policy and Practice in Primary Education*, London: Routledge.

Alexander, R., Rose, J. and Woodhead, C. (1992) *Curriculum Organisation and Classroom Practice in Primary Schools*, London: Department of Education and Science.

Askew, M. and Wiliam D. (1995) *Recent Research in Mathematics Education 5–16*, London: HMSO for Ofsted.

Askew, M., Brown, M., Rhodes, V., Johnson, D. and Wiliam, D. (1997) *Effective Teachers of Numeracy*, London: Kings College for the Teacher Training Agency.

Assessment Reform Group (1999) *Assessment for Learning: Beyond the Black Box*, Cambridge: Cambridge School of Education.

Atkin, J., Bastiani, J. and Goode, J. (1988) *Listening to Parents*, London: Croom Helm.

Barnes, R. (1999) *Positive Teaching, Positive Learning*, London: Routledge.

Bennett, N.S. and Blundell, D. (1983) 'Quantity and quality of work in rows and classroom groups', *Educational Psychology* 3 (2): 93–105.

Bennett, N.S. and Dunne, E. (undated) *Action and Abstract Talk in Classroom Groups,* Exeter: University of Exeter, mimeograph.

Bennett, S.N. (1976) *Teaching Styles and Pupil Progress*, London: Open Books.

Bennett, S.N. and Kell, J. (1989) *A Good Start? Four-Year-Olds in Infant Schools*, Oxford: Basil Blackwell.

Bennett, S.N., Desforges, C., Cockburn, A. and Wilkinson, B. (1984) *The Quality of Pupil Learning Experiences*, London: Lawrence Erlbaum Associates.

Bennett, S.N., Wragg, E.C., Carre, C.G. and Carter, D.S.G. (1992) 'A longitudinal study of primary teachers' perceived competences and concerns about National Curriculum implementation', *Research Papers in Education* 7: 53–78.

Brophy, J. and Good, T. (1986) 'Naturalistic studies of teacher expectation effects', in Hammersley, M. (ed.) *Case Studies in Classroom Research*, Buckingham: Open University Press.

Bruner, J.S. (1985) 'Vygotsky: a historical and conceptual perspective', in Wertsch, J.V. (ed.) *Culture, Communication and Cognition: Vygotskian Perspectives*, Cambridge: Cambridge University Press.

Carrington, B. and Short, G. (1989) *Race and the Primary School*, Windsor: NFER-Nelson.

Chazan, M., Laing, A. and Harper, G. (1987) *Teaching Five to Eight-Year-Olds*, Oxford: Blackwell.

Cleave, S., Jewett, J. and Bate, M. (1982) 'Local education authority policy on admission to infant/first school', *Educational Research* 27: 40–3.

Cohen, A. and Cohen, L. (eds) (1988) *Early Education: The School Years: A Source Book for Teachers*, London: Paul Chapman Publishing.

Collis, M. and Lacey, P. (1996) *Interactive Approaches to Teaching*, London: David Fulton.

Cooper, P. and MacIntyre, D. (1996) *Effective Teaching and Learning: Teachers' and Students' Perspectives*, Buckingham: Open University Press.

Cortazzi, M. (1991) *Primary Teaching: How it is*, London: David Fulton.

Crane, W.D. and Mellon, D.M. (1978) 'Causal influences of teachers' expectations on children's academic performance: a cross lagged panel analysis', *Journal of Educational Psychology* 70: 39–49.

Cullingford, C. (1995) *The Effective Teacher*, London: Cassell.

Davie, R., Butler, N. and Goldstein, H. (1972) *From Birth to Seven*, Harlow: Longman.

Dean, J. (2000) *Improving Children's Learning: Effective Teaching in the Primary School*, London: Routledge.

Delamont, S. (ed.) (1987) *The Primary School Teacher*, London: Falmer.

Department for Education and Employment (1999) *The National Numeracy Strategy Framework*, London: Department for Education and Employment.

Department of Education and Science (1967) *Children and their Primary Schools (The Plowden Report)*, London: HMSO.

Department of Education and Science (1982) *Mathematics Counts (The Cockcroft Report)*, London: HMSO.

Department of Education and Science (1985) *Committee of Enquiry into the Education of Children from Ethnic Minority Groups: Education for All (Swann Committee Report)*, Cmnd 9453, London: HMSO.

Department of Education and Science (1988) *National Curriculum Task Group on Assessment and Testing*, London: Department of Education and Science.

Desforges, C. (1985) 'Matching tasks to children's attainments', in Bennett, N.S. and Desforges, C. (eds) *Recent Advances in Classroom Research*, Edinburgh: Scottish Academic Press for the *British Journal of Educational Psychology*, monograph series no. 2.

Docking, J. (ed.) (1990) *Education and Alienation in the Junior School*, London: Falmer.

Douglas, J.B. (1964) *The Home and the School*, London: MacGibbon and Kee.

Dunne, E. and Bennett, N.S. (1990) *Talking and Learning in Groups: Activity Based In-Service and Pre-Service Materials*, London: Routledge.

Edwards, A. and Knight, P. (1994) *Effective Early Years Education: Teaching Young Children*, Buckingham: Open University Press.

Edwards, D. and Mercer, N. (1987) *Common Knowledge*, London: Methuen.

Evans, M. and Wilson, M. (1980) *Education of Disturbed Pupils*, Schools Council working paper no. 56, London: Methuen Educational.

Galton, M. (1989) *Teaching in the Primary School*, London: David Fulton.

Galton, M. and Delafield, A. (1981) 'Expectancy effects in primary classrooms', in Simon, B. and Willcocks, J. (eds) *Research and Practice in the Primary Classroom*, London: Routledge and Kegan Paul.

Galton, M. and Simon, B. (1980) *Progress and Performance in the Primary School Classroom (The Oracle Study)*, London: Routledge and Kegan Paul.

Galton, M., Simon, B. and Croll, P. (1980) *Inside the Primary Classroom (The Oracle Study)*, London: Routledge and Kegan Paul.

Gardner, H. (1983) *Frames of Mind: The Theory of Multiple Intelligences*, New York: Basic Books.

Giaconia, R. and Hedges, L. (1982) 'Identifying features of effective open education', *Review of Educational Research* 52: 579–602.

Gillborn, D. and Mirza, H.S. (2000) *Educational Inequality: Mapping Race, Class and Gender, a Synthesis of Research Evidence*, London: Ofsted.

Gipps, C. (1992) *What we Know about Effective Primary Teaching*, London: The Tufnell Press, The London File: Papers from the Institute of Education, London.

Goleman, D. (1996) *Emotional Intelligence*, London: Bloomsbury.

Hargreaves, A. (1994) 'Foreword', in Tickle, L. (ed.) *The Induction of New Teachers: Reflective Professional Practice*, London: Cassell.

Hargreaves, L. (1990) 'Teachers and pupils in small schools', in Galton, M. and Patrick, H. (eds) *Curriculum Provision in the Small Primary School*, London: Routledge.

Harlen, W. (1985) *Teaching and Learning Primary Science*, London: Paul Chapman Publishing.

Hay McBer (2000) *Research into Teacher Effectiveness*, London: Hay McBer.

HMI (1978) *Primary Education in England: A Survey by HM Inspectors of Schools*, London: HMSO.

HMI (1983) *9–13 Middle Schools: An Illustrative Survey*, London: HMSO.

HMI (1996–7) *Standards in the Primary Curriculum*, London: Ofsted.

HMI (1997) *The Teaching of Number in Three Inner-urban LEAs*, London: Ofsted.

HMI (1999a) *The National Literacy Strategy: An Interim Evaluation*, London: Ofsted.

HMI (1999b) *The National Literacy Strategy: An Evaluation of the First Year of the National Literacy Strategy*, London: Ofsted.

HMI (2000) *The National Numeracy Strategy: An Interim Evaluation*, London: Ofsted.

Holt, J. (1984) *How Children Fail*, Harmondsworth: Penguin.

Houlton, D. (1988) 'Teachers and diversity', in Cohen, A. and Cohen, L. (eds) *Early Education: The School Years: A Source Book for Teachers*, London: Paul Chapman Publishing.

Hughes, M. (1986) *Children and Number: Difficulties in Learning Mathematics*, Oxford: Basil Blackwell.

Inhelder, B. and Piaget, J. (1958) *The Growth of Logical Thinking from Childhood to Adolescence*, New York: Basic Books.

Jackson, K.F. (1975) *The Art of Solving Problems*, London: Heinemann.

Kelly, A. (1988) 'Gender differences in teacher–pupil interaction: a meta-analytic review', *Research Papers in Education* 39: 1–23.

Kerry, T. (1980) *Effective Questioning*, Teacher Education Project, Nottingham: University of Nottingham School of Education.

Kounin, J. (1970) *Discipline and Group Management in Classrooms*, New York; Holt, Rinehart and Winston.

Kyriacou, C. (1991) *Essential Teaching Skills*, Oxford: Blackwell.

Lewin, K. (1951) *Field Theory and Social Science*, London: Harper.

Medwell, J., Wray, D., Poulson, L. and Fox, R. (1998) *Effective Teachers of Literacy: A Report Commissioned by the Teacher Training Agency*, Exeter: University of Exeter.

Mortimore, P., Sammons, P., Stoll, L., Lewis, D. and Ecob, R. (1988) *School Matters*, London: Open Books.

National Advisory Committee on Creative and Cultural Education (1999) *All Our Futures, Creativity, Culture and Education*, London: Department for Education and Employment.

Neill, S. and Caswell, C. (1993) *Body Language for Competent Teachers*, London: Routledge.

Ofsted (1998) *Teacher Assessment in the Core Subjects at Key Stage 2: Policy and Practice*, London: Ofsted.

Osterman, K. and Kottkamp, R. (1994) 'Rethinking professional development', in Bennett, N., Glatter, R. and Levacic, R. (eds) *Improving Educational Management through Research and Consultancy*, London: Paul Chapman.

Palardy, J.M. (1969) 'What teachers believe – what children achieve', *Elementary School Journal* 69: 370–4.

Parsons, J.E., Ruble, D.N., Hodges, K.L. and Small, A.V. (1976) 'Cognitive-developmental factors in emerging sex differences in achievement-related expectancies', *Journal of Social Issues* 32 (3): 47–61.

Piaget, J. (1952) *The Origins of Intelligence in Children*, New York: International Universities Press.

Pollard, A. and Tann, S. (1987) *Reflective Teaching in the Primary School*, London: Cassell Education.

Qualifications and Curriculum Authority (1999) *Assessment and Reporting Arrangements at Key Stage 2*, London: Qualifications and Curriculum Authority Publications.

Rae, G. and McPhillimy, W.N. (1985) *Learning in the Primary School* (2nd edn), London: Hodder and Stoughton.

Rosenthal, R. and Jacobson, L. (1968) *Pygmalion in the Classroom*, New York: Holt, Rinehart and Winston.

Rutter, M., Maughan, B., Mortimore, P. and Ouston, J. (1979) *Fifteen Thousand Hours*, London: Open Books.

Sammons, P. and Mortimore, P. (1990) 'Pupil achievement and pupil alienation in the junior school', in Docking, J. (ed.) *Education and Alienation in the Junior School*, London: Falmer.

Sammons, P., Hillman, J. and Mortimore, P. (1995) *Key Characteristics of Effective Schools: A Review of Effectiveness Research*, London: Institute of Education and Ofsted.

SEAC (School Examinations and Assessment Council) (1990) *Assessing the National Curriculum*, London: SEAC.

Southgate, V., Arnold, H. and Johnson, S. (1981) *Extending Beginning Reading*, London: Heinemann Educational Books for the Schools Council.

Sylva, K., Roy, C. and Painter, M. (1980) *Child Watching at Playgroup and Nursery School*, London: Grant McIntyre.

Tizard, B. and Hughes, M. (1984) *Young Children Learning: Talking and Thinking at Home and at School*, London: Fontana.

Tizard, B., Blatchford, P., Burke, J., Farquhar, C. and Lewis, I. (1988) *Young Children at School in the Inner City*, London: Lawrence Erlbaum Associates.

Topping, K. and Wolfendale, S. (eds) *Parental Involvement in Children's Reading*, London: Croom Helm.

Vygotsky, L.S. (1978) *Mind in Society: The Development of Higher Psychological Processes*, Cambridge, MA: Harvard University Press.

Webb, R. and Vulliamy, G. (1996) *Roles and Responsibilities in the Primary School*, Buckingham: Open University Press.

Wells, C.G. (1985) *Language, Learning and Education: Selected Papers from the Bristol Study: Language at Home and at School*, Slough: NFER-Nelson.

Wheldall, K. and Glynn, T. (1989) *Effective Classroom Learning*, Oxford: Blackwell.

Wheldall, K. and Merritt, F. (1984) *Positive teaching: The Behavioural Approach*, London: Unwin.

Whyte, J. (1988) 'The "hidden curriculum"', in Cohen, A. and Cohen, L. (eds) *Early Education: The School Years: A Source Book for Teachers*, London: Paul Chapman Publishing.

Wragg, E.C. (1984) *Classroom Teaching Skills*, London: Croom Helm.

Wragg, E.C. and Brown, G. (1993) *Explaining*, London: Routledge.

Index